Constitutional Law in Latvia

Constitutional Law in Latvia

Kristīne Krūma †
Dita Plepa

This book was originally published as a monograph in the International Encyclopaedia of Laws/Constitutional Law.

General Editors: Roger Blanpain, Frank Hendrickx
Volume Editors: André Alen, David Haljan

Wolters Kluwer

Published by:
Kluwer Law International B.V.
PO Box 316
2400 AH Alphen aan den Rijn
The Netherlands
Website: www.wklawbusiness.com

Sold and distributed in North, Central and South America by:
Wolters Kluwer Legal & Regulatory U.S.
7201 McKinney Circle
Frederick, MD 21704
United States of America
Email: customer.service@wolterskluwer.com

Sold and distributed in all other countries by:
Turpin Distribution Services Ltd.
Stratton Business Park
Pegasus Drive, Biggleswade
Bedfordshire SG18 8TQ
United Kingdom
Email: kluwerlaw@turpin-distribution.com

ISBN 978-90-411-8275-3

This title is available on www.kluwerlawonline.com

The Authors

Dr iur. Kristīne Krūma was born in 1974. Dr Kruma studied law at the University of Latvia. She obtained an M.I.L. at the Lund University (Sweden), where she subsequently obtained her LL.D. degree in international law in 2012.

She has worked at the Ministry of Foreign Affairs during 1995–1999. Since 1999 she has focused on her academic career, lecturing at the Faculty of Law of the University of Latvia and Riga Graduate School of Law. In 2007, Dr Kruma was elected a judge of the Constitutional Court of Latvia. Since 2015 she has been a pro-rector of the Riga Graduate School of Law.

She was also an arbitrator with the OSCE Court of Arbitration and Reconciliation (2007), an ad hoc judge at the European Court of Human Rights (2012), a member of the European Commission against Racism and Intolerance of the Council of Europe (2012) and a member of the Scientific Committee of the Fundamental Rights Agency of the European Union (2013). She was a member of the Odysseus Network, the academic network for legal studies on immigration and asylum in Europe (2006) and a member of the Editorial Board of the Baltic Yearbook of International Law (2005).

Kristīne Krūma passed away on 4 July 2016.

The Authors

Mg. iur. Dita Plepa was born in 1987. Ms Plepa studied law at the University of Latvia. In 2011, she was awarded a master's degree in law. Her specialism is constitutional law and state law, as well as issues of legal theory. At present she is a doctoral student at the University of Latvia, Faculty of Law programme of legal science researching the procedure for managing State budget resources.

In 2008, Ms Plepa started working as the senior desk-officer with the Department of the Court of Justice of the European Union, Ministry of Justice of the Republic of Latvia. Since 2009 Ms Plepa has been working at the Constitutional Court of the Republic of Latvia.

In addition to this, since 2012 Ms Plepa has started teaching 'Legal Methods' at the Faculty of Law, Riga Stradins University.

Table of Contents

List of Abbreviations

CIS	Commonwealth of Independent States
EConvHR	European Convention on Human Rights and Fundamental Freedoms
ECtHR	European Court of Human Rights
EU	European Union
ILC	International Law Commission
Latvian SSR	Latvian Social Socialist Republic
MP	Member of the Parliament
OCMA	Office of Citizenship and Migration Affairs
Saeima	The Parliament of the Republic of Latvia
Satversme	Constitution of the Republic of Latvia
USSR	Union of Social Socialist Republics

For texts of legislative instruments and court decisions:

Likumi.lv/ ttc.

Baltic yearbook of IL.

List of Abbreviations

Preface

Latvia is a Baltic country situated in Northern Europe on the eastern shore of the Baltic Sea. It shares borders with Lithuania to the south, Estonia to the north, Russia to the east and Belarus to the southeast. The area of Latvia totals 64,000 square kilometres with 500 kilometres of coastline. Latvia is divided into four historical regions: Vidzeme, Kurzeme, Latgale and Zemgale. This has been set by Article 3 of the Constitution of the Republic of Latvia (hereinafter '*Satversme*') stating, 'The territory of the State of Latvia, within the borders established by international agreements, consists of Vidzeme, Latgale, Kurzeme and Zemgale.' The six largest cities and their population statistics are as follows: Riga (695,539), Daugavpils (98,922), Liepaja (80,763), Jelgava (62,800), Jurmala (57,463) and Ventspils (40,991).

There are 2,189,062 inhabitants in Latvia.[1] A majority of them are Latvians, Russians, and Byelorussians. Comparatively smaller numbers of Ukrainians, Poles and Lithuanians are also resident in Latvia. Most residents are Latvian citizens (1,829,192) with non-citizens totalling some 290,526.[2]

Latvia declared its independence on 18 November 1918. Before exercising its right to self-determination Latvia was a part of Russia. The *Satversme* was adopted on 15 February 1922 and can be recognized as one among the oldest constitutions in Europe.[3]

The *Satversme* is based on the text adopted in 1922. The legal force of the *Satversme* was suspended during the authoritarian regime of 1934–1940 and then

1. Statistics according to Population Register of the Office of Citizenship and Migration Affairs on 1 Jul. 2013. Available at http://www.pmlp.gov.lv/lv/assets/documents/statistika/IRD_01_07_2013/ISPV_Pasvaldibas_iedzivotaju_skaits_pagasti.pdf, accessed 27 Dec. 2013.
2. See statistics of the Office of Citizenship and Migration Affairs as of 1 Jul. 2013. http://www.pmlp.gov.lv/lv/assets/documents/statistika/IRD_01_07_2013/ISVP_Latvija_pec_VPD.pdf, accessed 27 Dec. 2013. See also Ch. 3 of Part I.
3. In Latvian legal terminology, the constitution is denoted with a special word '*Satversme*'. It was invented in 1869 and means that 'each state provides to its members, to its citizens refuge against one another and against strangers'. It was proposed for denoting the constitution by Kronvaldu Atis, one of the leaders of Latvian national awakening. The word '*Satversme*' has been derived from the verb '*tvert*' (to contain, to cover), because 'people have adopted laws because of that, so that in time of need they would have a place of containment'. Even the Latvian term used to denote constitution contains ideas of constitutionalism, i.e., that the constitution protects people and ensures the existence of the state. Karulis, K. *Latviešu etimoloģijas vārdnīca.* (Rīga, Avots, 1992), p. 159, Kronvalds A. *Kopotie raksti. I.* (Rīga, Valters un Rapa, 1937), p. 427. See also Rodiņa, A. & Pleps, J., *Constitutionalism in Latvia: Reality and Developments. New Millennium Constitutionalism: Paradigms of Reality and Challenges* 433 (Yerevan: NJHAR 2013).

subsequently de facto by the occupation regime of the Union of Social Socialist Republics (USSR) from 1940 to 1990.[4]

After Latvia regained its independence from USSR occupation in 1990, the *Satversme* became partially operational with the adoption of Declaration of Independence on 4 May 1990 and subsequently with the Constitutional Law on 21 August 1991. Latvian constitutional tradition is rooted in the concept of State continuity. It is taken as the basis to interpret the Latvian Constitution by acknowledging subsequent changes brought in by general developments of fundamental rights and general principles of law in European democracies.

The fact that the Republic of Latvia, after the restoration of independence at the beginning of the 1990s, did not draft a new constitution but renewed the *Satversme* can be seen as unique. This decision meant that the constitution, the operation and application of which had been stayed for more than fifty years, was reinstated.[5] No other State has conducted a constitutional experiment of this kind.[6] The restitution of the *Satversme* is an element in the doctrine of the continuity of the Republic of Latvia.[7]

The *Satversme* has been amended by Parliament (hereinafter '*Saeima*') several times. Apart from minor changes, the most important amendments concerned the provision on Latvian as the State language (Article 4), the insertion of Chapter 8 on fundamental rights, and provisions allowing Latvian accession to the EU (Articles 68 and 79).[8] The most recent addition is the adoption of the Preamble to the *Satversme* on 19 June 2014.

Latvia is a democratic republic based on the rule of law. According to Article 1 of the *Satversme,* Latvia is an independent democratic republic. Article 2 of the *Satversme* provides that the sovereign power of the State of Latvia is vested in the people of Latvia.

The *Satversme*'s character is to provide for the fundamental principles of the constitutional system of the Republic of Latvia in a concise way. It enumerates the most fundamental aspects of democratic system, the main powers and interrelationship between various branches of State power, and fundamental rights and freedoms.

Latvia is a unitary State and follows a Roman-Germanic system which is accepted in majority of European States. The decisions of the courts are not based on precedents. The Constitutional Court ('*Satversmes tiesa*') can declare provisions of statutes or other legal acts as void. The Supreme Court ('*Augstākā tiesa*') is dealing with cases as an instance of cassation in civil, criminal and administrative cases.

---

4. It should be noted that between 1 Jul. 1941–13 Oct. 1944 Latvia was under German occupation and there was specific regulation of governance and laws, See also Lēbers, D. A. (ed.), *Latvijas tiesību vēsture (1914-2000)* 49–367 (Rīga, Fonds Latvijas Vēsture, 2000).
5. Taube, C., *Constitutionalism in Estonia, Latvia and Lithuania. A study in comparative constitutional law* 46–55 (Upsala, Iustus Förlag 2001).
6. Rodiņa, A. & Pleps, J., *Constitutionalism in Latvia: Reality and Developments. New Millennium Constitutionalism: Paradigms of Reality and Challenges* 432 (Yerevan: NJHAR 2013).
7. Constitutional Court, Case No. 2007-10-0102, 29 Nov. 2007.
8. On 1 May 2004 Latvia became a Member State of the EU. Latvia joined the Euro area on 1 Jan. 2014.

The Constitutional Court of Latvia, by exploring different methods of interpretation,[9] *inter alia*, historic, evolutionary and teleological methods, has opened the possibility of adjusting the text of the *Satversme* to changing socio-political circumstances. The Constitutional Court has indicated that 'the *Satversme* is a short, laconic but at the same time a complicated document'.[10] So the specific codification style of the *Satversme*, which could be characterized as extreme brevity or textual laconism, is principally different from the expanded political declarations or detailed technical regulation typical of contemporary constitutions.[11]

Principles are applied on the basis of the same methodology as written norms. The main principles of the constitutional order of the Republic of Latvia are: the principle of State sovereignty, the principle of a democratic republic, the principle of the rule of law, the principle of a socially responsible State, and the principle of nation State and the principle of people sovereignty.[12]

---

9. Constitutional Court, Case No. 2000-03-01, 30 Aug. 2000, Constitutional Court, Case No. 2002-04-03, 22 Oct. 2002, Constitutional Court, Case No. 2006-04-01, 8 Nov. 2006, para. 15.3, Constitutional Court, Case, 2006-05-01, 16 Oct. 2006, para. 16, See also Pleps, J. *Satversmes iztulkošana.* (Rīga, Latvijas Vēstnesis, 2012), pp. 214–218.
10. Constitutional Court, Case No. 2005-12-0103, 16 Dec. 2005, para. 17.
11. Rodiņa, A. & Pleps, J., *Constitutionalism in Latvia: Reality and Developments. New Millennium Constitutionalism: Paradigms of Reality and Challenges* 432 (Yerevan: NJHAR, 2013).
12. *Ibid.*, pp. 439–442.

Preface

General Introduction

§1. Constitutional History

1. Before Latvia had exercised its right to self-determination it was part of both Czarist Russia and Germany.

2. In July 1917, the board of the Vidzeme Provisional Land Council (*Vidzemes pagaidu zemes padome*) summoned a conference to discuss the issue of the autonomy of Latvia. Fifty delegates from ten most important non-governmental organizations participated in the conference. They passed a resolution that provided that the Latvian people have a right to self-determination.[13]

3. Between 16 December 1917 and 19 December 1917, the Latvian Provisional National Council (*Latviešu pagaidu nacionālās padome*) adopted several acts regarding the future of Latvia.[14] The Council was against any division of the territory of Latvia and particularly against annexation or a joining of Kurzeme or all of Latvia to Germany. It also declared that Latvia should consist of Vidzeme, Kurzeme and Latgale as an autonomous entity within Russia. In the second sitting of the Latvian Provisional National Council, which took place in Petrograd on 15–18 January 1918, the decisive step was taken on the way to the independence of Latvia.[15] The tasks of the Latvian Provisional National Council were continued by the Latvian People's Council (*Latvijas Tautas Padome*).

4. On 18 November 1918, the Latvian People's Council proclaimed the independence of the Republic of Latvia.[16] The Latvian People's Council in the Proclamation Act concluded the stage of preparations for the statehood of Latvia, which had been initiated in the nineteenth century. During this period, the claim of the

13. Dišlers, K. *Ievads Latvijas valststiesību zinātnē.* (Rīga, A. Gulbis, 1930), pp. 56–59; Lēbers, D. A. (ed.), *Latvijas tiesību vēsture (1914-2000).* (Rīga, Fonds Latvijas Vēsture, 2000), pp. 147–148. See also Constitutional Court, Case No. 2007-10-0102, 29 Nov. 2007.
14. Constitutional Court, Case No. 2007-10-0102, 29 Nov. 2007, para. 18.3.
15. On details of the historical changes by German and Russian rule in Latvia preceding proclamation of independence, See also Lēbers, D. A. (ed.), *Latvijas tiesību vēsture (1914-2000).* (Rīga, Fonds Latvijas Vēsture, 2000), pp. 37–142.
16. The Latvian People's Council was formed on the basis of the Latvian Provisional National Council and Democratic Bloc by uniting representatives of Latvian political parties: Constitutional Court, Case No. 2007-10-0102, 29 Nov. 2007, paras 18.3 and 19.

Latvian people for broader rights developed into the idea of a national State. In the Proclamation Act, the Latvian People's Council declared:

> Latvia – united within the ethnographic borders (Kurzeme, Vidzeme and Latgale) – is an independent, democratically-republican State, the Constitution and relations with the foreign States of which shall be established by the Constitutional Assembly in the immediate future that is to be summoned on the basis of general, direct, equal, secret and proportional ballot by both genders.[17]

5. The period from the proclamation of independence until Latvia constituted itself as a state lasted from 1918 to 1920. The Latvian People's Council adopted its Political Platform on 17 November 1918. It was the first act of constitutional rank in Latvia. It was incomplete and drafted in a hurry. However, it was the first document which proclaimed Latvia as an independent republic, provided that it should be democratic, and that its institutions should be elected. The Platform also made provision to summon a Constitutional Assembly (*Satversmes Sapulce*).[18] It entrusted the People's Council with the appointment of a Provisional Government. The document was considered as transitional until the first Constitutional Assembly could be elected and subsequently adopt a Latvian Constitution proper.

6. De facto independence of Latvia was recognized by the United Kingdom (11 November 1918) and by Germany (26 November 1918). De facto activities of the Provisional Government were fragmented because of the presence of German and Russian military forces.[19]

7. Although the political situation was not stable, the Law on the Election of the Constitutional Assembly was adopted on 19 August 1919.[20] Voting rights were granted to everyone aged 21 and resident in Latvia. In order to organize elections, the Law on Citizenship was adopted on 23 August 1919.[21] The first elections took place on 17 and 18 April 1920 after the battles of the Latvian war of independence had been fought. On 1 May 1920, the Constitutional Assembly of Latvia started its activities. The main task for the Constitutional Assembly was to draft the *Satversme*. In order to fix the main principles of constitutional law, the Constitutional Assembly adopted two temporary legislative acts: the Declaration on the State of Latvia (27 May 1920) and the Transition Provisions on Latvian State Order (1 June 1920).[22]

---

17. *Ibid.*, para. 17.
18. On critical comments to the competence of the People's Council and counter-arguments See Lēbers, D. A. (ed.), *Latvijas tiesību vēsture (1914-2000).* (Rīga, Fonds Latvijas Vēsture, 2000), pp. 153–154.
19. Andersons, E. *Latvijas vēsture.* Ārpolitika. 1920–1940, Vol. I (Stockholm, Daugava, 1982), pp. 11–390.
20. Law on Elections to the Constitutional Assembly of 27 Sep. 1919.
21. Law on Citizenship of 23 Aug. 1919.
22. Lēbers, D. A. (ed.), *Latvijas tiesību vēsture (1914-2000).* (Rīga, Fonds Latvijas Vēsture, 2000). It should be noted that the Transition Provisions contained also provisions on human rights and freedoms.

8. Therefore, the formation of Latvia took place between 1918 and 1920 by a chain of events that started with the proclamation of the Republic of Latvia on 18 November 1918 and ended with adoption of the Declaration on the State of Latvia on 27 May 1920. Latvia received a wide support from foreign States. Independence from Russia and Germany was defended in the Battles for Independence.[23] The Peace Treaty between Russia and Latvia was concluded on 11 August 1920 by which Russia recognized the independence of Latvia.

9. Initial proposals provided that the *Satversme* should consist of two parts: a general system of the organization of governance and a part on human rights and freedoms. However, due to political disagreement on several provisions contained in the second part, only the first part was adopted.[24] The *Satversme* was adopted almost unanimously (with five abstentions) on 15 February 1922. It consisted of seven chapters and eighty-eight articles: general provisions, *Saeima*, State President, Cabinet of Ministers, Legislation, Courts, and State Audit.[25] The main emphasis was placed on the parliamentary republic: the *Saeima* was allocated higher rank in comparison to other institutions.[26] For instance, the *Saeima* has a power to elect and to dismiss the State President while the State President could dissolve the *Saeima* only by holding a referendum. The Cabinet of Ministers is responsible to the *Saeima*. The *Saeima* could also amend the *Satversme*, except for those articles laying a foundation for Latvia as a parliamentary republic – for which a referendum would have to be organized.[27]

10. The *Satversme* entered into force on 7 November 1922 and remained so until 15 May 1934, when an authoritarian regime was introduced after a coup. By introducing an emergency situation after a coup *Satversme* was suspended and after a coup *Saeima* was dissolved. The emergency situation was preserved until 15 February 1938. As a result of the coup all political parties were banned; no strikes and demonstrations were allowed, and voting rights were suspended. It lasted until after a coup occupation by the USSR in 1940.

11. On 23 August 1939, the USSR and Germany signed the Treaty of Non-Aggression and attached a secret additional protocol (the Molotov – Ribbentrop Pact). The secret protocol distinguished the spheres of interests of both parties and provided for 'territorially political rearrangements' in the Eastern Europe. According to it, the territory of Latvia was included in the sphere of interest of the

---

23. Constitutional Court, Case No. 2007-10-0102, 29 Nov. 2007, para. 19.2.
24. Lēbers, D. A. (ed.), *Latvijas tiesību vēsture (1914-2000).* (Rīga, Fonds Latvijas Vēsture, 2000), pp. 165–175.
25. Since most of the articles are preserved until present they will be discussed in detail under relevant chapters in this book.
26. Lēbers, D. A. (ed.), *Latvijas tiesību vēsture (1914-2000).* (Rīga, Fonds Latvijas Vēsture, 2000), p. 173.
27. The role of the *Saeima* became even stronger after four referenda organized before occupation failed because of lack quorum. See Lēbers, D. A. (ed.), *Latvijas tiesību vēsture (1914-2000).* (Rīga, Fonds Latvijas Vēsture, 2000), p. 174. At the same time there were non-implemented provisions – the ones on the Constitutional Court.

USSR.[28] Following this agreement Soviet forces were deployed in the territory of Latvia and the existence of the State of Latvia de facto was stopped on 17 June 1940.[29] The Constitutional Court of Latvia in its Judgment No. 2007-10-0102 analysed various bilateral, multilateral, customary norms as well as more recent rulings by international tribunals, doctrine, and International Law Commission (ILC) opinions. It concluded that: (i) the USSR unlawfully used force against Latvia, namely committing aggression in breach of international treaty rules; (ii) the USSR intervened in the internal affairs of Latvia, in breach of international treaty rules; and (iii) the USSR carried out an unlawful occupation of Latvia following the unlawful aggression. Latvia was incorporated into the Soviet Union in 1940 as a result of procedures which had the superficial appearance of a voluntary union, but which in reality amounted to a forced absorption by the Soviet Union: annexation.[30]

12. A USSR-friendly government took office on 21 June 1940. After adoption of the *Saeima* Election Law on 4 July 1940, elections were held on 14–15 July 1940. Only a few lists were registered. On 21 July 1940, after the coup, People's *Saeima* unanimously passed a declaration on joining the USSR.[31] The Latvian 'request' was accepted by the Supreme Council of the USSR on 5 August 1940 and the Constitution of the Latvian Soviet Socialist Republic (hereinafter 'SSR') was adopted on 25 August 1940.[32] No referendum was organized pursuant to the *Satversme*. Therefore, after the coup *Satversme* continued to be in force de iure but not de facto. While being one of the republics of the USSR, Latvia was governed by both the Constitution of the USSR and the Constitution of the Latvian SSR.

13. Claims to Latvian State continuity and the illegality of Soviet occupation were maintained by Latvians in exile.[33] The ambassadors residing abroad informed their host states that the annexation of Latvia was contrary to the *Satversme*. On 13 March and 3 April 1948, exiled judges of the highest judicial institution of Latvia – senators of the Latvian Senate – delivered an opinion on the illegality of the USSR actions on the basis of international law as well as the *Satversme*.[34]

---

28. Constitutional Court, Case No. 2007-10-0102, 29 Nov. 2007, para. 22.
29. *For details* See Constitutional Court, Case No. 2007-10-0102, 29 Nov. 2007, paras 24–27.
30. Jennings, R. & Watts, A (eds), *Oppenheim's International Law*. vol. I, 193 (9th ed. London: Longman 1992). It is recognized in international law that a request for annexation or intervention made by the puppet government of an admitted State is without international validity. The events that took place in the Baltic States in 1940 are to be considered from this perspective: Crawford, J., *Creation of States* 80 (New York: Oxford U. Inc., 2006).
31. *For details* See Constitutional Court, Case No. 2007-10-0102, 29 Nov. 2007, para. 28.
32. It should be noted that Constitution of the LSSR was not applied during occupation by Nazi Germany 1941–1945. At that time laws which existed prior to USSR occupation were applied as far as they complied with German interests or were not amended or repealed after 1 Jul. 1941, but laws adopted under the USSR regime were declared void. *For details* See Lēbers, D. A. (ed.), *Latvijas tiesību vēsture (1914-2000)*. (Rīga, Fonds Latvijas Vēsture, 2000).
33. Lerhis, A. *Latvijas Republikas ārlietu dienests. 1918-1941*. (Rīga Latvijas vēstures institūta apgāds, 2005), pp. 255–279.
34. Constitutional Court, Case No. 2007-10-0102, 29 Nov. 2007, para. 33.1–33.2.

14. Germany treated the Molotov – Ribbentrop Pact as void since 1 September 1939 by decision adopted in 1989. On 24 December 1989, the Second USSR People's Representatives' Congress passed a Resolution 'On the Political and Legal Assessment of the Treaty of Non-Aggression of Germany and USSR of 1939'. The Congress disapproved the fact that a 'secret additional protocol' was signed with Germany, and recognized this protocol as legally unsubstantiated and invalid as of the day of its signing.[35]

15. Adherence to the principle of State continuity was preferred and incorporated into the Declaration of Independence adopted by the Supreme Council of the Latvian SSR on 4 May 1990.[36] The Declaration renewed the main articles of the *Satversme* and established a transitional period until full recovery of independence. The Declaration was supported by 138 out of 201 MPs and by the international community.[37] The Supreme Council of Latvia passed the Constitutional Law when reacting to the attempted coup d'etat in the USSR on 19 August 1991, and declared the de facto restoration of independence of the Republic of Latvia.[38]

16. Upon the restoration of independence, Latvia reiterated that Soviet occupation had been illegal and that Latvia had never been part of the USSR de jure. This claim was based on the principle of State continuity, that is, the continuity or identity of States as legal entities under international law. It required the articulation of a set of claims in accordance with the applicable international legal rules and procedures when referring to statehood (*ex iniuria ius non oritur*).[39]

17. The Declaration of Independence established the de facto renewal of Latvian independence, thus confirming the doctrine of Latvian State continuity. 'The State continuity of Latvia […] is the backbone of the entire body of Latvian constitutional law.'[40] Indeed, this approach has been preserved in both internal and external relations.[41] The constitutional institutions of Latvia justify their position by the fact

35. *Ibid.*, paras 22.1, 22.2 and 22.3. See also Loeber. D. A, *Legal Consequences of the Molotov – Ribbentrop Pact for the Baltic States on the Obligation 'to Overcome the Problems Inherited from the Past'* Vol. 1, 131 (London, The Hague: Baltic Yearbook of International Law 2001).
36. The adoption of the Declaration was preceded by adoption of two decisions. On 28 Jul. 1989, the *Saeima* adopted the Declaration on the Sovereignty of the Latvian State. This Declaration proclaimed the supremacy of the laws of the Latvian SSR over the laws of the USSR: *Decision on Declaration on the Sovereignty of the Latvian State*, Official Reporter No. 32, 10 Aug. 1989. On 15 Feb. 1990, the Declaration on the Independence of the Latvian State was adopted. It authorized the establishment of a working group that would prepare restoration of independence of Latvia: *Decision on Declaration on the Independence of the Latvian State*, Official Reporter No. 9, 1 Mar. 1990.
37. Jundzis, T. *4.maijs. Rakstu, atmiņu un dokumentu krājums par neatkarības deklarāciju.* (Rīga, Fonds Latvijas Vēsture, 2000), pp. 654–658.
38. Both the Declaration and Constitutional Law have been declared as acts of constitutional rank: Constitutional Court, Case No. 2007-10-0102, 29 Nov. 2007, para. 60.1 and 60.2.
39. Ziemele, I., *State Continuity and Nationality: The Baltic States and Russia. Past, Present and Future as Defined by International Law* 118 (Leiden: Martinus Nijhoff Publishers, 2005). See also Constitutional Court, Case No. 2007-10-0102, 29 Nov. 2007, para. 32.2.
40. Endziņš, A. *Latvijas konstitūcijas apskats, kas rada šaubas un jautājumus.* (Rīga, Jurista Vārds, 1 May 2005, No. 8).
41. Ziemele, I. *Piezīmes pie sagatavotā lēmuma projekta.* (Rīga, Jurista Vārds, 30 Jan. 2007, No. 5).

that, after the events of 1940, Latvia as a subject of international law had not lost its status.[42]

18. The claim was supported by States which had never recognized Latvia's occupation and annexation as well as international organizations. The unlawful annexation of the Baltic States by the USSR was not recognized by more than fifty other world States, including the US, Germany, France, Italy, Canada, and Japan.[43] Upon restoration of its independence, Latvian claims to the State continuity principle were supported by, *inter alia*, Iceland, Belgium, Canada, Australia, Italy, the US, Estonia, Finland, Hungary, Romania, Chile, Czechoslovakia, and the Netherlands. The EU, the UN Security Council, and the Council of Europe referred to the restoration of the independence and sovereignty lost in 1940.[44]

19. Article 1 of the Declaration of Independence provided for the supremacy of the fundamental principles of international law over national law. Article 8 specified that all residents should be guaranteed human rights which are defined in international human rights instruments. This provision was further strengthened by the Declaration on the Accession of the Republic of Latvia to International Instruments Relating to Human Rights.[45] The Declaration contained a list of fifty-one international human rights instruments to which Latvia acceded, including twenty-three multilateral treaties, declarations, and other instruments of recommendatory character adopted by different international organizations.

20. According to Article 4 of the Declaration of Independence, the legal force of the *Satversme* was suspended until the adoption of the new Constitution, except for Articles 1, 2, 3 and 6 of the *Satversme* which set the constitutional basis for Latvia and could be amended only by the procedure envisaged in Article 77 of *Satversme* (by referendum). Article 6 on general, equal, and direct election of the *Saeima*, by secret ballot and by observing principle of proportionality, should have been applied upon the restoration of the institutions of an independent Latvia. Article 6 of the Declaration provided that during the period of transition, acts which were contrary to these Articles of the *Satversme* had to be considered as void.

---

42. Constitutional Court, Case No. 2007-10-0102, 29 Nov. 2007, para. 33.2.
43. William, H.J. & Hough, III, *The Annexation of the Baltic States and Its Effect on the Development of Law Prohibiting Forcible Seizure of Territory*, 6(2) (N.Y. L. Sch. J. Intl. & Comp. L. 391–446. The Parliamentary Assembly of the Council of Europe, in the Resolution of 29 Sep. 1960 No. 189 (1960) on the Situation in the Baltic States.
44. Feldmanis, I., Freimanis, A. A., Lerhis, A & Ziemele, I., *Latvijas valsts Okupacijas gados (1940-1991), Dokumenti par Latvijas valsts starptautisko atzisanu, neatkaribas atjaunosanu un diplomatiskajiem sakariem (1918-1998).* (Rīga, Latvijas arhivistu biedriba, Latvijas Republikas Arlietu ministrija, Latvijas Valsts vestures arhivs, NORDIK, 1999), pp. 127–183, pp. 174–135. See Constitutional Court, Case No. 2007-10-0102, 29 Nov. 2007, para. 34.2.
45. *Declaration on the Accession of the Republic of Latvia to International Instruments Relating to Human Rights*, Official Reporter No. 21, 24 May 1990. *For details* see Mits, M., *European Convention on Human Rights in Latvia. Impact on Legal Doctrine and Application of Legal Norms* 25–27 (Lund, Media Tryck 2010).

21. According to Article 2 on the Law on the Status of the Republic of Latvia (1991), Article 5 of the Declaration of Independence providing for a transition period during which Latvia would restore its independence de facto was declared void. According to Article 1, the *Satversme* became fully effective. As concluded by the Constitutional Court:

> In the elections of the fifth *Saeima* on 5 June 1993, the earlier work of the Supreme Council was accepted as consistent with the interests of the Republic of Latvia and its people. In these elections that were consistent with the requirements of Article 6 of the *Satversme* and standards of democratic elections, the Latvian people did not contest the necessity of restoration of independence of the Republic of Latvia and elected one hundred of its representatives, thus authorising them to continue the process of restoration of the State. Under the norms of the *Satversme*, the elected fifth *Saeima* took over the authority of the Supreme Council. By taking over the authority from the Supreme Council, the fifth *Saeima*, on behalf of the Latvian people, also accepted as legally binding the activities of the Supreme Council that is had carried out since the adoption of the Declaration of Independence in the interests of the Republic of Latvia.[46]

22. Therefore, restoration of de facto legal force of the *Satversme* was gradual, as determined by the existing situation of recovery after an occupation of fifty years. This has not left a significant imprint on further amendments or constitutional reforms.

23. Article 7 of the Declaration of Independence envisaged that a special commission should be established to amend the *Satversme* according to political, economic and social needs existing at the time of the restoration of independence. However, the amendments to the *Satversme* were not made as part of major constitutional reform. Over the years they have been rather incremental and in most cases came as a reaction to sporadic political and social developments, or were of technical nature. For instance, the right to vote was granted to voters who were 18,[47] and the term of convocation of the *Saeima* and State President was extended from three to four years.[48] The *Saeima* has adopted amendments to exclude candidates with dual nationality from running for the post of State President[49] and prolonged the term within which the President can refuse to sign a law and return it to the *Saeima* for reconsideration.[50]

46. Constitutional Court, Case No. 2007-10-0102, 29 Nov. 2007, para. 61.3.
47. Amendment to the *Satversme* of the Republic of Latvia, Art. 8, 27 Jan. 1994.
48. Amendment to the *Satversme* of the Republic of Latvia, Art. 10 and Art. 35, 4 Dec. 1997. The dates when the newly elected *Saeima* should convene and the term of convocation in cases of extraordinary elections have been amended accordingly (Arts 11 and 13). The same approach was followed by amending Art. 39 extending the maximum term in office for the State President from six to eight years.
49. Amendment to the *Satversme* of the Republic of Latvia, Art. 37, 4 Dec. 1997.
50. The term had been prolonged from seven to ten days. Amendment to the *Satversme* of the Republic of Latvia, Arts 69, 71, 72, 23 Sep. 2004.

24. In 2009, Latvia was hit by an economic crisis – one of the major systemic banks became bankrupt and over-expenditure in the State budget led to growing unemployment and the insolvency of many companies and private households. This generated social turbulence, which facilitated the adoption of amendments in the *Satversme*. According to the amendments to Article 14 of the *Satversme*, one-tenth of voters can initiate a referendum to dissolve the *Saeima*. The article further provides for quorum and when a referendum can take place. Procedural requirements on summoning the newly elected *Saeima* have been further particularized by amending Article 49 of the *Satversme*.[51]

25. Since elections of officials of higher rank had become non-transparent in the *Saeima*, MPs supported further amendments in the *Satversme* providing for an open voting procedure for the election of the judges of the Constitutional Court. According to amended Article 85 of the *Satversme*, judges of the Constitutional Court have to be elected by an open vote by a majority of MPs.[52]

26. Article 6(2) of the Declaration of Independence provided that disputes on the application of laws during the transition period should be resolved by the Constitutional Court. The idea of the Constitutional Court materialized after amendments to the *Satversme* were adopted in 1996.[53] The Court is entrusted with the review of compliance by laws with the provisions of the *Satversme* as well as other cases specified in the Law on the Constitutional Court. Also provided is that the Court can declare laws as well as other norms null and void. Judges of the Constitutional Court are elected by a majority of MPs. Judgments adopted by the Constitutional Court over the years serve as an important source for the interpretation and application of various provisions of the *Satversme*. The Court has also introduced a number of general principles which are derived from the articles of the *Satversme*.[54]

27. Several significant amendments to the *Satversme* were made in 1998.[55] First, Article 4 was amended to provide that Latvian is the State language of Latvia. This amendment was made as a compromise solution to reach majority support for the liberalization of the State Language Law. In addition, Article 77 has been amended to include reference to Article 4 among those articles which set the constitutional basis for Latvia. Therefore, Article 4 can be amended only by organizing an obligatory referendum. The status of the Latvian language was further strengthened by adopting amendments to the *Satversme* in 2002.[56] According to those amendments, MPs when taking up their duties should take an oath in which they, *inter alia*, promise to protect Latvian as the only State language. The working language in the *Saeima* and local governments should be Latvian only. Everyone has the right to receive an answer in Latvian from State or local institutions.

51. Amendment to the *Satversme* of the Republic of Latvia, Arts 14, 49, 8 Apr. 2009. Before the amendments the right to initiate dissolution of the *Saeima* was given only to the State President (Art. 49).
52. Amendment to the *Satversme*, Arts 85, 19 Sep. 2013.
53. Amendment to the *Satversme*, Art. 85, 5 Jun. 1996.
54. Cross reference Part I Ch. 2 and Ch. 5.
55. Amendment to the *Satversme*, Arts 4 and 77, as well as Ch. VIII, 5 Jun. 1996.
56. Amendment to the *Satversme*, Arts 18, 21, 101 and 104, 30 Apr. 2002.

28. Second, the *Satversme* was supplemented by Chapter VIII which includes twenty-eight articles on fundamental rights and freedoms. As a result of the adoption of Chapter VIII the Constitutional Law on the Rights and Obligations of a Citizen and a Person was repealed.[57] The adoption of Chapter VIII was preceded by a lengthy scholarly debate on the general approach to the hierarchy of Constitutional Laws in the Latvian legal system. It was only in 1997 that it was agreed that a Constitutional Law should be ranked between the *Satversme* and ordinary laws.[58] At the same time it was acknowledged that human rights in a modern democratic State should be protected at the constitutional level. Chapter VIII has become an important tool for human rights protection. It includes provisions on civil, political, social and economic rights. According to Article 89 of the *Satversme* the State shall recognize and protect fundamental human rights in accordance with this Constitution, laws and international agreements binding upon Latvia. The Constitutional Court has developed over the years substantive jurisprudence providing for the interpretation of Articles included in Chapter VIII.[59]

29. In 2003, the *Satversme* was amended to provide for procedures to accede to the EU.[60] The amendments were preceded by a scholarly debate whether amendments are required in Article 2 of the *Satversme* which provides that sovereign power is vested in the people of Latvia. Transfer of certain sovereign powers to the EU was questioned.

30. The *Saeima* opted for minimal amendments to the *Satversme* which provided for the procedure to be followed upon accession to the EU and in cases of fundamental changes in the requirements for membership in the EU. According to the amendments in Article 68 of the *Satversme*, the powers can be delegated to international institutions with an objective to strengthen democracy. This requires an affirmative vote of two-thirds of the MP, with two-thirds of the MPs being present. Membership in the EU should be decided by referendum upon initiative of the *Saeima*. In cases when half of the MPs consider that fundamental changes in the conditions of membership should take place, these changes shall be confirmed by referendum. In accordance with Article 79, membership in the EU and substantive changes in the membership conditions are confirmed by referendum if at least half of the voters who participated in the last *Saeima* elections vote and a majority of

57. Constitutional Law on the Rights and Obligations of a Citizen and a Person. Official Reporter No. 4, 30 Jan. 1992. An English translation is available in the *Latvian Human Rights Quarterly*, No. 1, 1997, 93–101. The Constitutional Law contained forty-four articles drafted along the lines of international human rights instruments. However, its effective implementation was hampered. There are two main reasons usually cited. First, the Constitutional Law was adopted in a post-Soviet environment when human rights instruments were treated as declaratory documents. Second, there was confusion caused by legal status of the Constitutional Law and courts were hesitant to apply it. Mits, M., *European Convention on Human Rights in Latvia. Impact on Legal Doctrine and Application of Legal Norms* 31–32 (Lund, Media Tryck 2010).
58. For detailed analysis of different options and arguments in favour of the present approach see Mits, M., *European Convention on Human Rights in Latvia. Impact on Legal Doctrine and Application of Legal Norms* 38–39 (Lund: Media Tryck 2010).
59. See also Part IV.
60. Amendment to the *Satversme* of the Republic of Latvia, Arts 68, 79, 8 May 2003.

votes are in favour of membership or substantial changes in the terms regarding such membership.[61]

31. The *Satversme* has been also amended on other occasions to comply with EU law. Article 98 of the *Satversme* was amended to implement Framework decisions on the European Arrest Warrant. The Article provides that Latvian citizen can be extradited in accordance with international agreements confirmed by the *Saeima* and if the human rights provided in the *Satversme* are observed. Article 101 of the *Satversme* was amended allowing EU citizens to vote in local elections and to take part in the work of local governments.[62]

32. Certain other amendments were made in response to national political developments. When reacting to the practice that the Cabinet of Ministers adopted an increasing number of regulations with the force of law, the *Saeima* decided to repeal Article 81 of the *Satversme*. Article 81 allowed the Cabinet to adopt between *Saeima*'s sessions regulations having force of law. These regulations were hierarchically equal to laws. These regulations lost their force if they were not submitted to the *Saeima* within three days of the next *Saeima* session.[63]

33. As a reaction to the LGBT Pride Movement, the *Saeima* rushed to amend Article 110 of the *Satversme*. According to these amendments, the State protects and supports marriage (as a union between a man and a woman), family, parents, and the rights of the child. Therefore, marriage between a man and a woman is the only form of marriage protected by the *Satversme*.[64]

34. The *Satversme* has been supplemented in 2014 with a Preamble. The draft of the Preamble has been debated among the scholars as well as MPs. The main idea of the Preamble is to strengthen the nation State idea of Latvia and the fundamentals of constitutional values. On 19 June 2014, the *Saeima*, with sixty-nine parliamentarians voting in favour and twenty-eight voting against, adopted amendments to the *Satversme* in the final reading to expand the constitution with a Preamble.[65]

35. The Preamble of the *Satversme* reads:

> The people of Latvia, in freely elected Constitutional Assembly, have adopted the following State Constitution: The State of Latvia, proclaimed on 18 November 1918, has been established by uniting historical Latvian lands and on the basis of the unwavering will of the Latvian nation to have its own State and its inalienable right of self-determination in order to guarantee the existence and development of the Latvian nation, its language and culture throughout the centuries, to ensure freedom and promote welfare of the people of

61. For details, including interpretation of the Constitutional Court, see Part II Ch. 6 s. 2.
62. Amendment to the *Satversme* of the Republic of Latvia, Arts 98, 101, 7 Oct. 2004.
63. Amendment to the *Satversme* of the Republic of Latvia, Art. 81, 3 May 2007.
64. Amendment to the *Satversme* of the Republic of Latvia, Art. 110, 15 Oct. 2005.
65. Amendment to the *Satversme* of the Republic of Latvia, 19 Jun. 2014.

Latvia and each individual. The people of Latvia won their State in the War of Liberation. They consolidated the system of government and adopted the Constitution in a freely elected Constitutional Assembly. The people of Latvia did not recognise the occupation regimes, resisted them and regained their freedom by restoring national independence on 4 May 1990 on the basis of continuity of the State. They honour their freedom fighters, commemorate victims of foreign powers, condemn the Communist and Nazi totalitarian regimes and their crimes. Latvia as democratic, socially responsible and national state is based on the rule of law and on respect for human dignity and freedom; it recognises and protects fundamental human rights and respects ethnic minorities. The people of Latvia protect their sovereignty, national independence, territory, territorial integrity and democratic system of government of the State of Latvia. Since ancient times, the identity of Latvia in the European cultural space has been shaped by Latvian and Liv traditions, Latvian folk wisdom, the Latvian language, universal human and Christian values. Loyalty to Latvia, the Latvian language as the only official language, freedom, equality, solidarity, justice, honesty, work ethic and family are the foundations of a cohesive society. Each individual takes care of oneself, one's relatives and the common good of society by acting responsibly toward other people, future generations, the environment and nature. While acknowledging its equal status in the international community, Latvia protects its national interests and promotes sustainable and democratic development of a united Europe and the world.

§2. Profile of the Form of Government

36. Article 3 of the *Satversme* provides, 'The territory of the State of Latvia, within the borders established by international agreements, consists of Vidzeme, Latgale, Kurzeme and Zemgale.' This provision defines the territory of Latvia and also mentions the ethnographic units (regions) that constitute the territory of Latvia.[66]

37. The drafting documents reveal that there was a clear idea of which territories should be included into the territory of Latvia.[67] Thus, for example, in the Proclamation Act, the Latvian People's Council declared, 'Latvia – united within the ethnographic borders (Kurzeme, Vidzeme and Latgale) – is an independent, democratically-republican State … .'[68] Therefore, Latvia was established on the basis of the self-determination of peoples inhabiting the historically ethnographic regions of Latvia.[69]

38. At the beginning of the twentieth century, the ethnographic regions of Latvia did not form a single administrative entity, but were part of three different provinces

66. See also General introduction s. 2.
67. Constitutional Court, Case No. 2007-10-0102, 29 Nov. 2007, para. 20.3.
68. Constitutional Court, Case No. 2007-10-0102, 29 Nov. 2007, para. 17.
69. Latvijas pilsoņiem! Pagaidu Valdības Vēstnesis, 14 Dec. 1918, No. 1. See also Constitutional Court, Case No. 2007-10-0102, 29 Nov. 2007, para. 20.

of Russia. The Kurzeme province included ten districts; the Vidzeme province, four Latvian and five Estonian districts; the Vitebsk province, three Latvian and eight Byelorussian and Russian districts. Such a division of territories into different provinces of the Russian Empire reflected historical struggles of superpowers over the territory of Latvia.

39. Article 3 of the *Satversme* takes note that these regions constitute the State of Latvia within those borders that were established in international treaties with neighbouring States. Thus, the reference in Article 3 of the *Satversme* to international agreements is used to establish normatively the borders provided for in border treaties.[70]

40. Article 3 of the *Satversme* provides for the basic principles of the Latvian State order and the form of government.[71] The Republic of Latvia is a unitary state. This has been confirmed by the Constitutional Court.[72] The same position is held by legal scholars.[73] However, it should be noted that there had also been proposals for a so-called Baltic Federation and Baltic United States.[74] This was a minority and unpopular position.

41. The Constitutional Court has introduced the concept of 'newly added territory' or 'newly acquired territory'. This concept is applicable to territories which were acquired as a result of negotiations on the Peace Treaty between Latvia and Russia on 11 August 1920. The inclusion of these territories in the territory of Latvia was linked to the success of negotiations on concluding the border treaty rather than uniting all parts of Latvia.[75]

42. The indivisibility of Latvia is considered to be a value to be protected by the *Satversme*. Since 2012 Article 83 of the Criminal Law provides for criminal charges in cases where a person acts against territorial integrity or seeks to effect the secession of parts of Latvia.

43. At the national level, governance is organized by the people and the *Saeima*.[76]

44. The *Saeima* has the power to form or establish the territorial divisions of Latvia and to define the status of different local organs. The *Saeima* establishes the

70. Constitutional Court, Case No. 2007-10-0102, 29 Nov. 2007, para. 42.3.
71. *Ibid.*
72. Decision of 20 Jan. 2009 by the Constitutional Court on Terminating Judicial Proceedings in Case No. 2008-08-0306, para. 16.
73. Balodis, R., *Latvia. Encyclopedia of World Constitutions. Volume II* 513–519 (G. Robbers ed. U.S. Facts on File 2007).
74. Cielēns, F. *Baltijas federācija.* (Latvju Ziņas, 10 Dec. 1947, No. 95), Pleps, J. *Baltijas vienotības ideja Latvijas valststiesiskajā domā* (Rīga, Jurista Vārds. 31 Jul. 2012, No. 31).
75. Constitutional Court, Case No. 2007-10-0102, 29 Nov. 2007, para. 50.
76. See Part II Ch. 4.

general regulations for the functioning of local governments, defines their competence and relations with the Cabinet of Ministers and ministries.[77] Latvia's administrative territorial structure consists of 119 units, the administration of which is implemented by local governments within the limits of their jurisdiction. There are local governments for the 9 largest cities and 110 regions in Latvia.[78]

45. Local governments are elected by citizens and the EU citizens residing in the respective administrative territory. The Constitutional Court has concluded that the principle of local government is derived from the principle of the democratic State, enshrined in Article 1 of the *Satversme* which 'comprises the minimum set of requirements with regard to organisation of local self-governance in a democratic State based on the rule of law'.[79]

§3. State Population

46. The Latvian population has always been multi-national. However, it should be noted that during the Soviet occupation, a large group of immigrants from former Soviet republics arrived in Latvia. Since restoration of its independence, Latvia has adhered to the State continuity principle which resulted in 673,398 people, or 28.2% of the total population being left in a legal limbo – persons with undetermined status. They were not entitled to Latvian citizenship and they had not opted for citizenship of another State, for instance Russia.[80]

47. By the beginning of the 1990s, the Lativan nation had almost become a minority, some 52%, with Russians and other non-Latvian nationalities comprising the other 48% of the population.[81] By comparison, in 1935, Latvians had comprised 75.5% of the total population. This made Latvians feel insecure about their State and identity.

48. Lack of coordination in domestic legislation among Russia, the various newly-independent CIS States, and the Baltic States presented an acute problem. Moreover, Russian military personnel (50,000–80,000 military personnel with more

77. Law on Local Governments of 19 May 1994.
78. Law on Administrative Territories and Populated Areas of 18 Dec. 2008.
79. Constitutional Court, Case No. 2009-04-06, 3 Nov. 2009, para. 7.4.
80. They could register as Russian citizens under the Citizenship Law of the Russian Federation, 28 Nov. 1991. According to Art. 13(1) all former USSR citizens could register as Russian citizens if they permanently resided in Russia, except if they explicitly refused acquisition of citizenship. Thus, Russia did not take over the whole responsibility as being successor to the occupying power but limited its responsibility to permanent residents only referring to them as compatriots. Another possible solution could have been to conclude an agreement with Russia. However, that was not politically possible.
81. Other sources suggest that the number of Latvians declined from 77% to 52%, while Eastern Slavs increased from 12% to 42%. See Report for the Parliamentary Assembly by Ole Espersen 'On the Application by Latvia for Membership of the Council of Europe' (Doc 7169, 6 Oct. 1994), available at http://assembly.coe.int/nw/xml/XRef/X2H-Xref-ViewHTML.asp?FileID=8059&lang=en, accessed 9 Feb. 2012.

than 22,000 retired Soviet military officers) remained in Latvia pending an inter-state withdrawal agreement, some of whom resorted to fictitious marriages and forged documents in an attempt to regularize their status in Latvia.[82] Initially the residence rights of non-citizens were regulated by the Law on the Entry and Residence of Foreigners and Stateless Persons which entered into force on 2 July 1992. Practice varied from one administrative district to another and the 1992 Law was applied retroactively.[83]

49. In order to secure the status of Soviet era settlers, Latvia created a specific category of persons, namely 'non-citizens'.[84] This was done in an attempt to strike a balance between the State continuity principles and to offer Soviet era settlers certain status. Therefore, Latvia introduced the special status of 'non-citizen' in 1995 by adopting the Law on the Status of Former Soviet Citizens who are not Citizens of Latvia or any Other State ('Former USSR Citizens Law').[85] The Law aimed to secure the rights of Soviet era settlers and to avoid criticism for creating stateless persons.[86] Initially, this status was seen as temporary because it was assumed that non-citizens would naturalize or eventually apply for citizenship of another State.[87]

Table 1 The Population of Latvia as of 1 July 2013

	Citizens	*Non-Citizens*	*Foreigners, Refugees or Stateless Individuals*	*Total*
Latvians	1,302,240	781	1,105	1,304,126
Russians	360,350	190,828	38,851	590,029
Byelorussians	30,579	39,483	4,896	74,958
Ukrainians	18,526	28,157	6,233	52,916
Poles	37,640	9,917	1,403	48,960

82. Latvia hosted the Soviet Army's Baltic region headquarters. Muižnieks, N., *Government Policy and the Russian Minority* in *Latvian-Russian Relations: Domestic and International Dimensions* 11–21, 15 (Muižnieks Nils ed., Rīga: LU Apgāds 2006); and Muižnieks, N., *Russian Foreign Policy Towards 'Compatriots' in Latvia* 119–130, 120 in the same volume.
83. Ziemele, I., *State Continuity and Nationality: The Baltic States and Russia. Past, Present and Future as Defined by International Law* 160–164 (Leiden: Martinus Nijhoff Publishers 2005).
84. For details on the status of non-citizen and attempts to foster their naturalization see the country report on Latvia available at http://eudo-citizenship.eu/docs/CountryReports/Latvia.pdf, accessed 13 Oct. 2013. Kruma, K., *Latvian Integration Policy: Lost in Translation* in *A Re-definition of Belonging? Language and Integration Tests in Europe* 241–270 (van Oers Ricky, Ersbøll Eva & Kostakopoulou Dora eds, Leiden: Martinus Nijhoff Publishers, 2010).
85. See also Part III.
86. See Art. 49 of the IV Geneva Convention Relative to the Protection of Civilian Persons in Time of War (1949). The article prohibits the occupying power from deporting or transferring parts of its own civilian population into the territory it occupies. Arts 85(4)(a) and 85 of Additional Protocol I and Art. 8(2)(b)(viii) of the ICC statute designate the transfer by the Occupying Power of parts of its own civilian population into the territory it occupies as a war crime. At the same time Latvia is a party to the Convention on the Reduction of Statelessness.
87. Kruma, K., *EU Citizenship, Nationality and Migrant Status. An Ongoing challenge* (Leiden: Martinus Nijhoff Publishers 2014).

	Citizens	*Non-Citizens*	*Foreigners, Refugees or Stateless Individuals*	*Total*
Lithuanians	18,111	7,501	2,630	28,242
Roma	7,815	417	59	8,291
German	2,200	1,133	1,589	4,922
Armenian	1,178	982	547	2,707
Estonians	1,375	425	483	2,283
Other (incl. undeclared or unknown)	49,178	10,902	11,548	71,628
TOTAL	**1,829,192**	**290,526**	**69,344**	**2,189,062**

Source: Office of Citizenship and Migration Affairs, http://www.pmlp.gov.lv/lv/assets/documents/statistika/IRD_01_07_2013/ISVN_Latvija_pec_TTB_VPD.pdf accessed on 27 December October 2013.

50. The Constitutional Court has analysed the adoption of the Former USSR Citizens Law in its historical and political context and has concluded that the opinion is unfounded that Latvia had a duty to grant nationality automatically to those individuals and their descendants who had never been Latvian nationals and who had arrived during the occupation. The Court acknowledged that the introduction of the status of non-citizen was a complicated political compromise as a result of which a category unknown in international law has been created. In its judgment, the Court defined the status of non-citizen in the following way: the status of non-citizens is not and cannot be considered as a mode of Latvian nationality. However, the rights given to non-citizens and the international obligations which Latvia has undertaken in relation to these persons, signify that the legal link of non-citizens to Latvia is recognized to a certain extent and based on it mutual obligations and rights have emerged.[88] The Constitutional Court therefore confirmed that non-citizens have a legal link with Latvia which entails mutual rights and obligations. Those are, however, different from the rights and obligations of nationals.

51. Latvia has consistently defended its position that non-citizens cannot be qualified as stateless persons and this view has been accepted by international human rights monitoring bodies.[89] For instance, the Human Rights Committee and the Committee on the Elimination of Racial Discrimination have accepted that non-citizens are not stateless persons. At the same time, they have emphasized the need to encourage the naturalization and integration of those persons. Therefore, they

88. Constitutional Court, Case No. 2004-15-0106, 7 Mar. 2005, paras 13 and 17.

89. Ziemele, I., Krūma, K., *Eiropas Savienības pilsonība un Latvijas nepilsoņi*. (Latvijas Vēstnesis, Jurista Vārds, 2003). See, for instance, UN Human Rights Committee, 'Concluding Observations on Latvia' (3 Oct. 1995), UN Doc CCPR/C/79/Add.53, which refers to non-citizens as 'permanent residents'. UN Committee on the Elimination of Racial Discrimination, 'Concluding observations. Latvia' (12 Apr. 2001), UN Doc CERD/304/Add.79 in paras 14 and 23 refers to 'non-citizens'.

have indirectly suggested that non-citizen status cannot become permanent by appealing to the fact that those people have been residing in Latvia for many years, if not their whole lives.[90] The EU Network of Independent Experts on Fundamental Rights has also acknowledged that non-citizens are neither citizens nor aliens. They are also not stateless persons. According to experts they belong to a category of persons unknown in international law.[91] However, the UN High Commissioner for Refugees qualifies non-citizens as stateless persons.[92]

52. There are sporadic initiatives to grant Latvian citizenship automatically or political rights to non-citizens.[93] Upon accession to the EU, the question of granting EU citizenship to non-citizens was raised by left-wing political parties. However, it was never debated in the ruling right-centre government coalitions. Over the years, the status of non-citizen in Latvia has been strengthened and is no longer treated as temporary.[94]

§4. State Language[95]

I. Language Policy

53. The basis for the Latvian Language policy is the State Language Law (1999) and the *Satversme* which, since 1998, has contained an article declaring Latvian the only official language.[96] The drafting of the Language Law was cumbersome since it took place just after the liberalization of the Citizenship Law. International experts

90. See UN Committee on the Elimination of Racial Discrimination, 'Concluding observations. Latvia' (12 Apr. 2001), UN Doc CERD/304/Add.79, paras 12–14, and UN Committee on Elimination of Racial Discrimination, 'Concluding Observations on Latvia' (10 Dec. 2003), UN Doc CERD/C/63/CO/7, paras 12–13. UN Human Rights Committee, 'Consideration of Reports Submitted by States Parties under Article 40 of the Covenant' (1 Dec. 2003), 79th Session, UN Doc CCPR/CO/79/LVA, paras 16–18.
91. Synthesis Report: Conclusions and Recommendations on the Situation of Fundamental Rights in the European Union and its Member States in 2003, 4 Feb. 2004, available at http://www.statewatch.org/news/2004/may/indexperts-synthesis-2003.pdf, accessed on 4 Apr. 2013, 90.
92. See for instance, http://www.unhcr.no/en/News/articles2011/article_110523-latvian-handbook.html, accessed 6 Jun. 2011. For the position of the Council of Europe See Report by Alvaro Gil-Robles, *Commissioner for Human Rights*, on his visit to Latvia, 5–8 Oct. 2003, CommDH(2004)3, 12 Feb. 2004, para. 30, http://ec.europa.eu/justice/fundamental-rights/files/cfr_cdf_synthesisrep2003_en.pdf, accessed 4 Apr. 2013.
93. On the last initiative See; Kruma, K., *Latvia: Comprehensive Citizenship Reform on the Agenda in Parliament and in a Referendum Campaign*, 2 Sep. 2012, available at http://eudo-citizenship.eu/news/citizenship-news/700-latvia-comprehensive-citizenship-reform-on-the-agenda-in-parliament-and-in-a-referendum-campaign-, accessed 8 Apr. 2013. Constitutional Court, Case No. 2013-06-01, 18 Dec. 2013.
94. On rights and status of non-citizens See Part III.
95. The English translation uses the term 'official language'. However, other laws and scholars emphasize that there is important difference between the term 'State language' and 'official language'. Therefore, in Latvian the usual term used is 'State language'. *Latvijas Republikas Satversmes komentāri. Ievads. I nodaļa. Vispārējie noteikumi.* Autoru kolektīvs prof. R. Baloža zinātniskā vadībā. (Rīga, Latvijas Vēstnesis, 2014), pp. 312.
96. Article 4 of the *Satversme*.

from the OSCE, EU and Council of Europe were involved. The Law includes general provisions for the use of Latvian in the public and private sectors. In addition to the Law, regulations also provide for language requirements for different professions. In the private sector, it remains the responsibility of employers to ensure adequate knowledge of the language by employees. If language inspectors establish that a person does not have sufficient knowledge to practice a certain profession, both the employee and the employer are fined.[97]

54. Since Latvia regained its independence, the education system in Latvia has undergone constant changes. Until the mid-1990s two different school systems – Latvian and Russian – existed in Latvia. Each of them had its own curriculum. When the new Language Law came into force, it was acknowledged that the education system had to be adjusted so that all graduates would have equal opportunities in the labour market. Since 1996, in Russian schools only one subject had been taught in Latvian at the elementary school level; two subjects in primary school, and in secondary school, three subjects. In 1999, bilingual education was introduced in primary schools, when each educational institution providing education in the Russian language chose one of the four ethnic minority primary education models developed by the Ministry of Education and Science. The bilingual curriculum had to be implemented in all national minority primary schools by the academic year 2002–2003.[98]

55. Further changes were introduced in the Education Law of February 2004. The new system envisaged that 40% of study time instruction should be in the minority language and 60% (or five subjects) in Latvian. This increase was phased in, starting with grade 10 in 2004, followed by grade 11 in 2005, and grade 12 in 2006. Primary school had to continue with the bilingual curriculum. Out of 1009 general education schools, only 149 had to implement the gradual transfer to 60% teaching in Latvian in 2005. In order to carry out the reform, substantial funds were allocated by the National Program of Latvian Language Training and the Foundation for the Integration of Society.[99]

II. Constitutional Framework

56. According to Article 4 of the *Satversme*, the Latvian language is the State language in the Republic of Latvia.[100] The reference to the Latvian language was

97. Kruma, K., *Latvian Integration Policy: Lost in Translation,* in *A Re-definition of Belonging? Language and Integration Tests in Europe* 241–269 (van Oers Ricky, Ersbøll Eva & Kostakopoulou Dora eds, Leiden: Martinus Nijhoff Publishers 2010).
98. *Ibid.*, pp. 256–257.
99. *Ibid.*, pp. 241–269, p. 257.
100. The English translation uses the term 'official language'. However, other laws and scholars emphasize that there is important difference between the term 'State language' and 'official language'. Therefore, in Latvian the usual term used is 'State language'. *Latvijas Republikas Satversmes komentāri. Ievads. I nodaļa. Vispārējie noteikumi.* Autoru kolektīvs prof. R. Baloža zinātniskā vadībā. (Rīga, Latvijas Vēstnesis, 2014), pp. 312.

inserted in Article 4 on 15 October 1998. One of the main reasons for this amendment was the fact that the Latvian Language Law was liberalized, allowing the use of other languages by people working in the private sector. At the same time Latvians feared that Latvian was still not sufficiently practiced and protected after Soviet occupation. Therefore, a compromise was reached following recommendations made by the OSCE and the Council of Europe.

57. It was long debated in which part of the *Satversme* reference to language should be included. The choice was made to include the Latvian language as one of the fundamental values of democratic State order. In addition, Article 77 of the *Satversme* was amended to ensure that any amendments in Article 4 can be adopted only by referendum.[101]

58. References to the Latvian language appear also in other articles of the *Satversme* including the Preamble. References to language are included in Articles 18 (text of the oath of MPs which *inter alia* refers to the promise to strengthen the Latvian language), 21 (Latvian as the working language of the *Saeima*), 101 (Latvian as the working language of local governments), 104 (the right to receive a reply from State and local government institutions in the Latvian language) and 114 (rights of ethnic minorities to preserve and develop their language).[102]

59. The first sentence of Article 4 of the *Satversme*, pursuant to which the Latvian language is the official language, has been in force since 6 November 1998. The Constitutional Court has already recognized that 'the constitutional status of the official language legally strengthens the rights and also the obligation of Latvia's inhabitants to use the Latvian language in both oral and written communication'.[103] On 24 May 2002, the third sentence of Article 101(2) of the *Satversme* entered into force, providing that the working language of local governments is the Latvian language.

60. The second part of Article 101 of the *Satversme* provides:

> Local governments shall be elected by Latvian citizens and citizens of the EU who permanently reside in Latvia. Every citizen of the EU who permanently resides in Latvia has the right, as provided for by law, to participate in the work of local governments. The working language of local governments is the Latvian language.

101. For details on drafting history *Latvijas Republikas Satversmes komentāri. Ievads. I nodaļa. Vispārējie noteikumi.* Autoru kolektīvs prof. R. Baloža zinātniskā vadībā. (Rīga, Latvijas Vēstnesis, 2014), pp. 304. Cross reference to para. 77.
102. It should be noted that when ratifying Framework Convention for the Protection of National Minorities Latvia had submitted declarations concerning the use of minority languages under Art. 10(2) (use of minority language with authorities) and 11(3) (display of local signs in minority language) of the Convention.
103. Constitutional Court, Case No. 2005-02-0106, 14 Sep. 2005, para. 151.

The State has the obligation not only to guarantee to a citizen formal right to participate, but also to create preconditions for citizens' participation in the work of the State and local government, moreover, doing that in an informed way and understanding the essence of participation.[104] The Constitutional Court has held that 'the obligation to know and to use the official language to the extent needed for performing duties of office is one the preconditions that every citizen should take into consideration when participating in the work of the State and local governments.'[105] The Court has also acknowledged:

> The requirement, that the third sentence in the second part of Article 101 of the *Satversme* contains that the working language of local governments is the Latvian 17 language is enshrined also in the law 'On Local Governments'. Article 3(3) of this Law provides that the working language of a local government council and the authorities and institutions established by it is the Latvian language. Thus, the requirement to use the Latvian language in the work of local governments, which comprises also the obligation of the local government council members to know the official language and to use it, is constitutionally enshrined and does not restrict a person's fundamental rights defined in Article 101 of the *Satversme*.[106]

61. The Constitutional Court has noted that the need to protect the official language and its use is closely connected with the democratic order of the State of Latvia:[107]

> Article 4 of the *Satversme,* by establishing that the Latvian language is the official language in the Republic of Latvia, grants it constitutional status. ... In view of the fact that the Latvian language has been enshrined in the *Satversme* as the official language, as well as the fact that under conditions of globalization Latvia is the only place in the world, where the existence and development of the Latvian language and, thus, also the Latvian nation can be guaranteed, narrowing the use of the official language within the territory of the State must be also considered as threat to the democratic order of the State.[108]

The European Court of Human Rights (ECtHR) has recognized that the State is interested in ensuring that its system of institutions functions normally, and, thus,

104. *Latvijas Republikas Satversmes komentāri. VIII nodaļa. Cilvēka pamattiesības.* Autoru kolektīvs prof. R. Baloža zinātniskā vadībā. (Rīga, Latvijas Vēstnesis, 2011), pp. 384–385, 394.
105. Constitutional Court, Case No. 2012-24-03, 7 Nov. 2013, para. 14. The case originated from the constitutional complaint by the elected deputies to local government. They did not possess a certificate proving level of knowledge of Latvian at the sufficient level (C) for practicing as deputies in local government. They claimed that their human right to be represented at local government have been violated. The applicants considered that by setting certain level of knowledge of State language is in proportionate restriction for them to perform functions in local government where they had been lawfully elected.
106. *Ibid.*
107. See Constitutional Court, Case No. 2005-02-0106, 14 Sep. 2005, para. 15.1 and para. 15.2.
108. Constitutional Court, Case No. 2001-04-0103, 21 Dec. 2001, para. 3.2.

the requirement set for deputy candidates regarding their proficiency in the official language has a legitimate aim.[109]

62. The Constitutional Court has emphasized that:

> stable and effective functioning of State institutions that have been properly legitimized is one of the preconditions for the existence of a democratic order. Therefore comprehensive and consistent use of the official language on appropriate level in the work of these institutions is necessary. If the representatives were to participate in the work of local government council only formally, without knowing and using the official language on the level and degree necessary for performing duties of office due performance of local government functions defined in law would not be ensured.[110]

It has also noted that the scope of a deputy's obligations proves his or her importance in the development and implementation of local government policy. Therefore, persons who have received a mandate from voters should be able to perform the duties of office entrusted to them. Similarly, the ECtHR has also noted that every person has the right to demand from public institutions communications in the official language.[111]

63. On the importance of language the Constitutional Court has said:

> Taking into account the historical features and the fact that the numerical structure of the Latvians in the state territory has decreased during the 20th century and in the biggest cities, including Riga Latvians are a minority and that the Latvian language only recently has regained its status as the state language, the necessity of protecting the state language and strengthening its usage is closely connected with the state of Latvia democratic system. Taking into consideration that the Latvian language as the state language has been fixed in the *Satversme* and the fact that in the era of globalization Latvia is the only place in the world where the existence and development of the Latvian language and together with it the existence of the main nation may be guaranteed. Limitation of the usage sectors of the Latvian language as the state language in the state territory shall be regarded as the threat to the democratic system.[112]

64. The Court has also ruled on the issue of transcription of family names in Latvian. In a case concerning the transcription of a surname, the Court acknowledged that Article 96 of the *Satversme* determines the right of everyone to

109. See judgment by ECHR in Case 'Podkolzina v. Latvia', No. 46726/99, para. 34, ECHR 2002-II, 9 Apr. 2002.
110. Constitutional Court, Case No. 2012-24-03, 7 Nov. 2013, para. 17.
111. See judgment by ECHT in Case 'Jutta Mentzen alias Mencena v. Latvia', No. 71074/01, 6 Apr. 2005.
112. Constitutional Court, Case No. 2001-04-0103, 21 Dec. 2001, para. 3.2.

the inviolability of private life and the use of their name.[113] The Court further noted that the Latvian language has constitutional status. This in turn strengthens the legal justification of its usage in documents issued by Latvia. Since the passport of a Latvian citizen is an official document, it is not only identifying the person but also confirming the continuous legal ties between the person and the State. Thus, a person's name and surname had to be written in the State language.[114]

65. The Constitutional Court had no doubt that it was not possible to isolate the spelling of a person's name (surname) in documents from other aspects of language use. That would threaten the quality of the Latvian language and, consequently, the functions of the Latvian language in Latvian society.[115] The Constitutional Court held that the threat to the functioning of the Latvian language as a unified system if the spelling of foreign personal names in official documents was allowed only in their original form, was much greater than the discomfort a person might experience in the case where their surname in a passport was reproduced according to the traditions of the Latvian language. Under the above circumstances, the functioning of the Latvian language as a unified system was a social necessity in Latvia and not a voluntary caprice of State power.[116]

66. The references to the role of the State language can be found in decisions of other Supreme Court Department decisions as well. They have emphasized the role of the Latvian language as basis for integration.[117]

III. Recent Developments

67. In 2011, one-tenth of voters submitted a draft proposal to the *Saeima* for amending the *Satversme* to provide that State languages in Latvia are both Latvian and Russian. On 2 February 2012, the *Saeima* adopted a declaration that Latvian

113. See Judgment by ECtHR in Case 'Jutta Mentzen alias Mencena v. Latvia', No. 71074/01, 6 Apr. 2005. On 13 Jul. 2001 Juta Mencena submitted a constitutional claim at the Constitutional Court, because after joining in matrimony with the citizen of the German Federative Republic *Ferdinand Carl Friedrich Mentzen* the Department of Citizenship and Migration Affairs issued the passport spelling her surname *Mencena.* On p. 14 it was indicated in English that the original form of the surname was *Mentzen*. Before that on 3 Dec. 1999, the applicant, holding that the Latvian version of her surname noticeably differs from her husband's surname, which could create additional problems in proving the personal identity, addressed a claim on illegal activity of an official to the Riga Centre District Court. On 31 Jan. 2001 the cassation court reached the decision that the appellate court had had ground for declaring that the private and family life of the applicant was not violated. As the cassation claim did not incorporate any vitally new arguments, on the basis of which the appellate court decision could be revalued, the case was dismissed.
114. Constitutional Court, Case 2001-04-0103, 21 Dec. 2001, para. 3.2.
115. *Ibid.,* para. 4.1.
116. *Ibid.,* para. 4.1.
117. Judgment of the Administrative Cases Department of the Supreme Court in Case No. SA/-1/2014, 12 Feb. 2014, para. 36.

has an official function. The subsequent referendum which took place on 18 February 2012 rejected the proposed amendments to the *Satversme*. Of those who participated, 74.8% voted against the amendments.[118]

68. As a result of the initiative to amend Article 4, a special commission was established to draft the Preamble to the *Satversme*. The Preamble was adopted in 2014. At present the Preamble refers to the Latvian language when stating the purpose for establishing an independent Latvia was *inter alia* to guarantee the existence and development of the Latvian language. The Preamble (reproduced above at paragraph 35) proclaims that the identity of Latvia in the European cultural space has been shaped by the Latvian language and that, among other things, the Latvian language as the only official language comprises the foundations of a cohesive society.

118. See http://www.cvk.lv/pub/public/30256.html, accessed 27 Jul. 2015. See also decision of the Constitutional Court in case No. 2012.-03-01, 19 Dec. 2012. The Constitutional Court was asked to rule on the legitimacy of the referendum. The Court refused to verify whether draft law submitted by voters corresponds to *Satversme* because of the lack of competence according to Art. 85 of the *Satversme* and Arts 1 and 16 of the Law of the Constitutional Court.

Part I. Sources of Constitutional Law

69. The *Satversme* does not deal with hierarchy issues. Laws refer to situations of collision between international and national law, but judges would tend to prefer to apply international law.[119] The general approach adopted by the Constitutional Court is one of consistent interpretation. Thus, Latvia can be classified as de facto monist.

70. The Constitutional Court has been proactive in developing the concept of general principles of law. Since its jurisprudence has equal force to the law, it has served as a catalyst for the development of Latvian legal system.

119. Mits, M., *Internationalisation of Public Law: the Case of Latvia*, 18(1) Revue Européenne de Droit Public 421–442, 429 (2006).

Chapter 1. Treaties

71. According to the Law of the Constitutional Court, the Court is entitled to review the constitutionality of international agreements ratified by Latvia. Article 68 of the *Satversme* also provides for the competence of the *Saeima*, namely '[A]ll international treaties, which settle matters to be decided by the legislative process, shall require ratification by the *Saeima.*' The requirement to ratify international treaties in the *Saeima* is included in the *Satversme* with a view to avoiding those international obligations which would seek to regulate issues to be decided in a legislative process without the consent of the *Saeima*.

72. Latvia is the State Party to the Vienna Convention on the Law of the Treaties. The Constitutional Court has stated:

> Validity of rules of international law, as well as the rights and duties of States that undertake international obligations are dealt with by international law itself, and in the first instance by the Vienna Convention and the rules of customary international law (see: judgment of May 13, 2005 by the Constitutional Court in the case No. 2004-18-0106, Para 8.1 of the Concluding Part). … States, in the international relations, must primarily comply with the rules of international law, but the rules of domestic law are to be applied only insofar they are permitted by international law. Consequently, Article 68 (1) of the *Satversme* imposes an obligation on the authorities of Latvia, *inter alia* the *Saeima*, to observe in the international relations not only the requirements of the rules of *Satversme* and other domestic legal rules, but also rules of international law. If the institutions of Latvia, when undertaking international obligations, have not observed the rules of international law for the drafting, signature and ratification of international treaties, then the first part of Article 68 of the *Satversme* has also not been complied with.[120]

73. In certain cases, the Constitutional Court has given direct effect to international law norms.[121] The Court has stated that the text of the European Convention on Human Rights and Fundamental Freedom (EconvHR) and the practice of the ECtHR serve as means of interpretation on the level of constitutional law to determine the contents and scope of fundamental rights and the principle of the rule of law.[122] Further, the Court also applied directly the International Convention on Elimination of Racial Discrimination, International Covenant on Civil and Political Rights and the Convention on the Rights of the Child.

120. Constitutional Court, Case No. 2007-10-0102, 29 Nov. 2007, para. 75.1.
121. Constitutional Court, Case No. 2004-18-0106, 13 May 2005, para. 5.
122. Constitutional Court, Case No. 2000-03-01, 30 Aug. 2000, para. 5 and Constitutional Court, Case No. 2001-08-01, 17 Jan. 2002, para. 3.

74. The Court has stated:

> Upon entering into international agreements, Latvia, with the purpose of strengthening democracy, may delegate a part of its State institution competencies to international institutions. The *Saeima* may ratify international agreements in which a part of State institution competencies are delegated to international institutions in sittings in which at least two-thirds of the members of the *Saeima* participate, and a two-thirds majority vote of the members present is necessary for ratification. Substantial changes in the terms regarding the membership of Latvia in the EU shall be decided by a national referendum if such referendum is requested by at least one-half of the members of the *Saeima*.

Furthermore, Article 68(1) of the *Satversme* prescribes that all international agreements, which settle matters that may be decided by the legislative process, shall require ratification by the *Saeima*.[123]

75. Rules on ratification of international treaties have been spelled out in the Law on International Treaties; but the hierarchy treaties, in the Law on Administrative Procedure. According to Article 15(4) of the Law on Administrative Procedure, EU law should be applicable according to the hierarchy of normative acts. When applying EU law provisions, the relevant institution and court should observe the case law of the EU Court of Justice. The Supreme Court has provided that EU Court of Justice rulings should be applied when interpreting provisions according to an historical and systemic interpretation.[124]

---

123. Constitutional Court, Case 2009-43-01, 21 Dec. 2009, para. 30.1.

124. Judgment of Department of Administrative Cases of the Senate of the Supreme Court of the Republic of Latvia in Case No. SKA-216, 23 Nov. 2004, para. 10 and Judgment Department of Administrative Cases of the Senate of the Supreme Court of the Republic of Latvia in Case No. 162/2007 of 10 May 2007, para. 8.

Chapter 2. Constitution

76. The *Satversme* is a written and codified regulatory enactment. The *Satversme* is a short and laconic, yet complex, document. The Constitutional Court has acknowledged that no provision of the *Satversme*, or any part, or even a single word may be regarded as superfluous, because such an interpretation would compromise the structure of the *Satversme*.[125] Accordingly the key elements of the *Satversme* can be summarized thus:

(1) Protection of fundamental principles and values of democracy and the rule of law.
(2) Functioning of parliamentary democracy.
(3) Guarantees for national sovereignty.[126]
(4) Protection of fundamental rights and freedoms.[127]
(5) Functioning of the division of powers.[128]

77. The text of the *Satversme* includes constitutional regulation. However, the Constitutional Court has noted that alongside the *Satversme*, there are other acts of constitutional rank. For instance, the Act on Proclaiming the Republic of Latvia of 18 November 1918, the Declaration on the State of Latvia of 27 May 1920, the Declaration 'On Restoration of the Independence of Latvia' of 4 May 1990 and the constitutional law 'On Statehood of the Republic of Latvia'.[129] The Constitutional Court has also concluded that those laws, which have been adopted in procedures envisaged by Article 68(2) of the *Satversme*, are to be considered as being constitutional level acts. Thus, the written constitution of Latvia consists of a number of constitutional acts.

125. Constitutional Court, Case No. 2005–12–0103, 16 Dec. 2005, para. 17.
126. Constitutional Court, Case No. 2008-35-01, 7 Apr. 2009, para. 14.
127. According to the Constitutional Court, the provisions of Ch. 8 require threefold obligations: to respect, to protect and to fulfil individual rights. It should be noted that more than 80% of all cases reviewed by the Constitutional Court concern provisions of Ch. 8.
128. The Constitutional Court has derived this principle by interpreting Art. 1 of the *Satversme* This principle ensures balance and mutual control which fosters temperance of power. Constitutional Court, Case No. 03-05(99) of 1 Oct. 1999, para. 1.
129. Constitutional Court, Case No. 2007-10-0102, 29 Nov. 2007, para. 62.

Chapter 3. Legislation and Equivalent Legislative Rules

78. A number of laws define the hierarchy of external regulatory enactments in Latvia.[130] The following hierarchy of the legal force of external regulatory enactments must be complied with in applying regulatory enactments:

(1) the *Satversme*;
(2) laws;
(3) cabinet regulations;
(4) binding regulations of local governments.

79. Taking into account that the wording of the *Satversme* is not detailed and enshrines mainly procedural issues, the *Saeima* is authorized to specify regulations in a law. The purpose of the law is to embody the provisions of the *Satversme*.[131] According to its Chapters 2 and 5, the *Saeima* is the main institution in relations with other constitutional bodies. This means that the *Saeima* is the directly democratically legitimated body to decide on the most important issues for Latvia.

80. Articles 74 and 79 of the *Satversme* provide that the electorate can use legislative powers in cases where at least half of the voters who participated in the last parliamentary elections vote in a referendum. Article 78 of the *Satversme* provides that voters amounting to not less than one-tenth of the electorate, have the right to submit a fully elaborated draft of an amendment to the *Satversme* or of a law to the President, who shall present it to the *Saeima*. If the *Saeima* does not adopt it without change to its content, it shall be submitted to a national referendum. The initiative is adopted if at least 50% of those participating vote in its favour.

81. There are several provisions of the *Satversme* which cannot be adopted without the consent of the people of Latvia. According to Article 77 of the *Satversme*, in cases where the *Saeima* amends Articles 1, 2, 6 or 77, these amendments become effective only if confirmed by referendum. According to Article 79, an amendment to the Constitution submitted for referendum shall be deemed adopted if at least half of the electorate has voted in its favour.

82. Article 64 of the *Satversme* provides that law is an act adopted by the *Saeima* or the people which has been passed in accordance with the legislative procedures established by the *Satversme* and which contains the most important norms of a general nature. Thus, in the case concerning cuts to pensions, the Constitutional Court has confirmed:

130. Law On Official Publications and Legal Information of 31 May 2012, Art. 9, Administrative Procedure Law of 25 Oct. 2001, Art. 15.
131. Decision of 19 Dec. 2012 by the Constitutional Court on Terminating Judicial Proceedings in Case No. 2012-03-01, para. 15.

> [The] principle of separation of powers delimits the authority of the Cabinet of Ministers. In accordance with this principle, the Constitution confers the law-making powers – namely, the powers to decide the most important matters for the State – to the *Saeima* in particular, and, in individual cases, to citizens of the Republic of Latvia. ... Although the Cabinet of Ministers is entitled to adopt regulatory enactments, the latter are not permitted to contain such provisions that cannot be deemed as aids for the implementation of the provisions of the law. Thus, the *Saeima* is obliged to decide all the most important matters of the State and public life by itself through legislation.[132]

83. The legislative procedure in the *Saeima* proceeds in accordance with the norms of the *Satversme* and the Rules of Procedure of the *Saeima*. The Rules of Procedure of the *Saeima* provide that a draft law is adopted if it has been discussed in three readings at *Saeima* sittings, and has obtained the majority of votes of the MP's present. Draft laws, which are recognized as being urgent, draft State budget and amendments to the State budget, as well as draft laws that envisage ratification of international agreements are adopted in two readings.[133]

84. Local governments, to ensure fulfilment of their functions and in cases stipulated by law, adopt external regulatory enactments – binding regulations.[134]

85. The Cabinet of Ministers may adopt external regulatory enactments (Cabinet regulations)[135] only in the following cases:

(1) if the Cabinet has been especially authorized to do so by law. The authorization outlines the main content of this act;
(2) to ratify an international treaty or a draft treaty, to denounce an international treaty or to suspend it, unless the *Satversme* or the law provides otherwise;
(3) if it is necessary for applying the legal acts of the EU and if the particular issues have not been regulated by law. Such regulations may not restrict the fundamental rights of a private person.[136]

132. Constitutional Court, Case 2009-43-01, 21 Dec. 2009, para. 30.1.
133. See Part II Ch. 3.
134. Law on Local Governments of 19 May 1994, Arts 14 and 41.
135. See Part II Ch. 4.
136. Law on the Structure of Cabinet of 15 May 2008, Art. 31.

Chapter 4. Jurisprudence

86. In Latvia, the concept 'case law' comprises a totality of court rulings which are publicly accessible.[137] Case law comprises rulings by courts of all instances; however, 'the rulings by higher instance courts – the Supreme Court – are more authoritative'.[138]

87. Every court has the right and the obligation to interpret law and take into account provisions of international treaties binding on Latvia, as well as the *Satversme*. The Constitutional Court has repeatedly emphasized, 'any party applying the law must apply the *Satversme* directly'.[139] Therefore, besides the cases of the Constitutional Court, the scope and application of the provisions of the *Satvermse* can also be found in the rulings of Latvian courts of general jurisdiction. It should be noted, however, that interpretation by the courts of general jurisdiction of the *Satversme*, while an authoritative source, are without legally binding effect.

88. It is the Constitutional Court which has the exclusive jurisdiction to recognize legal norms as being incompatible with norms of higher legal force and as being invalid. These norms of higher legal force include not only the *Satversme* but also international treaties binding on Latvia.

89. The Law on the Constitutional Court envisages that the interpretation of legal norms given by the Constitutional Court in its judgments or decisions on terminating legal proceedings is mandatory for all State and local government institutions (including other courts) and for officials and other persons. Hence, the interpretation given by the Constitutional Court in a judgment or decision on terminating legal proceedings has *erga omnes* force.

90. The Constitutional Court is obliged to abide by the findings expressed in its rulings. This ensures the stability of the legal system, continuity, the rule of law, and equality. However, on those occasions when the contested norm is incompatible with actual social reality or collides with the legal relationships which in the course of social development have become dominant, the constitutionality of this norm can be reviewed.[140] Thus, no judgment by the Constitutional Court provides a final interpretation of a norm of the *Satversme*: with the emergence of new cases the case law of the Constitutional Court in interpreting a specific norm of the *Satversme* expands and adjusts.[141]

137. Neimanis, J. *Judikatūra un tās saistošais spēks*. (Rīga, Jurista Vārds, 8 Mar. 2005. No. 9).
138. Levits, E. *Aktuālās judikatūras apskats*. (Rīga, Likums un Tiesības 2005, No. 1), p. 27.
139. Constitutional Court, Case No. 2013-06-01, 18 Dec. 2013, para. 15.2.
140. Constitutional Court, Case No. 2011-01-01, 25 Oct. 2011, para. 18.3.
141. Pastars E., Pleps J., *Satversmes lasīšana Satversmes tiesā* (Rīga, Jurista Vārds, 20 Nov. 2007, No. 42).

Chapter 5. Customary Law, Unwritten Law, General Principles of Law

91. In Latvia's constitutional system, conventional norms and the constitutional tradition are granted importance.[142] A conventional norm is based upon a precedent: actions by an organ of State power in deciding on issue in implementing the State power for the first time. This precedent forms a conventional norm, if the subjects of legal relations invoke this precedent under similar circumstances in the future, if the particular practice does not comprise conflicting precedents, and if it is possible to establish and clearly construct the constitutive elements of the legal norm.

92. A number of conventional norms evolved during the interwar period, regulating the procedure for exercising the powers of some bodies of the State power. For instance, the conventional norm that the President of the State convenes and chairs the first of the Cabinet of Ministers developed during this period.[143]

93. The Constitutional Court has recognized conventional norms as a source of constitutional law, noting:

> the Rules of Procedure [of the *Saeima*] do not prohibit from examining cases in compliance with parliamentary customs, insofar this is not contrary to the Rules of Procedure. However, one of the fundamental principles of parliamentary work requires that, before such cases are examined, the procedure for examining them should be clear. In the absence of established customs, the *Saeima*, prior to commencing discussing the particular case, shall establish the procedure for examining it.[144]

94. The fact that the Presidium of the *Saeima* is a collegial institution can be considered to be a constitutional tradition. This tradition requires representatives of different factions to be members of the Presidium of the *Saeima*, thus ensuring that the opposition parties are represented in the Presidium and may participate in organizing the routine work of the *Saeima*. During the sessions of several initial *Saeimas*, there arose an agreement that one of the Secretaries of the *Saeima* had to be an MP nominated by ethnic minorities.[145]

95. The constitutional tradition in Latvia is a broader concept of State law than conventional norms or constitutional customs, since the latter are to be considered as unwritten legal norms which have evolved in the practice by applying the

142. Pleps, J. *Latvijas valsts konstitucionālie pamati.* 'Latvieši un Latvija', III sējums 'Atjaunotā Latvijas valsts'.(Rīga, Latvijas Zinātņu akadēmija, 2013), p. 117.
143. Dišlers, K. *Konvencionālas normas valststiesību novadā.* (Rīga, Tieslietu Ministrijas Vēstnesis, 1933, No. 11/12), p. 252.
144. Constitutional Court, Case No. 03-04-(98), 30 Jul. 1998.
145. Kusiņš, G. *Parlamentārās tradīcijas Latvijā.* (Rīga, Jurista Vārds, Dec. 25 2012, No. 52).

Satversme. Alongside conventional norms or constitutional customs, a constitutional tradition has also been shaped. This had been influenced by opinions of constitutional law scholars.[146]

96. In the course of time many of the constitutional traditions in Latvia have been included in the Rules of Procedure of the *Saeima* and in other laws. However, a number of them continue to exist in the forms of oral agreement, concepts, and opinions.

97. Conventional norms are not binding upon the Constitutional Court. The Court should examine the compatibility of such conventional norms with the *Satversme*.[147]

98. The Constitutional Court has emphasized that the 'State's obligation to abide in its actions by the fundamental principles of a State based on the rule of law follows from the concept of a democratic republic embedded in Article 1 of the *Satversme*.'[148]

99. Principles are not codified by the *Satversme*. However, in a considerable number of judgments, the Constitutional Court has derived constitutional principles on the basis of the term 'democratic republic' as enshrined in Article 1 of the *Satversme*. Over the years, more than thirty principles have been declared of constitutional rank. For instance, the concept 'the rule of law' is not expressly mentioned in the *Satversme*. However, it has been derived by the Constitutional Court as one of the principles enshrined in Article 1 of the *Satversme*. The other principles include the division of powers, proportionality, legal certainty (legal expectations), good governance, as well as others.[149]

100. The rights enshrined in the *Satversme* as well as the principles derived therefrom are directly applicable: each court can rely on the provisions of the *Satversme* irrespective of the provision of the specific law.[150]

---

146. Pleps, J. *Latvijas valsts konstitucionālie pamati*. 'Latvieši un Latvija', III sējums 'Atjaunotā Latvijas valsts'. (Rīga, Latvijas Zinātņu akadēmija, 2013).
147. Pleps, J. *Satversmes iztulkošana*. (Rīga, Latvijas Vēstnesis, 2012), p. 40.
148. Constitutional Court, Case No. 03-04-(98), 30 Jul. 1998.
149. Constitutional Court, Case No. 2008-09-0106, 16 Dec. 2008, para. 4.2. and Constitutional Court, Case No. 2012-02-0106, 18 Oct. 2012, para. 11.2. and Constitutional Court, Case No. 2004-06-01 of 11 Oct. 2004, para. 21.
150. The Supreme Court in administrative cases as well as civil cases has acknowledged that the *Satversme* should be applicable directly. For instance, Department of Civil Cases of the Senate of the Supreme Court of the Republic of Latvia in Case No. SKC 12/2009, 29 Apr. 2009 (not publicly available), Department of Administrative Cases of the Senate of the Supreme Court of the Republic of Latvia in Case No. SKA-68/2013, 22 Feb. 2013 available at http://www.tiesas.lv/februaris-10, accessed 6 Feb. 2014).

Chapter 6. Administrative Regulations and Orders

101. Article 1 of Administrative Procedure Law envisages that an administrative act is a legal instrument directed externally. It is issued by an institution in an area of public law with regard to an individually indicated person or individually indicated persons establishing, altering, determining, or terminating specific legal relations or determining a fact. Administrative acts are also decisions regarding the establishing, alternating, or terminating of the legal status of, or the disciplinary punishment, of employees of or persons specially subordinate to the institution, as well as other decisions if they significantly limit the human rights of the employees or of persons specially subordinate to the institution.

102. Decisions or other types of actions of an institution in the sphere of private law, and internal decisions which affect only the institution itself, bodies subordinate to it, or persons subordinate to it, are not administrative acts. Political decisions (political announcements, declarations, invitations, election of officials, and so on) by the *Saeima*, the President, the Cabinet, or local government, city councils (district and parish councils), as well as decisions regarding criminal proceedings and court adjudications are not administrative acts.[151]

103. An action is an action of an institution in the sphere of public law in any way other than by issuing an administrative act, if a private person has a right to such action or such action results or may result in infringement of the rights or legal interests of the private person. An action is also the failure to act by an institution, if the institution had or has a duty to perform some action in accordance with the norms of law, as well as if it ought to issue a certificate.[152]

104. In administrative proceedings, especially in adopting decisions on the merits, institutions and courts shall, within the scope of the applicable norms of law, facilitate the protection of the rights and legal interests of private persons.[153]

105. The basic objectives of Administrative Procedure Law are as follows:

(1) to ensure the observance of fundamental principles of a democratic State based on the rule of law, especially human rights, in specific public legal relations between the State and a private person;
(2) to subject actions of executive power relating to specific public legal relations between the State and a private person to the control of an independent, impartial and competent judicial power; and
(3) to ensure just, accurate, and effective application of the norms of law in public legal relations.[154]

151. Administrative Procedure Law of 25 Oct. 2001, Art. 1.
152. *Ibid.*, Art. 89.
153. *Ibid.*, Art. 5.
154. *Ibid.*, Art. 2.

106. Article 11 of Administrative Procedure Law envisages that an institution may issue an administrative act or perform an action detrimental to a private person on the basis of the *Satversme*, laws, or the provisions of international law. Cabinet regulations or binding regulations of local governments may be a basis for such administrative act or action only if the *Satversme*, law, or the provisions of international law either directly or indirectly contain an authorization for the Cabinet or local government to issue binding regulations or to provide for such administrative acts or actions. If the *Satversme*, law, or provisions of international law have authorized the Cabinet, then the Cabinet may, in its turn, by adopting regulations authorize local governments for further action.

107. There exist two pathways for administrative proceedings: administrative proceedings before institutions and administrative proceedings before the courts.[155] The fundamental duty of an institution in an administrative proceedings is – within its authorized competences – to ensure legal, effective, and accurate application of legal norms, impartial clarification of actual and legal circumstances, as well as to take the decision most conformable thereto.

108. The Administrative Procedure Law is applied to administrative proceedings before institutions to the extent that special norms of law do not provide otherwise.[156] An administrative matter shall be adjudicated by an institution in accordance with the competences conferred on it by regulatory enactment.[157]

109. An administrative matter to be heard by an institution shall be initiated:

(1) on the basis of a submission;
(2) on the basis of an initiative of the institution; or
(3) on the basis of an order by a higher institution or of a notification by another authority.[158]

110. If the applicable norm of law prescribes an administrative act of specified content to be issued (an obligatory administrative act), an institution must issue such an administrative act.[159]

111. If the norm of law to be applied allows an institution the discretion whether or not to issue an administrative act, and in the event it is issued, prescribes the specific content thereof (issue choice administrative act), the institution shall consider the usefulness of issue. If the institution comes to the conclusion that the administrative act is to be issued, it shall issue the administrative act with such content as

155. Judgment of the Constitutional Court in the Case No. 2004-16-01, 4 Jan. 2005, para. 10.
156. Administrative Procedure Law of 25 Oct. 2001, Art. 3.
157. *Ibid.*, Art. 51.
158. *Ibid.*, Art. 55.
159. *Ibid.*, Art. 65(1).

is provided for by the norm of law to be applied. If the institution concludes that the issue of an administrative act is not useful, it shall close the matter.[160]

112. If the norm of law to be applied prescribes that an administrative act is to be issued, but does not prescribe the specific content thereof (content choice administrative act), an institution shall issue such act, observing the limits laid down by the norm of law, and within this framework, on the basis of considerations of usefulness, shall determine the content of the administrative act.[161]

113. If the norm of law to be applied allows an institution the discretion whether or not to issue an administrative act and, in the event of issue, does not determine its specific content (free administrative act), the institution shall first consider the usefulness of issue. If the institution concludes that the administrative act is to be issued, it shall issue such act, observing the limits laid down by norms of law and, within this framework, on the basis of considerations of usefulness, determine the content of the administrative act. If the institution concludes that the issue of the administrative act is not useful, it shall close the matter.[162]

114. When considering the usefulness of the issue of, or of the content of an administrative act, an institution must determine:

(1) the necessity of the administrative act for the attaining of a legal (legitimate) goal;
(2) the suitability of the administrative act for the attaining of the relevant goal;
(3) the need for the administrative act, that is, whether it is possible to attain such goal by means which are less restrictive of the rights and legal interests of the participants in the administrative proceeding; and
(4) the conformity of the administrative act, comparing the infringement of the rights of a private person and the benefits to the public interest, taking into account that substantial restriction of the rights of a private person may only be justified by a significant benefit to the public.[163]

115. Any restriction of human rights which in substance deprives the addressee of those rights, their benefit is not proportionate in any case.[164]

116. Article 70 of Administrative Procedure Law provides that, if not otherwise stipulated in an external regulatory enactment or the administrative act itself, an administrative act shall come into effect at the time the addressee is notified of it. The manner in which the addressee is notified of the administrative act – in writing, orally or otherwise – shall not affect its coming into effect.

160. *Ibid.*, Art. 65(2).
161. Administrative Procedure Law of 25 Oct. 2001, Art. 65(3).
162. *Ibid.*, Art. 65(4).
163. *Ibid.*, Art. 66(1).
164. *Ibid.*, Art. 66(2).

117. An administrative act shall be in effect, but may be disputed if:

(1) the legal duty imposed on the addressee (specific actions or prohibition of specific actions) or rights granted, approved or refused to the addressee may not be unambiguously construed therefrom;
(2) this Law or other norms of law, which determine the procedure for issue of the relevant administrative act, have not been observed in the course of administrative procedure (procedural error); or
(3) it is, in accordance with its substance, in conflict with the norms of law, or the institution has incorrectly applied the norms of law (or has relied upon erroneous facts), or it has not observed the hierarchy of the legal force of norms of law or has erred regarding considerations of usefulness (mistakes regarding substance).[165]

118. An administrative act is legal if it complies with the norms of law, but illegal, if it does not comply with the norms of law.[166]

119. Administrative proceedings are commenced by filling a complaint with the institution which has issued the act contested or performed a contested action. Once proceedings before the institution have concluded, an applicant has the right to submit the complaint to the administrative court.[167]

120. Administrative proceedings before the courts take place in accordance with Administrative Procedure Law.[168] Judicial proceedings in an administrative matter take place in accordance with the norms of the law of administrative procedures which are in effect at the time of the adjudication of the matter, the performance of individual procedural actions, or execution of a court judgment.[169]

121. The substance of the administrative proceedings before the court is a judicial review of the legality and validity of the administrative acts issued by institutions or the actual actions of institutions within the scope of freedom of action, as well as the determination of public legal duties or the rights of private persons, as well as the adjudication of disputes arising from public legal contracts.[170]

---

165. Administrative Procedure Law of 25 Oct. 2001, Art. 70.
166. *Ibid.*, Art. 84.
167. On administrative courts See Part II Ch. 6 s. B.
168. Administrative Procedure Law of 25 Oct. 2001, Art. 3.
169. *Ibid.*, Art. 102.
170. *Ibid.*, Art. 103.

Chapter 7. Codification, Interpretation and Publication

122. The Constitutional Court has emphasized that 'only such legal situation complies with the *Satversme*, where at least one constitutional institution of the State power or an institution of public administration established by it has the obligation to ensure that the provisions of the *Satversme* are complied with'.[171]

123. The interpretation of the norms of the *Satversme* means deciding on relevant issues pertaining to the limits of the jurisdictions of the State power and the openness of the constitution to changes in social relationships. These issues are first of all decided upon by the totality of citizens or the directly elected representatives – the *Saeima*.[172]

124. In 1996, by amending Article 85 of the *Satversme*, the decision on establishing a Constitutional Court was adopted. Thus, Article 1 of the *Satversme* in connection with Article 85 of the *Satversme* grants the Constitutional Court the jurisdiction to assess the compatibility of legal norms with the *Satversme*, and thus the right to interpret the norms of the *Satversme*.

125. The norms of the *Satversme* are to be interpreted in accordance with the methodology that the Constitutional Court has developed in its judgments. Simultaneously, methods for interpreting the norms of the *Satversme* have also been developed in legal scholarship. The main approach for interpreting the *Satversme* is that the wording of the norms of the *Satversme*, their interconnection, and the intent of the constitutional legislator are applied. For the interpretation of the basic principles of the *Satversme* and fundamental rights, the teleological method of interpretation is used.

126. According to the Constitutional Court, to reveal the content of particular norms of the *Satversme* more fully and more objectively, these must be interpreted in connection with the content of other norms of the *Satversme*, since the *Satversme* is a unified whole, and the norms included in it are closely interconnected.[173]

127. The Constitutional Court has also recognized that on the level of constitutional law the norms of international human rights binding upon Latvia and the practice of their application serve as a means of interpretation to define the content and scope of fundamental rights and the principles of a judicial State envisaged by the *Satversme*, insofar as this does not lead to a decrease or restriction of the fundamental rights included in the *Satversme*.[174]

---

171. Constitutional Court, Terminating Judicial Proceedings in Case No. 2012-03-01, 19 Dec. 2012, para. 19.2.
172. Pleps J. *Satversmes iztulkošana* (Rīga, Latvijas Vēstnesis, 2012), p. 125.
173. Constitutional Court, Case No. 2005-12-0103, 16 Dec. 2005, para. 13.
174. Constitutional Court, Case No. 2004-18-0106, 13 May 2005, para. 5.

128. The Constitutional Court has emphasized that the importance of the institutions of judicial power in interpreting the *Satversme* is constantly growing, since:

> in a democratic and judicial State every institution of the State power has the obligation to comply with the norms and principles of the *Satversme*. Moreover, every issue, where an institution of the State power has applied law, is subject to the control by the judicial power, which guarantees application of legal norms in compliance with the *Satversme*.[175]

129. In construing the norms of law, institutions and courts must apply the following basic methods of interpretation:

(1) a grammatical (linguistic) interpretation method, ascertaining the meaning of the norm of law linguistically;
(2) an historical interpretation method, ascertaining the meaning of the norm of law considering the circumstances on the basis of which it has been created;
(3) a systemic interpretation method, ascertaining the meaning of the norm of law in relation to other norms of law; and
(4) a teleological (meaning and purpose) interpretation method, ascertaining the meaning of the norm of law on the basis of the useful and equitable purposes to be attained pursuant to the relevant norm of law.[176]

130. If there is a conflict between a legal norm of international law and a norm of Latvian law of the same legal force, the legal norm of international law is to be applied.[177]

131. In applying the legal norms of the EU, institutions and courts must take into account EU Court of Justice case law.[178]

132. The Constitutional Court in its rulings has provided a number of insights into the construing of legal norms as a process, providing thus certain methodological guidelines. For example, the Constitutional Court has recognized that in the interests of reaching a fair outcome, the party applying legal norms has the obligation to interpret a norm in compliance with legal norms of higher legal force. The application of legal norms in compliance with the *Satversme* is comprised of the identification of the legal norm to be applied and the use of appropriate methods of interpretation, an assessment of intertemporal and hierarchical applicability, the use of national and international case law and doctrine, as well as considerations of the evolution of law.[179]

---

175. Constitutional Court, Terminating Judicial Proceedings in Case No. 2012-03-01, 19 Dec. 2012, para. 23.
176. Administrative Procedure Law of 25 Oct. 2001, Art. 17(1).
177. Administrative Procedure Law of 25 Oct. 2001, Art. 15(3).
178. *Ibid.*, Art. 15(4).
179. Decision of 8 Mar. 2011 by the Constitutional Court on Terminating Judicial Proceedings in Case No. 2010-52-03, para. 7.

133. The procedure of publishing external regulatory enactments is first and foremost regulated by Article 69 of the *Satversme*. 'The President shall proclaim laws passed by the *Saeima* not earlier than the tenth day and not later than the twenty-first day after the law has been adopted. A law shall come into force fourteen days after its proclamation unless a different term has been specified in the law.'

134. Article 90 of the *Satversme* envisages that everyone has the right to know his or her rights. The requirements that apply to codification and publication of legal norms also follow from this norm.[180] Essentially, Article 90 of the *Satversme* imposes upon the State the obligation to ensure that laws and other regulatory enactments are published in an official printed publication.

135. *Latvijas Vēstnesis* is the official gazette of the Republic of Latvia and the information published therein is an official publication. Information in the official gazette must be published electronically on the website www.vestnesis.lv in accordance with the procedures laid down in law. The official publication must be publicly reliable and binding. No one can plead not knowing the legal acts or official notices published in the official gazette.[181]

136. In extraordinary cases, the President or the Speaker of the *Saeima* as the case may be, is entitled to proclaim a law, reading it in public electronic mass media or, if that is not available, then in another electronic mass media form upon the choice of the proclaimer. A law thus proclaimed must be, without delay, published in the official gazette, indicating the way and time of proclamation of the law.[182]

137. The procedure by which legal norms are codified and systematized in Latvia, is regulated by law. The law envisages that the State agency must ensure systematization of legal acts on the website www.likumi.lv. The Cabinet must determine the minimum requirements and procedures for systematization of legal acts. If a contradiction is detected between the systematized legal act and the official publication of legal act, the official publication is to be taken into account.[183]

138. The Constitutional Court has concluded that Article 90 of the *Satversme* also defines certain requirements with regard to the wording of the text of legal norms and applies also to the interpretation of legal norms. In this regard, the Constitutional Court has noted that the principle of legal certainty follows from the requirement that a legal norm, which establishes restrictions to a person's fundamental rights, must be clear and precise. That is, it is the obligation of the *Saeima* to ensure that legal norms are worded sufficiently unambiguously so that they can

180. *Latvijas Republikas Satversmes komentāri. VIII nodaļa. Cilvēka pamattiesības.* Autoru kolektīvs prof. R. Baloža zinātniskā vadībā. (Rīga, Latvijas Vēstnesis, 2011), p. 68.
181. Administrative Procedure Law of 25 Oct. 2001, Art. 2.
182. *Ibid.*, Art. 8(1).
183. Administrative Procedure Law of 25 Oct. 2001, Art. 16(1).

be interpreted correctly, and that an individual, in the case of necessity by seeking appropriate advice, could regulate his or her actions accordingly.[184]

SELECTED FURTHER READING

Balodis, R. *Evolution of Constitutionality of the Republic of Latvia: from 1918 – 2006.* Jahrbuch des öffentlichen Rechts der gegenwart. Neue Folge/Band 56, 2006, S. 269–278.

Balodis, R., A. Kārkliņa & E. Danovskis. 'The Development of Constitutional and Administrative Law in Latvia after the Restoration of Independence'. *Rīga, Journal of the University of Latvia Law* 5 (2013): 44–120.

Iļjanova, D. *The Republic of Latvia. Constitutional Law of 10 EU Member States.* The Hague, London, Boston, Kluwer Law International, 2006, pp. V-1–V-65.

Pleps, J. *Conventional Norms as a Source of Latvian Constitutional Law.* Vilnius: Mokslinés minties švente, Mykolo Romerio Universitetas, 2006, pp. 325–332.

Rodiņa, A. & J. Pleps. *Constitutionalism in Latvia: Reality and Developments. New Millennium Constitutionalism: Paradigms of reality and challenges.* Yerevan: NJHAR, 2013, pp. 431–471.

Ziemele, I. *State Continuity and Nationality: The Baltic States and Russia. Past, Present and Future as Defined by International Law.* Leiden, Martinus Nijhoff Publishers, 2005.

Levits, E. *General Clauses and Discretionary Power of Administrative Institutions and Courts.* Law and Justice, 2004, pp. 2–24.

Rezevska, D. 'The Republic of Latvia'. In *Constitutional Law of the EU Member States*, edited by Kortmann C., J. Fleuren & W. Voermans, 2nd revised ed. The Hague, London, Boston: Kluwer Law International, Deventer, 2007, pp. 969–102.

184. Constitutional Court, Case No. 2010-44-01, 20 Dec. 2010, para. 11.

Part II. Form of Government

Chapter 1. General

§1. Introduction

139. Article 1 of the *Satversme* is the legal basis for Latvia's statehood.[185] It provides, 'Latvia is an independent democratic republic.' Pursuant to the *Satversme*, Latvia has been created as a democratic parliamentary republic. The central institution of the State power is the Parliament – the *Saeima*, which is elected in free, direct elections by all Latvian citizens having the right to vote.

140. The *Saeima* elects the President of Latvia. The *Saeima* also approves the Cabinet of Ministers upon the proposal of the President. Judges are also confirmed by the *Saeima*.

141. The Constitutional Court has noted that it follows from the concept of a democratic republic included in Article 1 of the *Satversme* that all State institutions have the obligation in their actions, in particular in adopting regulatory enactments, to abide by law, the division of powers, and to perform reciprocal supervision in conformity with the subjection of public power to law – the rule of law and associated principles, as well as the principles of proportionality and legal certainty.[186]

142. The Constitutional Court has ruled that the principle of the division of powers, which follows from Article 1 of the *Satversme*, should be linked to the objective of preventing the centralization of power in the hands of one institution or one official.[187] Moreover, the Constitutional Court has also noted that the principle of the division of powers embedded in Article 1 of the *Satversme* requires that all constitutional institutions of State power, *inter alia*, the Constitutional Court, must abide by the limits on jurisdiction as defined in law.[188] Likewise, the Constitutional Court has also held that the people, in exercising the rights granted to them by the *Satversme*, do not have the right to violate the *Satversme*.[189]

185. Constitutional Court, Case No. 2007-10-0102, 29 Nov. 2007, para. 40.2.
186. Constitutional Court, Case No. 04-07(99), 24 Mar. 2000, para. 3.
187. Constitutional Court, Case No. 03-05(99), 1 Oct. 1999, para. 1.
188. Constitutional Court, Case No. 2008-03-03, 24 Sep. 2008, para. 9.2.
189. Constitutional Court, Terminating Judicial Proceedings in Case No. 2012-03-01, 19 Dec. 2012.

143. The *Satversme* divides jurisdiction among the constitutional institutions that it refers to: the totality of Latvia's citizens, the *Saeima*, the President of the State, the Cabinet of Ministers, the State Audit Office, and the Constitutional Court. The *Satversme* establishes an exhaustive division power among these constitutional institutions. Hence, any powers of the State not granted to any constitutional institution of the State cannot exist, whereas the totality of powers of all the constitutional institutions of State power constitutes the total jurisdiction of the State.[190]

144. The Constitutional Court has provided the following explanation of the concept of a democratic republic included in Article 1 of the *Satversme*. Democracy is founded upon the freely expressed will of the people, defining the political, economic, social and cultural system of the State. Participation in the parliamentary election is one of the most important forms of the manifestation of the citizens' political will.[191] It is the participation of society in decision-making that ensures the legitimacy and effectiveness of a democracy.[192]

145. In the second half of the nineteenth century, the first Latvian National Awakening began among ethnic Latvian intellectuals, a movement that partly reflected similar nationalistic trends elsewhere in Europe. The Latvian National Awakening movement promoted Latvian identity in the context of Russian political domination and Baltic German economic power. This movement was the first source which inspired Latvian elites later to seek national independence. In the 1880s and 1890s, a russification policy aimed to reduce the autonomy of the Baltic provinces. Growing urbanization and industrialization promoted leftist ideas and Latvia in the early twentieth century saw popular discontent explode in the 1905 Revolution. Russian authorities were able to suppress protests yet they did promote some economic liberalization. During World War I, Latvian territory was divided between Russia and Germany with about 800,000 Latvians in exile. Only after the Revolutions in Russia and Germany did Latvian political organizations pursue the idea of national independence as a serious political option. The post-war confusion was a suitable opportunity for the development of an independent nation. Latvia proclaimed its independence shortly after the end of World War I, on 18 November 1918. A series of conflicts within the territory of Latvia from 1918 to 1920 is commonly known as the Latvian War of Independence. In April 1920, elections to the Constitutional Assembly were held. In May 1922, the Constitution of Latvia, and in June the new Law on Elections were passed, opening the way to an elected parliament.

146. The first act which contains a reference to the political system of Latvia is the platform of 17 November 1918 of the People's Council of Latvia. Article 1 of

190. Constitutional Court, Case No. 2006-05-01, 16 Oct. 2006, para. 10.3 and 10.4.
191. Constitutional Court, Case No. 2002-08-01, 23 Sep. 2002, para. 2.
192. Constitutional Court, Case No. 2004-18-0106, 13 May 2005, para. 7.

the second chapter 'The form of the State and relations with other nations' declares 'A republic on democratic foundations.'[193]

147. In the period from 1918 to 1934, a democratic system managed to evolve. It flourished in the 1920s and underwent a crisis in the 1930s. On 15 May 1934, a coup d'état occurred leading to the establishment of an authoritarian regime. The development of democracy and the statehood of Latvia were violently disrupted by occupation in 1940, which established a totalitarian regime.[194]

148. Since 1993 (when the first *Saeima* election was held after the restoration of independence), eight *Saeima* elections have already taken place, of which one (of the eleventh *Saeima*) was an extraordinary election, and eighteen governments – the Cabinets of Ministers – have been formed.

149. Latvia, in general, is characterized by a high level of political pluralism. There are approximately fifty registered political parties, of which more than twenty have also traditionally run for *Saeima* election.[195]

150. When dealing with contemporary Latvian democracy, it is stated that Latvia, after the end of the Soviet occupation, has succeeded in creating a full-fledged democratic regime, which has its strengths and weaknesses.[196] Latvia can be characterized as having a democratic electoral process, a developed civil society and independent media, local and national democratic governance, as well as the rule of law.

§2. Political Parties

151. Article 102 of the *Satversme* provides that 'everyone has the right to form and join associations, political parties and other public organisations'. Thus, the *Satversme* refers to political parties only in the Chapter on fundamental human rights.

152. The Constitutional Court has noted that by exercising the fundamental rights defined in Article 102 of the *Satversme*, a person gains the possibility of participating in democratic processes. Hence everyone's right to join a political party is an essential prerequisite for the existence of a democratic State order.[197]

153. After the restoration of independence, the regulation on political parties was set into the law of 1992 On Civic Organisations and Associations. In 2006, a

193. *Latvijas Republikas Satversmes komentāri. Ievads. I nodaļa. Vispārējie noteikumi.* Autoru kolektīvs prof. R. Baloža zinātniskā vadībā. (Rīga, Latvijas Vēstnesis, 2014), p. 231.

194. *For details* See General introduction.

195. Ijabs, I. *Demokrātija Latvijā.* 'Latvieši un Latvija', III sējums 'Atjaunotā Latvijas valsts'. (Rīga, Latvijas Zinātņu akadēmija, 2013), p. 145.

196. *Ibid.*, p. 133.

197. Constitutional Court, Case No. 2012-16-01, 10 May 2013, para. 17.

new law – 'Law on Political Parties' – was drafted. The latter law had the purpose of ensuring the legal grounds for the activities of political parties: to regulate the procedure for establishing them and the principles of their activities.[198]

154. The *Satversme* does not provide an explanation of the concept 'political party'. The definition of a political party is included in 'Law on Political Parties'. Article 2(1) of this Law provides that a party is an organization which is established in order to perform political activities, to participate in election campaigns, to nominate candidates for deputy positions, to participate in the work of the *Saeima*, local government councils, the European Parliament, and to implement the party programme with the intermediation of deputies, as well as to be involved in the establishment of public administrative bodies.[199]

155. The Constitutional Court has provided the following interpretation of the concept political party:

> A political party is a union of persons, the members of which hold similar political views, which has a definite ideology and the principal aim of which is gaining political power in order to implement it, in accordance with the aims and principles included in the programme of the party.[200]

156. A political party can be founded by Latvian citizens who have reached the age of 18. The number of founding members must be at least 200.[201] To establish a party, founding members must adopt a decision on establishing a political party. They also approve the programme and the articles of association of the party. Party members elect a board and an audit institution for economic and financial activities. The procedure of the meeting founding a political party must be certified by a sworn notary.[202]

157. The Law on Political Parties specifies which issues must be regulated by the articles of association of the party. The law also envisages that other rules, which are not contrary to the law, may be included in the articles of association of the party. If the articles of association are incompatible with law, then provisions of law are applicable.[203]

158. The parties are registered in a special register. Within three months of the decision on founding a political party, the founders or the board submit to the relevant registry institution an application on entering the political party into the register of parties.[204] The law provides that the following information is entered into the register of parties: the name of the party, the legal address of the party, the aim

198. Law on Political Parties of 22 Jun. 2006, Art. 1.
199. *Ibid.*, Art. 2.
200. Constitutional Court, Case No. 2012-16-01, 10 May 2013, para. 19.
201. Law on Political Parties of 22 Jun. 2006, Art. 12.
202. *Ibid.*, Art. 13.
203. *Ibid.*, Art. 14.
204. *Ibid.*, Art. 16.

of the party's activities, the territorial structural units of the party (if such exist), the date of the decision establishing the political party, the full names of the board members, and indicating whether they have right to represent the political party individually or jointly; the term for the party's activities (if the party has been established for a fixed term) and any other information required by law.[205] This information must be published in *Latvijas Vēstnesis*. A decision taken by the official of the registry institution can be contested and appealed in accordance with administrative law procedures.[206]

159. Article 17 of the Law on Political Parties provides that everyone has the right to familiarize himself or herself with the entries of the party register and the documents submitted to the registry institution. Upon submitting a request in writing and payment of any fee, a person may receive a statement from the Register of Political Parties or an extract or a copy of any document held in the Register of Political Parties.

160. When a party is entered into the Register of Political Parties, it acquires the status of a legal person.[207] Henceforth it is the entire property of the party which is available to discharge its debts and liabilities. At the same time the legislator has thereby also envisaged a consequent limited liability: a party is not responsible for the liabilities of its members, and a member is not responsible for the liabilities of the party.[208] To reach the aim defined in its constitutive statutes, a party has the right to engage in economic activities on its own behalf, which do not have the nature and purpose of gaining profit. The revenues obtained by political parties as the result of such economic activities may not be divided among members generally or the founding members.[209]

161. Parties are prohibited from arming their members or other persons, from organizing military training or forming paramilitary units.[210]

162. Article 29 of Law on Political Parties provides a general regulation on the rights and obligations of party members, for example, the right to participate in decision-making, to elect the board of a party, and to freely express their views. The articles of association of a party may also prescribe other rights and obligations for its members, providing they are not incompatible with the Law.

163. In order to coordinate their activities and reach the objectives defined in their articles of association, several parties may register alliances of political parties in accordance with the procedures set out in the Law on Political Parties. An alliance of political parties may be established by two or more parties that have been

205. *Ibid.*, Art. 18.
206. *Ibid.*, Art. 20.
207. *Ibid.*, Art. 3.
208. *Ibid.*, Art. 4.
209. Law on Political Parties of 22 Jun. 2006, Art. 8.
210. *Ibid.*, Art. 9.

registered in accordance with the Law.[211] An alliance of political parties is prohibited from establishing, in its turn, another alliance of political parties.[212] The regulation regarding political parties set out in the Law on Political Parties is applicable to alliances of political parties, insofar the law does not provide otherwise.[213]

164. The rules on financing political parties and the admissible amount of pre-election expenditure are regulated by a separate law, the Law on Financing of Political Organisations. The Law provides that the parties may be financed by membership and joining fees, gifts (donations) from natural persons, the income earned from the economic activities of the relevant political organization (party), and the State budget (in cases determined by law).[214] Funding from the State budget is granted to a political organization (party) which received more than 2% of all votes during the previous *Saeima* elections.[215] The implementation of the Law on Financing of Political Organisations (Parties) is monitored by the Bureau for Preventing and Combating Corruption.[216]

165. The Constitutional Court has noted that the State, in regulating the activities of political parties and the participation of persons in them, must ensure that the chosen solutions are established by law, justified by a legitimate aim, and are proportional. The intervention by the State into the activities of political parties should be assessed as a restriction on a person's fundamental rights.[217]

166. The Law 'On Judicial Power' prohibits judges from joining political parties. The Constitutional Court examined the compliance of this prohibition on a judge becoming a member of party with norms of higher legal force (the *Satversme*). The Constitutional Court concluded that this regulation created certainty in society that a judge did not represent the opinion of a political party. It helps to prevent situations which might raise doubts regarding a judge's ability to administer justice in an unbiased and independent way. However, the rejection or recusing of a judge helps to dispel justified and reasonable doubts regarding a judge's ability to administer justice in an unbiased way.[218] In view of the fact that this kind of regulation helps to strengthen the authority of judicial power and that the existence of the restriction established by it is beneficial to society, the Constitutional Court held the prohibition on judges joining political parties to be compatible with the *Satversme*.

167. The activities of lobby groups are not regulated in Latvian law. While there have been a number of initiatives to do so, none of them have materialized.

211. *Ibid.*, Art. 9.
212. *Ibid.*, Art. 12.
213. *Ibid.*, Art. 2.
214. Law on Financing of Political Organisations (Parties) of 19 Jul. 1995, Art. 2.
215. *Ibid.*, Art. 71.
216. *Ibid.*, Art. 13.
217. Constitutional Court, Case No. 2012-16-01, 10 May 2013.
218. Constitutional Court, Case No. 2012-16-01, 10 May 2013, paras 29.3 and 30.1.

§3. MISCELLANEOUS

168. The first part of Article 101 of the *Satversme* provides that 'every citizen of Latvia has the right, as provided for by law, to participate in the work of the State and of local government, and to hold a position in the civil service'.

169. The Constitutional Court has recognized that Article 101 of the *Satversme* establishes a right which serves as a safeguard for the existence of a democratic order and is aimed at ensuring the legitimacy of a state order.[219] The civil service comprises all state offices established in the institutions of legislative, executive, and judicial power.[220]

170. The right established by Article 101 of the *Satversme* is not absolute, since Article 101 comprises the provision 'as provided by law'. Thus the *Satversme* provides that the mode of exercising this right must be defined by law.[221]

171. Only Latvian citizens are entitled to vote and be elected in parliamentary elections and vote in referenda. EU citizens can participate in local elections and elections for the European Parliament. Third country nationals do not enjoy any voting rights, irrespective of the length of residence in Latvia. There are different conditions set for citizens residing outside Latvia depending on the type of elections.

172. The *Satversme* prescribes four ways for citizens to implement their will, namely:

(1) direct election of their representatives into the State legislative organ – the *Saeima* (Articles 6–9 and Article 14 of the *Satversme*);
(2) functioning as legislators (by referendum), except when adopting laws and amendments to the *Satversme* (Articles 64, 65, 78–80 of the *Satversme*);
(3) deciding upon laws or amendments to the *Satversme* adopted by the *Saeima* (Articles 72–75, 77, 79, 80 of the *Satversme*);
(4) deciding upon other issues provided for by the *Satversme* that are submitted to a national referendum (Article 48 and the third and the fourth part of Article 68 of the *Satversme*).[222]

173. The voting system has not been subject to major changes since its introduction, except for relatively new provisions on the rights of EU citizens. There have been proposals to change the voting system from a proportional to a plurality system in parliamentary elections and to elect the President in direct elections. The debates are ongoing.

219. Constitutional Court, Case No. 2000-03-01, 30 Aug. 2000, para. 1.
220. Constitutional Court, Case No. 2012-16-01, 10 May 2013, para. 31.1.
221. See Part IV Ch. 3.
222. Constitutional Court, Case No. 2008-40-01, 19 May 2009, para. 11.

174. Latvian citizens have the right to vote in all elections and referenda if they are 18 years of age or more. The age threshold to run as a candidate differs. In national parliamentary elections and elections for the European Parliament, the minimum age is 21, whereas in local elections 18 years is the minimum age requirement to run as a candidate.

175. Mentally disabled person can be disenfranchised (Articles 3 and 5 of the Law on Elections to the European Parliament; Articles 2 and 5 of the Parliamentary Election Law (applicable also in cases of referenda), Articles 6 and 9 of the Law on Local Elections).

176. In European Parliament elections, convicted persons have active voting rights. However, according to Article 5, a person cannot run as a candidate if she or he:

(1) is serving a prison sentence;
(2) has been convicted of a severe crime and has a criminal record which has not been extinguished or set aside, except when the person is rehabilitated;
(3) has been in a mentally disabled condition or state of limited responsibility when committing a crime or, also, after committing the crime has become mentally ill such that the person is deprived of their ability to understand their actions or to control them and, as a result, has been subjected to compulsory medical treatment or the case has been dismissed without applying such a compulsory measure;
(4) has been punished by a prohibition to stand as a candidate for Parliament, the European Parliament, or local elections, except if the person is deemed to be rehabilitated or the penalty is set aside or expunged.

177. According to Article 7^1 of the Law on Referenda, Legislative Initiatives and Initiative of European citizens, persons who are criminal suspects, accused, or on trial and who are arrested may participate in the collection of signatures to initiate a referendum. According to Article 20(4) of the Law, they can also vote in a referendum according to the same procedure which is used in the case of parliamentary elections. Prisoners and persons under arrest can take part in parliamentary elections. Prisoners are not entitled to vote in local elections according to Article 6 of the Laws on Elections of Major City Council and Municipality Council. Groups of persons excluded from the right to stand as candidates in local and parliamentary elections are quite similar: for instance, a person who has been employed by the USSR, the Latvian SSR, or another country's state security, intelligence or counter-intelligence services, a person who has been punished by prohibition to run for elections of the *Saeima*, the European Parliament, city councils and municipality councils, except if they have been exonerated or their criminal record has been expunged or annulled.[223]

223. See Kruma, K., *Access to Electoral Rights.* Latvia, European University Institute, Florence, Robert Schuman Centre for Advanced Studies (EUDO Citizenship Observatory, June 2013, available at http://cadmus.eui.eu/bitstream/handle/1814/29816/ER_2013_14-Latvia-FRACIT.pdf?sequence=1), accessed 6 Apr. 2015, p. 4.

178. For referenda and parliamentary elections, there is no specific registration procedure. Those who vote are registered at the polling station and their passport is stamped to prevent voting in another polling station (Article 22(3) of the Parliamentary Elections Law).

179. In case of voting outside Latvia for its parliamentary elections, voters receive lists of candidates for the Riga voting district (Article 44(1) of the Parliamentary Elections Law). In local and European Parliament elections, voters should register and vote in their respective (foreign) municipality.

SELECTED FURTHER READING

Auers, D. 'An Electoral Tactic? Citizens' Initiatives in Post-Soviet Latvia'. In *Citizens' Initiatives in Europe*, edited by Maija Setala & Theo Schiller. London: Palgrave Macmillan, 2012, pp. 53–68.

Ijabs, I. 'Strange Baltic Liberalism: Paul Schiemann's Political Theory Revisited'. *Journal of Baltic Studies* 40 (2009).

Kruma, K. *Access to Electoral Rights*. Latvia, European University Institute, Florence, Robert Schuman Centre for Advanced Studies, EUDO Citizenship Observatory, June 2013, available at http://cadmus.eui.eu/bitstream/handle/1814/29816/ER_2013_14-Latvia-FRACIT.pdf?sequence=1, accessed 6 April 2015.

Chapter 2. Head of State

180. In the period from 1920 to 1922, the Provisional Rules of the Regime of the State of Latvia envisaged that the President of the Constitutional Assembly would also perform the functions of Head of State.[224] It is considered that the origins of the institution of the President of the State are to be found in those Provisional Rules.[225] Yet scholarship has suggested that already from 1918 to 1920, the Chairman of the People's Council of Latvia was performing the functions of Head of State.[226]

181. When the Constitutional Assembly decided on the provisions of the *Satversme* applicable to the Head of State, discussions arose regarding both the scope of the President's jurisdiction and election procedures.[227] At the same time, an opinion existed that the special institution of a President was not necessary.[228] The Constitutional Assembly decided to establish the special institution of the State President. A possible explanation of this could be that the chairperson of the Parliament, due to his dual status, could not perform the functions of the Head of State to their fullest extent.[229]

182. Latvia's constitutional experience has witnessed cases where the functions of the Head of State were performed by the Chairman of the Parliament. For example, following the restoration of independence, the functions of Latvia's Head of State were fulfilled by the Chairman of the Supreme Council. Moreover, pursuant to Article 52 of the *Satversme*, if the President resigns from office, dies, or is removed from office before the end of his mandate, the Chairperson of the *Saeima* assumes the duties of the President until the *Saeima* has elected a new President. Similarly, the Chairperson of the *Saeima* assumes the duties of the President if the latter is absent from Latvia or if, for any other reason, is unable to fulfil the duties of office.

183. When the Chairperson takes up the duties of the President, this does not include the right to exercise the President's authority in full. The scope of rights may differ between those cases of replacing an existing President and those with one no longer existing.[230]

---

224. Pleps, J., Pastars, E., Plakane, I. *Konstitucionālās tiesības. Papildināts un pārstrādāts izdevums.* (Rīga, Latvijas Vēstnesis, 2014), p. 180.
225. Lazdiņš J. *Valsts prezidenta institūta tapšana Latvijā.* (Likums un Tiesības, 2001, No. 6), p. 170.
226. Pleps, J., Pastars, E., Plakane, I. *Konstitucionālās tiesības. Papildināts un pārstrādāts izdevums.* (Rīga, Latvijas Vēstnesis, 2014), p. 181.
227. *Latvijas Satversmes Sapulces stenogrammu izvilkums (1920–1922). Latvijas Republikas Satversmes projekta apspriešana un apstiprināšana.* (Rīga, Tiesu namu aģentūra, 2006), p. 20.
228. *Ibid.*, p. 5.
229. Pleps, J., Pastars, E., Plakane, I. *Konstitucionālās tiesības. Papildināts un pārstrādāts izdevums.* (Rīga, Latvijas Vēstnesis, 2014), p. 181.
230. Pleps, J. *Bīskaps Rancāns un Satversme. Valsts prezidenta vietas izpildīšana.* (Jurista Vārds, 3 Mar., 2009, No. 9).

184. The institution of President of the State of Latvia was first established on 14 November 1922, when ninety-two members of the *Saeima* voted for electing the first President of the State of the Republic of Latvia, Jānis Čakste.

185. Chapter III of the *Satversme* 'The President' regulates the competences and functions, the rights and obligations, of the President, as well as the procedure for electing the President of the State. Some issues pertaining to the procedure in which the President of the Sate fulfils his or her functions are regulated by law.

§1. A State Institution

186. The *Satversme* contains no references as to the implementation of the principle of the division of powers, including the place of the President in the system of state institutions.

187. The Constitutional Assembly, when drafting the regulation on the State President, emphasized that 'the neutral and balancing power, the task of which is, in certain cases, to maintain the balance between other powers of the State, is vested in the President of the State'.[231] The view is that the State President has the function of an arbiter, and it has been called a 'residual power' in the contemporary theory of constitutional law:

> The arbiter's function for the President means that in the case of a political dispute between the constitutional institutions of the State, it is the task of the President to attempt to achieve compromise or to resolve the dispute. The President's residual function means that the President of the State starts acting only as the last instance, if it has been impossible to eliminate the dispute by other means.

Hence the State President is the institution which can try to deal with situations involving a serious parliamentary crisis.[232]

188. In the Latvian constitutional system, the State President has been given a role in the executive, legislative, and the judicial branches of power. Hence, he or she is involved in exercising all three aspects of public power.[233] For example, the State President proposes the candidate for the office of the Prime Minister, which is the initial stage in the process of forming the government (Article 56 of the

231. *Latvijas Satversmes Sapulces stenogrammu izvilkums (1920–1922). Latvijas Republikas Satversmes projekta apspriešana un apstiprināšana.* (Rīga, Tiesu namu aģentūra, 2006), *Latvijas Satversmes sapulces IV sesijas 1921.gada 20.septembra sēdes (1.sēde) stenogramma.*
232. Valsts prezidenta Konstitucionālo tiesību komisijas 2008.gada 30.aprīļa viedokļa *'Par Saeimas priekšlaicīgu vēlēšanu mehānisma pilnveidošanu'.* Valsts prezidenta Konstitucionālo tiesību komisija. Viedokļi: 2008-2011 (Rīga, Latvijas Vēstnesis, 2011), p. 55.
233. Valsts prezidenta Konstitucionālo tiesību komisijas 2011.gada 10.maija viedokļa *'Par Valsts prezidenta funkcijām Latvijas parlamentārās demokrātijas sistēmas ietvaros'* Valsts prezidenta Konstitucionālo tiesību komisija. Viedokļi: 2008-2011 (Rīga: Latvijas Vēstnesis, 2011), p. 112.

Satversme). The President may initiate a draft law in the *Saeima*, which is the initial stage of the legislative procedure (Article 47 of the *Satversme*). The President of the State may grant clemency to convicted persons, which, conditionally, is the last stage of judicial proceedings (Article 45 of the *Satversme*).

§2. Legal Status

189. By Article 37 of the *Satversme,* 'Any person who enjoys full rights of citizenship and who has attained the age of forty years may be elected President. A person with dual citizenship may not be elected President.' The Law on Elections of the President of the State regulates further the specifics foreseen by the *Satversme*. It provides that only a citizen of Latvia with an unimpeachable reputation may be elected to the office of the President of the State.[234]

190. In 2007, following prolonged public discussions, the *Saeima* adopted the Law on Elections of the President of the State. This regulates the procedure for electing the President. Prior to the adoption of this, normative acts did not regulate the procedure for electing the President in any great detail, and the issues pertaining to elections were decided by the Council of Factions of the *Saeima*, in accordance with the *Saeima* Rules of Procedure.[235]

191. The Law provides that the following persons may not be elected to the office of the State President:

(1) persons by law declared as incapacitated;
(2) persons serving a custodial sentence;
(3) persons having a criminal record for intentional criminal offences, unless formally rehabilitated or whose record has been expunged or set aside;
(4) those held by law to be mentally ill or in a state of reduced mental capacity, at the time of committing an offence or becoming so thereafter, and to whom compulsory measures of a medical nature have been applied (or where the matter has been terminated without the application of such a compulsory measures);
(5) persons who are or have been employed by the security services, intelligence services, or counter-intelligence services of the USSR, Latvian SSR, or foreign countries;
(6) those active after 13 January 1991 in the Communist Party of USSR (Latvian SSR), the International Front of the Working People of the Latvian SSR, the United Council of Labour Collectives, the All-Latvian Salvation of Society Committee or its regional committees;

234. Law on Electing the President of the State of 3 May 2007, Art. 2.

235. Balodis, R., Kārkliņa, A. *Divdesmit gadi kopš Latvijas Neatkarības deklarācijas: valststiesību attīstības tendences un risinājumi* (Jurista Vārds, 27 Apr., 2010, No. 17/18).

(7) persons penalized by a ban on running for election to the *Saeima*, the EU Parliament, a Republic city or regional council, unless formally rehabilitated or whose convictions have been expunged or set aside.[236]

192. The *Saeima* Mandate, Ethics and Submissions Committee verifies whether a Presidential candidate complies with the prerequisites established in the law. A decision to reject a candidate is adopted by the *Saeima*.[237]

193. A proposal for candidacy for the office of the State President should be submitted in writing to the Presidium of the *Saeima* no earlier than fifty days and no later than forty-five days before the term of office of the incumbent President expires.[238]

194. Article 36 of the *Satversme* reads, 'The President shall be elected by secret ballot with a majority of the votes of not less than fifty-one members of the *Saeima*.' It should be noted that the issue of who elects the State President –the *Saeima* or the people – has always been relevant, both at the time of drafting the *Satversme* and after the restoration of independence. It remains so at present: a number of proposals regarding a popularly-elected President have been submitted to the *Saeima*.

195. If, during the last round of voting, none of the candidates has obtained the majority necessary for election, new elections are organized. The candidates for this new round of elections are proposed no later than five days after the previous one.[239]

196. By Article 35 of the *Satversme*, 'The *Saeima* shall elect the President for a term of four years.' Article 39 of the *Satversme* sets out that the same person 'shall not hold office as President for more than eight consecutive years'.

197. A extraordinary election for President is held if the incumbent President of the State:

(1) resigns from office;
(2) dies; or
(3) is removed from office.[240]

198. Article 51 of the *Satversme* prescribes that, upon a proposal of not less than half of all of the members of the *Saeima*, the *Saeima* may decide, in closed sitting and with a majority vote of not less than two-thirds of all of its members, to remove a sitting President from office.

236. Electing the President of the State of 3 May 2007, Art. 3.
237. *Ibid.*, Art. 7.
238. *Ibid.*, Art. 9.
239. Law on Electing the President of the State of 3 May 2007, Art. 9.
240. *Ibid.*

199. Articles 48–50 of the *Satversme* provide a unique regulation on what happens if the State President loses his or her office. In those cases the President is entitled to propose the dissolution of the *Saeima*. Following this proposal, a national referendum must be held. If in the referendum more than half of the votes are cast in favour of dissolution, the *Saeima* is considered dissolved and new elections are called. These elections should be held no later than two months after the date of the dissolution of the *Saeima*.[241] If the *Saeima* has been dissolved or recalled, the mandate of the MPs continue to be effective until the convening of the newly elected *Saeima*. The former *Saeima* may only hold sittings upon the request of the President. The President determines the agenda of such sittings of the *Saeima*. New elections must take place not earlier than one month and not later than two months after the *Saeima* has been dissolved.[242] If at the national referendum more than a half of the votes cast are against the dissolution of the *Saeima*, the President of the State is to be considered dismissed and the *Saeima* elects a new State President for the President's remaining term in office.[243]

200. Articles 48–50 of the *Satversme* present a way of dealing with a constitutional conflict between the *Saeima* and the State President. On 28 May 2011, the President of the State, Valdis Zatlers, adopted Order No. 2, initiating a national referendum on the dissolution of the *Saeima*. As the result of that national referendum the tenth *Saeima* was dissolved.

201. One prerequisite to taking office is the giving of an oath or a solemn promise. Article 40 of the *Satversme* stipulates the oath/solemn promise:

> The President, upon taking up the duties of office, at a sitting of the *Saeima*, shall take the following solemn oath: 'I swear that all of my work will be dedicated to the welfare of the people of Latvia. I will do everything in my power to promote the prosperity of the Republic of Latvia and all who live here. I will hold sacred and will observe the Constitution of Latvia and the laws of the State. I will act justly towards all and will fulfil my duties conscientiously.'

202. By Article 38 of the *Satversme*, 'The office of the President shall not be held concurrently with any other office. If the person elected as President is a member of the *Saeima*, he or she shall resign his or her mandate as a member of the *Saeima*.'

203. The first sentence in Article 53 of *Satversme* sets out that political responsibility for the fulfilment of presidential duties shall not be borne by the President. In the parliamentary system, responsibility for the President's activities rests with the government. All orders of the President must be jointly signed by the Prime Minister or by the appropriate Minister, who thereby assumes full responsibility for such orders, except in the cases specified in Articles 48 (dissolution of the *Saeima*)

241. Article 48 of the *Satversme*.
242. *Ibid.*, Art. 49.
243. *Ibid.*, Art. 50.

and 56 (inviting the candidate for the office of the Prime Minister to form the Government).

204. Article 54 of the *Satversme* provides that the President may be subject to criminal liability if the *Saeima* consents thereto by no less than two-thirds majority.

§3. Competences

205. The President of the State has been granted representative functions (Article 41 of the *Satversme*). The President represents the State in international relations, appoints the diplomatic representatives of Latvia, and also receives diplomatic representatives of other States. The President implements the decisions of the *Saeima* concerning the ratification of international agreements.

206. According to Article 42 of the *Satversme,* 'The President shall be the Commander-in-Chief of the armed forces of Latvia. During wartime, the President shall appoint a Supreme Commander.' The President declares war on the basis of a decision of the *Saeima.*[244] The President has the right to take whatever steps are necessary for the military defence of the State should another State declare war on Latvia or an enemy invade its borders. Concurrently and without delay, the President must convene the *Saeima*, which shall decide as to the declaration and commencement of war.[245] The commencement and declaration of war is the prerogative of the *Saeima.*

207. Article 8 of National Security Law imposes the duty on the President to chair the National Security Council. The Council ensures coordination of actions taken by Latvia's higher security institutions in accordance with the national security interests of Latvia. The President of the State also proposes for the *Saeima*'s approval the candidate for the Commander of National Armed Forces, as well as requests the *Saeima* to dismiss the Commander from office.[246]

208. Article 56 of the *Satversme* defines the prerogative of the State President to choose the person who is to form the Cabinet of Ministers. The State President single-handedly adopts the order on inviting a person to form the Cabinet of Ministers, and, pursuant to Article 53 of the *Satversme*, this order does not require countersigning. Article 59 of the *Satversme* envisages that in order to fulfil their duties, the Prime Minister and other Ministers should have the confidence of the *Saeima.* It is mandatory for this candidate for the office of the Prime Minister, invited by the President of the State, to obtain the confidence of the *Saeima.*

209. It should be noted that a tradition has evolved in Latvia that, prior to nominating the candidate for the office of the Prime Minister, the President of the State

244. Article 43 of the *Satversme.*
245. *Ibid.*, Art. 44.
246. Law on Emergency Situation and State of Exception, 7 Mar. 2013, Art. 14(1).

holds consultations with the political parties elected to the *Saeima* regarding possible candidates for the office. Even though the *Satversme* does not envisage the right of the State President to approve the candidates for Ministers' offices or appoint the members of the Cabinet, over a number a years a practice has evolved that the candidate for the Prime Minister's office, selected by the President, asks the approval of the President for the possible candidates for the offices of the Minister for Foreign Affairs and the Minister for Defence. The reason for this is that these Ministries are linked with the implementation of the President's function of international representation of the State and the defence of the State.[247]

210. The authorization granted to the President of the State in connection with the legislative process covers all three stages in the legislative process: (1) legislative initiative,[248] (2) review in the *Saeima*, and (3) promulgation.[249] Moreover, the State President has the right to seek an opinion from the Constitutional Court.[250] This right of the President to subject a law for review or examination by the Constitutional Court has the purpose of increasing the political expediency and legal quality of a law.[251]

211. Article 48 of the *Satversme* provides that the President has the right to initiate legislation. The President may also submit a draft law to the *Saeima*.[252] The *Satversme* envisages also the involvement of the President in implementing the people's right to legislative initiative. Voters, comprising not less than one-tenth of the electorate, have the right to submit to the President a fully detailed draft of an amendment to the Constitution or of a law, and the President must present it to the *Saeima*.[253]

212. In the legislative process, the President also has the following rights and obligations. The *Satversme* sets out the President's duty to promulgate laws adopted by the *Saeima*. Article 71 of the *Satversme* provides that within ten days after the adoption of a law by the *Saeima*, the President, by means of a written and reasoned request to the Chairperson of the *Saeima*, may require that a law be reconsidered. If the *Saeima* does not amend the law, the President may not then raise objections a second time.

213. Article 72 of the *Satversme* defines certain other rights and obligations of the State President. The President has the right to suspend the proclamation of a law

---

247. Valsts prezidenta Konstitucionālo tiesību komisijas 2011.gada 10.maija viedokļa *'Par Valsts prezidenta funkcijām Latvijas parlamentārās demokrātijas sistēmas ietvaros'* Valsts prezidenta Konstitucionālo tiesību komisija. Viedokļi: 2008-2011 (Rīga, Latvijas Vēstnesis, 2011), p. 112.
248. Article 48 and Art. 66 of the *Satversme*.
249. *Ibid.*, Art. 69.
250. Constitutional Court Law of 5 Jun. 1996, Art. 17.
251. Valsts prezidenta Konstitucionālo tiesību komisijas 2011.gada 10.maija viedokļa *'Par Valsts prezidenta funkcijām Latvijas parlamentārās demokrātijas sistēmas ietvaros'* Valsts prezidenta Konstitucionālo tiesību komisija. Viedokļi: 2008-2011 (Rīga, Latvijas Vēstnesis, 2011), p. 112.
252. Article 65 of the *Satversme*.
253. *Ibid.*, Art. 78.

for a period of two months. The President shall suspend the proclamation of a law if so requested by not less than one-third of the members of the *Saeima*. This right may be exercised by the President, or by one-third of the members of the *Saeima*, within ten days of the adoption of the law by the *Saeima*. The law thus suspended must be put to a national referendum if so requested by not less than one-tenth of the electorate. If no such request is received during the aforementioned two-month period, the law then must be proclaimed after the expiration of such period. A national referendum must not take place, however, if the *Saeima* again votes on the law and not less than three-quarters of all members of the *Saeima* vote for the adoption of the law.

214. Article 20 of the *Satversme* envisages that the Presidium must convene sittings of the *Saeima* if requested by the President, the Prime Minister, or not less than one-third of the members of the *Saeima*. Article 22 of the *Satversme* defines the right of the President to request an *in camera* sitting.

215. The *Satversme* envisages also two special cases with regard to convening and conducting *Saeima* sittings. First, only the President of the State has the right to convene a sitting of the *Saeima* to decide on commencing or declaring a war (Article 44 of the *Satversme*). Second, the State President sets the agenda and convenes the sittings of a dissolved *Saeima* (Article 49 of the *Satversme*).

SELECTED FURTHER READING

Pleps, J. *The Application of Article 48 of the Constitution of Latvia*. (Poland, Rozważania nad problemami współczesnych społeczeństw demokratycznych. Płock: Szkoła Wyższa im. Pawła Włodkowica w Płocku, 2010), pp. 205–217.

Chapter 3. The Legislature

§1. The Organ of State

216. Article 64 of the *Satversme* reads, 'The *Saeima*, and also the people, have the right to legislate, in accordance with the procedures, and to the extent, provided for by this Constitution.'

217. As the Constitutional Court has explained, 'The legislator is entrusted to pass laws, i.e., the right to regulate some issue by law.'[254] Moreover, laws may be adopted only in compliance with the *Satversme* and the general principles of law.[255]

218. The legislation process is a special procedural order, according to which the *Saeima* or the people achieve the transformation of a draft law prepared in advance into a law: a normative act that takes a certain place in the system of normative acts. The process of legislation can be divided into the following stages: legislative initiative, discussing a draft law, adopting a law, and publishing the law. Only after having undergone all these stages does a draft law become a law.[256]

219. Passing ordinary legislation is the task of the representatives elected by the people – the *Saeima*. This body is the representation of the totality of citizens, where various thoughts, ideas, and interests, which exist among the people, become crystallized.[257]

220. The Constitutional Court has noted that the adoption of any law is the outcome of a political compromise.[258] Even though regulating all issues in law in a detailed and comprehensive way would not be appropriate, the legislator should nevertheless consider these issues.[259] The drafting, examination, and adoption of legal regulations which affect the exercise of a person's fundamental rights is the first and foremost task of the legislator. The considerations of a private person should not influence the rights and obligations of the *Saeima* to decide itself on the legal regulations that affect protecting, exercising, or ensuring the fundamental rights of other persons.[260]

221. The Constitutional Court has held that requiring only the legislator itself to regulate all issues in the State is hard to implement in the wide variety of complicated situations which affect modern society. In order to ensure an effective exercise of State power, it is possible to deviate from the strict requirement that the

254. Constitutional Court, Case No. 2005-12-0103, 16 Dec. 2005, para. 12.
255. Constitutional Court, Case No. 2010-40-03, 11 Jan. 2011, para. 6.
256. Constitutional Court, Case No. 2008-40-01, 19 May 2009, para. 9.
257. Pleps, J., Pastars, E., Plakane, I. *Konstitucionālās tiesības. Papildinātais un pārstrādātais izdevums*, (Rīga, Latvijas Vēstesis, 2014) p. 226.
258. Constitutional Court, Case No. 2007-01-01, 8 Jun. 2007, para. 16.
259. Constitutional Court, Case No. 2010-40-03, 11 Jan. 2011, para. 11.
260. Constitutional Court, Case No. 2009-05-01, 7 Oct. 2009, para. 11.

legislator itself should regulate all issues. Such efficiency is observed when the legislator regulates all the most important issues in the process of lawmaking, but delegates the drafting of more detailed legal norms to the Cabinet of Ministers or another State organ, within the limits of delegated power.[261]

222. Thus, Article 64 of the *Satversme* only enumerates the bodies which have the right to adopt laws in the narrowest meaning of this term. Laws in a broader sense also entail external regulatory enactments, and these may also be passed by institutions of executive power which have been authorized to do so by law. For instance, these include the Cabinet of Ministers, local government councils, and some institutions of public administration.

§2. The People's Legislative Initiative

223. The fundamental rules for exercising the electorate's legislative initiative are found in Articles 78–80 of the *Satversme*. Article 77 of the *Satversme*, in its turn, applies to those cases where citizens can implement their will by deciding on the laws adopted by the *Saeima* or on amendments to the *Satversme*.[262]

224. Article 78 of the *Satversme* prescribes:

> Voters, comprising no less than one tenth of the electorate, have the right to submit a fully elaborated draft of an amendment to the Constitution or of a law to the President, who shall present it to the *Saeima*. If the *Saeima* does not adopt it without change as to its content, it shall then be submitted to national referendum.

225. The Constitutional Court has noted that the *Saeima* enjoys a discretion in establishing the procedure for a national referendum, to the extent it is not contrary to the norms of the *Satversme*. Likewise, the *Saeima* has a broad discretion which laws to include in the relevant regulation.[263]

226. The Constitutional Court has emphasized that the legislator's constitutional obligation to define sufficiently clear regulations regarding the electorate's legislative initiative and the implementation of a national referendum stems from Article 78 of the *Satversme* in connection with the principle of legal certainty.[264]

227. The Constitutional Court has held that a specific procedure has been provided for in the Law on National Referendum, Legislative Initiative and European Citizens' Initiative. This Law aims at implementing the right envisaged in Article

261. Constitutional Court, Case No. 2007-04-03, 9 Oct. 2007, para. 15.
262. Constitutional Court, Terminating Judicial Proceedings in Case No. 2012-03-01, 19 Dec. 2012, para. 14.
263. *Ibid.*, para. 16.
264. *Ibid.*, para. 17.

78 of the *Satversme*.[265] This procedure specifies the rights of one-tenth of the electorate, and defines the rights and obligations of the Central Election Commission in the process of implementing these rights.[266]

228. The Law on National Referendum, Legislative Initiative and European Citizens' Initiative sets out that not less than 10,000 Latvian citizens with voting rights have the right to file a fully drawn-up draft law or draft amendments to the *Satversme* with the Central Election Commission, indicating their full names and respective personal identity numbers. Each signature must be certified by a sworn notary or at the local government institution carrying out notarial activities, not earlier than twelve months before filing the draft law or draft *Satversme* amendments with the Central Election Commission.[267]

229. The Law on Referenda, Legislative Initiatives and Initiative of European Citizens has been recently amended. The main amendments concern the number of signatures that need to be collected in order to initiate a referendum. Before amendment, only 10,000 signatures of voters were required to initiate collections of signatures for a referendum. The amendments raised the number of signatures required for the first round to 30,000.[268] After the number of signatures is collected, the Central Election's Committee proceeds with organizing general referendum.

230. An initiative group shall be set up to collect signatures in support of a draft law or draft amendments to the *Satversme*. The initiative group may consist of:

(1) a political party or association of political parties;
(2) an association of at least ten voters, set up and registered in accordance with the procedures stipulated in the Law on Associations and Foundations.[269]

231. The initiative group may appeal the decision of the Central Election Commission to refuse registration of the draft law or draft *Satversme* amendments before the Department of Administrative Cases of the Senate of the Supreme Court. This Court reviews the matter as a court of first instance, with a panel of three judges. The Court must examine the matter and issue a ruling within one month from the date of receipt of the petition. If necessary, the Court may extend the term for issuing its ruling, but for no more than one month. The appellant-applicant must support the petition with reasoned justification. The burden of proof lies with the participants to the administrative proceedings.[270]

265. Constitutional Court, Case No. 2008-40-01, 19 May 2009, para. 9.
266. Constitutional Court, Terminating Judicial Proceedings in Case No. 2012-03-01, 19 Dec. 2012, para. 16.
267. Law on a National Referendum, Legislative Initiative and European Citizens' Initiative of 31 Mar. 1994, Art. 22.
268. The law was adopted on 8 Nov. 2012, published on 27 Nov. 2012, in force since 11 Dec. 2012.
269. Law on a National Referendum, Legislative Initiative and European Citizens' Initiative of 31 Mar. 1994, Art. 23.
270. *Ibid.*, Art. 231.

232. The Central Election Commission counts the votes and establishes the result of the referendum, following which, not later than within three days, it reports them to the President, also sending the draft law or draft *Satversme* amendments submitted by the voters. If the draft law or draft *Satversme* amendments are supported by the signatures of at least one-tenth the number of citizens with voting rights in the previous *Saeima* elections, the President must submit such draft law or draft amendments to the *Satversme* to the *Saeima*.[271]

233. The Constitutional Court has noted that the *Satversme* envisages:

> that the President of the State has the right and obligation to present to the *Saeima* only a draft law, which 1) has been submitted by at least one tenth of the electorate; 2) is fully elaborated. There are no grounds to consider that the requirement included in this norm should be given narrow grammatical interpretation.[272]

234. If the President of the State disagrees with the Central Election Commission opinion regarding the compliance of the draft law prepared by electorate with the criterion 'fully elaborated', then pursuant to the functions of the President of the State defined in the *Satversme* and by employing the lawful means at his disposal, the President must see to it that the norms and principles of the *Satversme* are complied with.[273]

235. According to Article 81 of the *Saeima* Rules of Procedure, a draft law which has been submitted to the *Saeima* in accordance with the procedure set out in the Law On National Referendum, Legislative Initiative and European Citizens' Initiative, must be submitted to a national referendum if the *Saeima* rejects submitting it to *Saeima* committees, rejects it as a whole, or adopts if with changes to its content.[274]

236. The Constitutional Court has explained that:

> voters, exercising the right of legislative initiative, participate in the legislative process and not only enjoy the legislator's right established in the *Satversme*, but also assume the obligations set for the legislator. Thus, in exercising the right to legislative initiative, the same limits to discretion, which the norms and principles of the *Satversme* set for the legislator, have to be complied with.

---

271. Law on a National Referendum, Legislative Initiative and European Citizens' Initiative of 31 Mar. 1994, Art. 24 and Art. 25.
272. Constitutional Court, Terminating Judicial Proceedings in Case No. 2012-03-01, 19 Dec. 2012, para. 21.
273. Constitutional Court, Terminating Judicial Proceedings in Case No. 2012-03-01, 19 Dec. 2012, para. 21.
274. *Ibid.*, para. 22.

The Constitutional Court noted further:

> [T]he principle of legality provides that law and rights are binding to all institutions of State power, including the legislator itself. Consequently, not only the legislator which exercises the legislative rights permanently – the *Saeima* – but also the legislator which exercises the legislative right on separate occasions – the people – are obliged to comply with the norms of higher legal force and respect the constitutional values enshrined in them. Thus, a party submitting a draft law can predict that a draft law, which, in case it was adopted, would collide with the norms, principles and values contained in the *Satversme*, cannot be recognised as being fully elaborated. None of the constitutional institutions, also people, in exercising their rights, are allowed to violate the *Satversme*.[275]

237. In a national referendum pursuant to Article 77 of the *Satversme*, the 'mandatory referendum', the people express their support for or rejection of the amendments to the *Satversme* initiated by the *Saeima*. Article 77 of the *Satversme* provides that Articles 1, 2, 3, 4, 6 or 77 of the *Satversme* may be amended only if at least half of Latvian citizens having the right to vote agree to the amendments adopted by the *Saeima*.[276]

238. For the law adopted by the *Saeima* on amendments to Articles 1, 2, 3, 4, 6 or 77 of the *Satversme* to come into force, it should be passed by a national referendum.[277]

239. A national referendum on such a law adopted by the *Saeima* shall be arranged not earlier than one month and not later than two months after adopting the law in the *Saeima*.[278]

240. The Constitutional Court has also noted that the people, in expressing their opinion, decide themselves whether the submitted draft law is compatible with the values of a democratic and judicial State.[279]

§3. The Legislative Rights of the *Saeima*

I. Introduction

241. The first legislator elected by the people of Latvia was the Constitutional Assembly. Elections were held on 17 and 18 April 1920. The Constitutional

275. *Ibid.*, para. 18.3.
276. *Ibid.*, para. 14.
277. Law on a National Referendum, Legislative Initiative and European Citizens' Initiative of 31 Mar. 1994, Art. 4.
278. *Ibid.*, Art. 4.
279. Constitutional Court, Terminating Judicial Proceedings in Case No. 2012-03-01, 19 Dec. 2012, para. 14.

Assembly drafted and adopted the *Satversme*, as well as other laws (e.g., the law on agrarian reform and Law on Electing the *Saeima*). The Constitutional Assembly functioned until 7 November 1922, when the *Satversme* came into force and the *Saeima* convened for its first sitting.

242. From 1922 to 1934, four convocations of the *Saeima* were elected. On 15 May 1934, as the result of coup d'état, the sitting of the fourth *Saeima* was suspended, and the Cabinet of Ministers assumed the functions of the *Saeima*.

243. On 18 March 1990, the election of the Supreme Council of the Republic of Latvia was held. For the only time during the period of occupation, candidates from several political movements were allowed to run. The Supreme Council established a transitional period for the de facto restoration of State power, which concluded with the convening of the *Saeima* of the Republic of Latvia.

244. On 6 July 1993, with the convening of the fifth *Saeima*, the *Satversme* was reinstated.

245. On 28 May 2011, President Valdis Zatlers, by Order No. 2 based on Article 48 of the *Satversme*, proposed for the first time in the history of Latvia the dissolution of the *Saeima*. On 23 July 2011, a national referendum on the dissolution of the tenth *Saeima* was held. In accordance with the results of this referendum, more than half of the voters supported the dissolution of the tenth *Saeima*.

246. The noun '*Saeima*' in the Latvian language derives from the verb 'iet' – 'to go'. Juris Alunāns created the neologism 'saeims' with the meaning 'council of State'. Later the word '*Saeima*' was used with an expanded meaning of 'meeting, convention, conference'.[280] Since 1922, *Saeima* is the official name of the Parliament of the Republic of Latvia.

II. Organization of the *Saeima*'s Work

247. Article 15 of the *Satversme* provides that the *Saeima* holds its sittings in Riga, and only in extraordinary circumstances may it convene elsewhere.

248. Article 50 of the *Saeima* Rules of procedure stipulates, 'Consideration of matters at the sittings of the *Saeima* and at its committee meetings shall be held in the official language.'

249. Article 16 of the *Satversme* provides, 'The *Saeima* shall elect a Presidium that shall be composed of a Chairperson, two Deputies and Secretaries. The Presidium shall function continuously during the mandate of the *Saeima*.'

280. Karulis, K. *Latviešu etimoloģijas vārdnīca*. (Rīga, Avots, 1992), p. 141.

250. The Speaker represents the *Saeima* and maintains order during its sittings. In the Speaker's absence and upon mutual consent, the Speaker's duties are fulfilled by one of the Deputy Speakers. The Speaker and the Deputy Speakers divide among themselves responsibilities, including the duty of chairing *Saeima* sittings.[281]

251. The Presidium of the *Saeima* organizes the work of the *Saeima* – the process of legislation – and it also performs a number of managerial functions linked to human resources and material infrastructure. The following are the significant tasks of the Presidium:

(1) to give opinions on documents submitted and forward these documents as prescribed by the Rules of Procedure of the *Saeima*;
(2) in coordination with the Council of Parliamentary Groups, to resolve issues which cannot be settled through the Rules of Procedure of the *Saeima* and the decisions of the *Saeima*;
(3) to appoint a *Saeima* representative in the Constitutional Court if the *Saeima* has not ruled otherwise.[282]

252. Article 17 of the *Satversme* provides, 'The first sitting of the newly elected *Saeima* shall be opened by the Chairperson of the preceding *Saeima* or by another MP of the Presidium at the direction of the Presidium.'

253. The Presidium shall convene sessions of the *Saeima* and schedule regular and extraordinary sittings.[283]

254. The *Saeima* Rules of Procedure envisage that the sittings of the *Saeima* are regular and extraordinary. There are three regular annual sessions: autumn, winter, and spring. Between sessions and in accordance with necessity, an extraordinary sitting of the *Saeima* may be convened at any time.

255. Article 20 of the *Satversme* reads, 'The Presidium shall convene sittings of the *Saeima* if requested by the President, the Prime Minister, or not less than one-third of the MPs of the *Saeima*.'

256. Sittings of the *Saeima* shall be public. The *Saeima* may decide by a majority vote of no less than two-thirds of MPs present to sit in closed sitting, if so requested by ten MPs, or by the President, the Prime Minister, or a Minister.[284]

257. Article 23 of the *Satversme* sets out that sittings of the *Saeima* may take place if at least half of the MPs of the *Saeima* participate therein.

281. Rules of Procedure of the *Saeima* of 27 Jul. 1994, Art. 20 and Art. 21.
282. *Ibid.*, Art. 23.
283. *Ibid.*, Art. 19.
284. Article 22 of the *Satversme*.

258. The *Saeima* makes decisions by an absolute majority of votes of the MPs present at the sitting, except in cases specifically set out in the *Satversme*.[285]

259. The *Saeima* establishes committees and determines the number of MPs for them and their duties. Committees have the right to request information and clarifications from Ministers or local government authorities which is necessary for the work of the committees. They also have the right to invite to their sittings representatives from the relevant ministries or local government authorities to furnish explanations. Committees may also carry on their work between sessions of the *Saeima*.[286]

260. The *Saeima* can appoint special commissions or sub-commissions under regular/permanent commissions.

261. Article 26 of the *Satversme* provides, 'The *Saeima* shall appoint parliamentary investigatory committees for specified matters if not less than one-third of its MPs request it.'

262. Article 27 of the *Satversme* reads:

> The *Saeima* shall have the right to submit to the Prime Minister or to an individual Minister requests and questions which either they, or a responsible government official duly authorised by them, must answer. The Prime Minister or any Minister shall furnish the relevant documents and enactments requested by the *Saeima* or by any of its committees.

263. If consideration of a draft law has not been completed during the term of office of one *Saeima* although it has been considered in one or two readings, the next *Saeima*, upon the recommendation of the President, the Cabinet of Ministers, a *Saeima* committee, or at least five MPs of the *Saeima*, decides during its first session whether to continue consideration of that draft law. If the *Saeima* decides to continue consideration of the draft law, it appoints a committee responsible for it and sets a deadline for submitting proposals. A draft law thus assigned to the committee responsible is regarded as passed at its first reading.[287]

III. Legislative Proceedings in the *Saeima*

264. Article 5 of the *Satversme* stipulates legislative procedures. Article 21 of the *Satversme* provides that the *Saeima* 'shall establish rules of order to provide for its internal operations and order'. The *Saeima* sets its own agenda. The purpose of the *Saeima* Rules of Procedure is to set down such an agenda or the parliamentary

285. *Ibid.*, Art. 24.
286. Article 25 of the *Satversme*.
287. Rules of Procedure of the *Saeima* of 27 Jul. 1994, Art. 98(3).

procedure which, implementing the will of majority, at the same guarantees also minority rights and ensures the effective work of the *Saeima*.[288]

265. The *Saeima* may exercise its right to adopt, amend, or supplement laws and other regulatory enactments, or to recognize them as being invalid by complying with the procedure established by the *Satversme* and the principles included in the *Satversme*.[289] The *Saeima* has the discretion to choose the law in which a concrete regulation is included. Also the *Saeima* enjoys great discretion regarding the issues linked to legal technique in the framework of a law.[290]

266. Article 65 of the *Satversme* provides, 'Draft laws may be submitted to the *Saeima* by the President, the Cabinet or committees of the *Saeima*, by not less than five MPs of the *Saeima*, or, in accordance with the procedures and in the cases provided for in this Constitution, by one-tenth of the electorate.'

267. Pursuant to Article 47 of the *Satversme,* the President is entitled to submit legislative initiatives, which do not have to be in the form of draft laws.[291]

268. The Presidium reports to the *Saeima* on the draft laws received and on its opinion regarding their further progress. The *Saeima* rules whether to forward the draft law to the committees and to appoint a responsible committee or to reject it.[292]

269. The submitted draft laws must be made available to MPs at least seven days before the Presidium reports on them to the *Saeima*. If necessary, the Presidium may shorten this term.[293]

270. The *Saeima* Rules of Procedure envisage that the committees to which the *Saeima* has forwarded a draft law may prepare their alternative draft law to be considered on first reading.[294] No draft law may be tabled and considered at a *Saeima* sitting before it has been considered by the committee responsible.[295]

---

288. Constitutional Court, Case No. 2009-04-06, 30 Oct. 2009, para. 11.
289. *Ibid.*
290. *Ibid.*, para. 11.5.
291. For example, President Andris Bērziņš has consulted with representatives of the country's government and the Roman Catholic Church and decided to submit a draft law to the *Saeima* on amending the current treaty between the Republic of Latvia and the Holy. See The purpose is to assure that norms in the treaty are implemented in an equal way. President Bērziņš signed the original law on 28 Feb. 2013, thus addressing a number of major issues: announcements about the appointment of bishops, the way in which third parties can learn about those who have the right to represent the relevant church institution, and the way in which bishops report on the church's legal representatives, clergymen who have the right to conduct weddings, and chaplains who provide spiritual care.
292. Rules of Procedure of the *Saeima* of 27 Jul. 1994, Art. 82(1).
293. *Ibid.*, Art. 82(4).
294. *Ibid.*, Art. 85(4).
295. *Ibid.*, Art. 86(4).

271. In accordance with the *Saeima* Rules of Procedure,[296] a draft law is examined in three readings, except for special cases, when a draft law is examined in two readings. The draft law on the State budget and draft laws that have been recognized as being urgent, as well as draft laws that envisage ratifying international agreements are examined in only two readings. In accordance with Article 88 of the *Saeima* Rules of Procedure, during the first reading of a draft law a general debate on its principles is held. During the second reading, in accordance with Article 99(1), a vote is taken 'on each subparagraph, an entire article or a group of articles'. Prior to this vote, the proposals regarding particular article of the draft law are examined. In the third reading, as provided for by Article 109 of the *Saeima* Rules of Procedure, 'only those articles for which proposals have been submitted after the second reading shall be considered and put to vote'. At the end of the first and the second reading, the MPs of the *Saeima* vote for the draft law in general, thus expressing their support for the wording of the draft law examined during the particular reading and thus deciding to transfer it to a next reading. Following a vote on the draft law by MPs in third reading, the draft law becomes a law.

272. The Constitutional Court has explained that, in accordance with the *Saeima* Rules of Procedure, during the course of examining a draft law, a particular article, a part thereof, or amendments to a legal norm may be included both in the second and in third reading. The aforementioned does not apply only in those cases when, in accordance with Article 76 of the *Satversme*, amendments to the *Satversme* are being examined. In such a case, during the second and third reading, proposals may be submitted only with regard to those articles (regarding amending or deleting these articles) which were in the draft law when it was adopted in the first reading.[297]

273. The Constitutional Court has also noted that in the course of elaborating a draft law the *Saeima* fulfils its duty of whose opinion to hear and to consider in the framework of the legislative process. To meet the requirements of a hearing, it is sufficient if the opinion of a particular person is made known orally during the sitting of the committee responsible or is made available in writing to the MPs of that committee. If the committee of the *Saeima* has discussed a problem in the framework of one draft law, it is not necessary to discuss it anew when technically implementing the already discussed solution in other draft laws.[298]

274. The *Saeima* Rules of Procedure mainly focus on the legislative process. Only compliance with the procedure allows the valid adoption of a law under due process, whereas deviations from the procedure allow the contesting of validity of such a law. However, a decision of this kind must be well-founded, since minor violations of procedure are not sufficient grounds to arrive at this conclusion.[299] The

296. Rules of Procedure of the *Saeima* of 27 Jul. 1994, Art. 86(4).
297. Constitutional Court, Case No. 2009-11-01, 18 Jan 2010, para. 11.5.
298. Constitutional Court, Case No. 2010-17-01, 29 Oct. 2010, para. 10.1.3.
299. Pleps, J., Pastars, E., Plakane, I. *Konstitucionālās tiesības. Papildinātais un pārstrādātais izdevums*, (Rīga, Latvijas Vēstnesis, 2014), p. 297.

Constitutional Court has noted that not every violation of the parliamentary procedure constitutes sufficient grounds to consider that the adopted act has no legal force. 'To recognise an act as being invalid because of violations of the parliamentary procedure, well-founded doubts should exist that in case, if the procedure had been complied with, the *Saeima* would have been taken a different decision.'[300]

275. Article 68 of the *Satversme* reads:

> All international agreements, which settle matters that may be decided by the legislative process, shall require ratification by the *Saeima*. Upon entering into international agreements, Latvia, with the purpose of strengthening democracy, may delegate a part of its State institution competencies to international institutions. The *Saeima* may ratify international agreements in which a part of State institution competencies are delegated to international institutions in sittings in which at least two-thirds of the MPs of the *Saeima* should participate, and a two-thirds majority vote of the MPs present is necessary for ratification. Membership of Latvia in the European Union shall be decided by a national referendum, which is proposed by the *Saeima*. Substantial changes in the terms regarding the membership of Latvia in the European Union should be decided by a national referendum if such referendum is requested by at least one-half of the MPs of the *Saeima*.

276. The Constitutional Court has noted that Article 68(4) of the *Satversme* and Article 79(2) of the *Satversme* confers rights on the people to decide issues regarding substantial changes in the terms of the membership of Latvia in the EU if it is requested by at least a half of the MPs of the *Saeima*. Such wording ensures the possibility of finding out the will of the people in the case where the EU changes its constitutional structure to the extent that it may raise doubts whether the people of Latvia would approve Latvia's continuing membership in the EU after such a significant change of form and structure. At the same time it is also guaranteed that a national referendum would only be held regarding very important issues regarding integration in the EU (for instance, substantial changes in the EU Fundamental Treaties). The present wording does not allow submitting just any issue to a national referendum (for instance, acts adopted by EU institutions, like directives, regulations, and so on).[301]

277. In general, the Constitutional Court has opted for an EU-friendly approach:

> Already before World War I, when analysing legal consequences that emerge when a state undertakes international liabilities, in international law sovereignty was evaluated as exercise of sovereign rights rather than restriction thereof. The right to undertake international liabilities is an element of State sovereignty. The Permanent Court of International Justice has indicated, 'The

300. Constitutional Court, Case No. 03-04(98), 13 Jul. 1998, para. 3.
301. Constitutional Court, Case No. 2008-35-01, 7 Apr. 2009, para. 19.4.

> Court declines to see in the conclusion of any treaty by which a State undertakes to perform or refrain from performing a particular act an abandonment of its sovereignty. But the right to enter into international engagements is an attribute of State sovereignty.' … When analysing international relations of states and international organizations, it has been admitted that international organizations are institutions, in the frameworks of which the States are merging their sovereignty and resources in order to solve common problems and find common solutions for them by thus acting in favour of their national interests The notion of sovereignty has always been related with the use of power in internal and foreign relations, and this use has always been subjected to sovereign values establishing it. Values attach normative character to sovereignty, which in our case means relations between the State and an international organization … The State may be a member to such international organizations, legal relations between the institutions and member states of which may differ, and in each particular case these relations would differently affect the respective constitutional norms, even if the organization is endowed with international legal personality.[302]

278. The guidelines provided in the rulings of the Constitutional Court have influenced the organization of the legislative process and the quality of law. However, the Constitutional Court has emphasized that:

> the *Satversme* does not grant to the Constitutional Court the right to interfere in the process of legislation. Pursuant to Article 85 of the *Satversme*, the Constitutional Court may only examine the constitutionality of the laws adopted by the *Satversme*, but may not decide, what laws should be examined by the *Saeima* and when these should be adopted.[303]

279. The Constitutional Court has held that the decision with respect to the request for loan from international financial institutions – its terms and conditions – is to be deemed as an important and significant matter of State and public life, and that, in compliance with the procedure established by the *Satversme*, it had to be decided by the legislator itself.[304]

280. The President must proclaim laws passed by the *Saeima* not earlier than the tenth day and not later than the twenty-first day after the law has been adopted. A law comes into force fourteen days after its proclamation unless a different term has been specified in the law.[305] The President proclaims adopted laws in the following manner. 'The *Saeima* (that is, the People) has adopted and the President has proclaimed the following law: (text of the law).'[306]

---

302. Constitutional Court, Case No. Case 2008-35-01, 7 Apr. 2009, para. 17.
303. Constitutional Court, Decisions on the Applicant's Request in Case No. 2007-10-0102, 10 May 2007 by the on.
304. Constitutional Court, Case 2009-43-01, 21 Dec. 2009, para. 30.1.
305. If law is adopted and promulgated in due procedure, than it has been established. Observance of the procedures of adoption of norms is a precondition for validity of a legal norm.
306. Article 69 and Art. 70 of the *Satversme*.

281. Within ten days of the adoption of a law by the *Saeima*, the President, by means of a written and reasoned request to the Chairman of the *Saeima*, may ask for reconsideration of the law. If the *Saeima* does not amend the law, the President may not then raise objections for a second time.[307]

282. Article 72 of the *Satversme* provides that the President has the right to suspend the proclamation of a law for a period of two months. The President must suspend the proclamation of a law if so requested by not less than one-third of the MPs of the *Saeima*. This right may be exercised by the President, or by one-third of the MPs of the *Saeima*, within ten days after the adoption of the law by the *Saeima*. The law thus suspended must be put to a national referendum if so requested by not less than one-tenth of the electorate. If no request is received during the aforementioned two-month period, the law must then be proclaimed after the expiration of such period. A national referendum must not be held, however, if the *Saeima* again votes for the law and not less than three-quarters of all MPs of the *Saeima* vote for the adoption of that law.

283. Should the *Saeima*, by not less than a two-thirds majority vote, determine a law to be urgent, the President may not then request reconsideration of the law. And it may not be submitted to a national referendum. The adopted law must be proclaimed no later than the third day after the President has received it.[308]

284. Article 72 of the *Satversme* envisages an optional referendum with a veto character. However, with regard to the institute enshrined in Article 72 of the *Satversme*, there are apparently no obstacles for the President to propose to citizens the repeal of a law adopted by the *Saeima*, on his or her own initiative or on a proposal submitted by at least one-third of the MPs of the *Saeima*. Moreover, the President, in exercising the right set out in Article 72 of the *Satversme* on his or her own initiative or on the proposal of at least one-third of the MPs of *Saeima*, must abide by Article 73 of the *Satversme*.[309]

285. Article 74 of the *Satversme* provides that a law adopted by the *Saeima* and suspended pursuant to the procedures specified in Article 72 should be repealed by national referendum if the number of voters is at least half of the number of voters who participated in the previous *Saeima* election and if the majority have voted for the repeal of the law.

286. Nevertheless and by contrast, Article 73 of the *Satversme* provides that the budget and laws concerning loans, taxes, customs duties, railroad tariffs, military conscription, the declaration and commencement of war, peace treaties, a declaration of a state of emergency and its termination, mobilization and demobilization,

307. *Ibid.*, Art. 71.
308. Article 75 of the *Satversme*.
309. Pleps, J., Pastars, E., Plakane, I. *Konstitucionālās tiesības. Papildinātais un pārstrādātais izdevums*, (Rīga, Latvijas Vēstnesis, 2014), pp. 313–315.

as well as agreements with other nations may not be submitted to a national referendum.

287. The *Saeima* may amend the *Satversme* in sittings at which at least two-thirds of the MPs of the *Saeima* participate.[310] The amendments shall be passed in three readings by a majority of not less than two-thirds of the MPs present. According to Article 77 of the *Satversme,* 'If the *Saeima* has amended the first, second, third, fourth, sixth or seventy-seventh Article of the Constitution, such amendments, in order to come into force as law, shall be submitted to a national referendum.'

IV. The Rights of the *Saeima* to Adopt the Budget

288. The Latvian Constitutional Court has expressed the view that the adoption of the annual State budget law is one of the most important decisions taken by the State.[311]

289. Article 66 of the *Satversme* provides:

> Annually, before the commencement of each financial year, the *Saeima* shall determine the State Revenues and Expenditures Budget, the draft of which shall be submitted to the *Saeima* by the Cabinet. If the *Saeima* makes a decision that involves expenditures not included in the Budget, then this decision must also allocate funds to cover such expenditures. After the end of the budgetary year, the Cabinet shall submit an accounting of budgetary expenditures for the approval of the *Saeima.*

This provision defines the procedure according to which the legislator deals with the State budget and financial issues, in interaction with the executive power.

290. The Constitutional Court has recognized that the budget is a tool for implementing State policy and that only the legislator can take decisions concerning the State budget.[312]

291. The adoption of the law on the State budget is an important function of the *Saeima*, which it fulfils as an institution directly responsible to the people of Latvia. Compared to other constitutional institutions involved in the drafting and adoption of the budget, the *Saeima* has the most important role from the point of view of constitutional law in fulfilling this constitutional task. This decisive role of the *Saeima*, *inter alia*, is also grounded on the condition that it has the task to control the fulfilment of the budget, which, in turn, is the government's task. Thus, the *Saeima*'s

310. Article 76 of the *Satverme.*
311. Constitutional Court, Case No. 2010-06-01, 25 Nov. 2010, para. 13.
312. Constitutional Court, Case No. 2009-11-01, 18 Jan. 2010, para. 8.1.

right in the budget process is one of the most important tools of the *Saeima* to exercise its constitutional control over implementation. Other institutions have the right to adopt decisions pertaining to the State budget only in cases envisaged by the *Satversme* or if the *Saeima* has granted permission to adopt such decisions and if the basic principles of a democratic State are abided by.[313]

292. The budget is the backbone for a sustainable functioning of the State and its future prosperity, The State budget is a policy-planning document of an economic nature, and it includes not just a calculation of expenditures and revenues taking into account available financial resources, but also the steps to be taken for distributing benefits among various groups in society. When approving the State budget, the legislature also amends other normative acts so as to harmonize the State's financial capabilities with the duties of the State which require certain expenditures.[314] Article 87^1 of the *Saeima* Rules of Procedure state that the package of budget laws consists of draft laws which determine or amend the budget, as well as ones which are related to the budget.[315] This means that in drafting the State budget, the government should establish plans for the spending of financial resources, and it should also approve the relevant normative regulations. This also makes it possible to claim that the national budget can be adopted as a set of normative acts.[316]

293. The legal definition of the State budget is provided in Article 1 of the Law on the Budget and Financial Management. Its first part provides, 'A budget is a means for the implementation of State policy through financial methods. The budget is the foundation for government financial activities and management.' The second part of this article reads:

> The purpose of a budget is to determine and substantiate the means required for the government, other State authorities and self-governments to fulfil such State duties the financing of which is determined by legislative acts, ensuring that within the period for which such funds are provided expenditures are covered by corresponding revenue. In formulating budgets, the necessity of ensuring an overall economic balance shall be taken into account.

The aforementioned law first and foremost regulates the procedure for drafting, adopting, and implementing the budget. Thus, the regulation included in the law expands and specifies the contents of Article 66 of the *Satversme*.[317]

313. Constitutional Court, Case No. 2011-11-01, 3 Feb. 2012, para. 10.
314. Constitutional Court, Case No. Case No. 2011-03-01, 20 Dec. 2011, para. 18.
315. Rules of Procedure of the Saeima, Art. 871.
316. Amolina D. *Legislation and Financial Issues in the State*. Publication presents a collection of research papers in conjunction with the international scientific conference 'The Quality of Legal Acts and its Importance in Contemporary Legal Space', 4–5 Oct. 2012 at the University of Latvia Faculty of Law, Riga.
317. Constitutional Court, Case No. 2011-11-01, 3 Feb. 2012, para. 10.

294. The Constitutional Court has also acknowledged that the budget is the economic plan for the State which, on the basis of laws that are in force, estimates the State revenue and expenditure for the financial year. It defines and substantiates the resources necessary for meeting the State's obligations in such a way that, during the period for which these resources are intended, expenditures are covered by appropriate revenues. All State institutions and authorities are linked to the State budget.[318]

295. The Law on the State Budget is in force for a limited time – one year. The Constitutional Court has already recognized that the Law on the State Budget is a special law, its validity being limited in time to the concrete fiscal year.[319]

296. The budget is submitted to the *Saeima* by the Cabinet of Ministers and subsequently approved by the *Saeima*. Initially, parts of the draft budget are elaborated by departments of the Ministries and other institutions and authorities. The main task of the Cabinet of Ministers is to collect them and harmonize the budgets of the individual institutions. The Cabinet should find a balance between competing interests in the State expenditure budget and the State revenue budget.[320] At this stage the views of the social partners are also taken into account.

297. The Constitutional Court has noted that the objectives of the State:

> are reflected in the budget as expenditure should be covered by appropriate revenue. Thus, the scope and content of the State budget reflects the general State politics. At the same time, the limited revenue defines the discretion of the government and the *Saeima* in deciding on the usage of the State financial resources. Since the State budget is based upon the revenue and expenditure estimates, the constitutional institutions have the discretion, when taking decisions concerning concrete budgetary items, to harmonise them with the general State politics and the already adopted legal acts.[321]

298. When addressing the case of reducing pensions due to austerity policies, the Constitutional Court emphasized the role of the *Saeima* in adopting the budget. During proceedings the *Saeima* and the Cabinet of Ministers relied on a Memorandum of Understanding between the Cabinet and the EU, as well as the IMF. The Court noted that it had not received any information:

> attesting that the international creditors stipulated the adoption of the impugned provisions as a prerequisite for granting the loan … . Besides, the principle of separation of powers delimits the authority of the Cabinet of Ministers. In accordance with this principle, the Constitution confers the

318. Constitutional Court, Case No. 01-05(98), 27 Nov. 1998, para. 1 and Constitutional Court, Case No. 2010-06-01, 25 Nov. 2010, para. 12.
319. Constitutional Court, Case No. 04-03(98), 10 Jun. 1998.
320. Dišlers, K. *Latvijas valsts varas orgāni un viņu funkcijas*. (Rīga, Tieslietu Ministrijas Vēstnesis, 1925) p. 121.
321. Constitutional Court, Case No. 2011-11-01, 3 Feb. 2012, para. 10.

> lawmaking powers – namely, the powers to decide the most important matters for the state – to the *Saeima* in particular, and, in individual cases, to full-fledged citizens of the Republic of Latvia. The other branches of power are obliged to implement these laws in practice … . Although the Cabinet of Ministers is entitled to adopt regulatory enactments, the latter are not permitted to contain such provisions that cannot be deemed as aids for the implementation of the provisions of the law … . Thus, it is permissible to delegate the drafting required for the implementation of a law in practice to the Cabinet of Ministers, whereas the *Saeima* is obliged to decide all the most important matters of the State and public life by itself through legislation. Furthermore, the first part of Article 68 of the Constitution prescribes that all international agreements, which settle matters that may be decided by the legislative process, shall require ratification by the *Saeima* … . In order to establish whether the *Saeima*'s argumentation for the infringement of the rights of persons, one should consider whether the Cabinet of Ministers was entitled to decide without the authorisation from the *Saeima* the matters pertaining to the international loans, or else the respective commitments are to be taken as settling the matters that had to be decided through legislation and, accordingly, needed the *Saeima*'s approval.[322]

Therefore, the international commitments assumed by the Cabinet of Ministers cannot by themselves serve as an argument for the restriction of the fundamental rights.

299. Article 114 of the *Saeima* Rules of Procedure prescribes that only two readings are required 'for adopting: a draft budget law and amendments thereto, the draft medium-term budget framework and amendments thereto'.

300. During the first reading, it is allowed to hold a debate on the whole package of draft budget laws, but a vote must be taken separately on each draft law.[323]

301. The persons referred to in Article 95 of the *Saeima* Rules of Procedure may submit proposals. The committee which is responsible for the draft budget law and budget-related draft laws shall compile the submitted proposals and immediately send them to the Cabinet. At the same time, it shall inform the Cabinet when the proposals will be considered by the committee.[324]

302. The *Saeima* Rules of Procedure envisage that during consideration of a draft budget law, debate may be held on several articles (paragraphs) simultaneously, if so required by the submitted proposal.[325] When considering a draft budget law, a vote must be taken on the entire proposal, amending several articles

322. Constitutional Court, Case No. 2009-43-01, 21 Dec. 2009, para. 30.1.
323. Rules of Procedure of the *Saeima* of 27 Jul. 1994, Art. 871.
324. *Ibid.*, Art. 95(4).
325. *Ibid.*, Art. 98(3).

simultaneously if necessary. If the proposal has been adopted or rejected, it is deemed adopted or rejected with regard to all the articles concerned.[326]

303. The order in which the proposals for a draft budget law are put to a vote is determined by the *Saeima* upon the recommendation of the committee responsible. A proposal is deemed adopted if it has received an absolute majority of votes of the MPs present.[327]

304. The *Saeima* Rules of Procedure state that if the annual draft budget submitted by the Cabinet is rejected by the *Saeima* at the first or second reading, 'it shall be regarded as a vote of no confidence in the Cabinet'.[328]

V. Electoral System

305. Article 6 of the *Satversme* envisages that the *Saeima* should be elected in general, equal, and direct elections, and by secret ballot based on proportional representation.

306. In the division of Latvia into separate electoral districts, the number of MPs of the *Saeima* to be elected from each district is proportional to the number of voters in each district.[329]

307. All citizens of Latvia who enjoy full rights of citizenship and who, on election day, have attained 18 years of age, are entitled to vote. Any citizen of Latvia who enjoys full rights of citizenship and who is more than 21 years of age on the first day of elections may be elected to the *Saeima*.[330]

308. The Law on the Election of the *Saeima* lists the groups of persons who cannot be included on the list of candidates and who are not eligible to be elected to the *Saeima*:

(1) those placed under statutory trusteeship by the court;
(2) those serving a court sentence in a penitentiary;
(3) those convicted of criminal offence committed with intent, except where rehabilitated or where their conviction has been expunged or vacated;
(4) those having committed a criminal offence set forth in the Criminal Law in a state of mental incapacity or of diminished mental capacity, or who, after committing a criminal offence, have developed a mental disorder and are thereby incapable of self-aware, conscious action and as a result have been subjected to

326. *Ibid.*, Art. 99(3).
327. *Ibid.*, Art. 101 and Art. 102.
328. Rules of Procedure of the *Saeima* of 27 Jul. 1994, Art. 30.
329. Article 7 of the *Satversme*.
330. Article 8 and Art. 9 of the *Satversme*.

compulsory medical measures, or whose cases have been dismissed without applying such compulsory medical measures;

(5) those belonging to the salaried staff of the State security, intelligence or counter-intelligence services of a foreign country or having been part of the salaried staff of the State security, intelligence or counter-intelligence services of the USSR or the Latvian SSR, excepting those who have been employed at the Planning, Finance or Administrative Departments of the Committee for State Security of the USSR or the Latvian SSR;

(6) those active after 13 January 1991 in the Communist Party of the Soviet Union (the Communist Party of Latvia), the International Front of the Working People of the Latvian SSR, the United Board of Working Bodies, the Organisation of War and Labour Veterans, the All-Latvia Salvation Committee, or its regional committees;

(7) those sentenced to a prohibition from standing as a candidate in the elections of the *Saeima*, European Parliament, city or municipality councils, unless otherwise rehabilitated or their conviction having been expunged or vacated.[331]

309. The ECtHR has confirmed the Latvian approach in relation to sixth group in the *Ždanoka* case where it stated:

> [I]n order to guarantee the stability and effectiveness of a democratic system, the State may be required to take specific measures to protect itself. … Every time a State intends to rely on the principle of 'a democracy capable of defending itself' in order to justify interference with individual rights, it must carefully evaluate the scope and consequences of the measure under consideration, to ensure that the aforementioned balance is achieved.[332]

310. A list of candidates may be submitted by a legally registered political party and legally registered alliance of political parties. Lists of candidates must be submitted to the Central Election Commission by the prescribed deadline and according to the procedure set out by the Commission. A list of candidates must be submitted by the person authorized by the decision-making body of the relevant political party or alliance of political parties.[333]

311. Voters registering for passive voting rights should be included in the list of candidates of a political party or a union of political parties. The lists should be submitted to the Central Election Commission eighty to sixty days before election day. The law sets out the requirements and procedures for submission, registration, verification, and publication of lists and party programmes.

---

331. Law on the Election of the Saeima of 25 May 1995, Art. 5.
332. Case of *Ždanoka v. Latvia* (Application No. 58278/00), judgment of 16 Mar. 2006. The judgment was adopted by the Grand Chamber by thirteen votes to four that there had been no violation of Art. 3 of Protocol No. 1 and by thirteen votes to four that it is not necessary to examine separately the applicant's complaints under Art. 11 of the EConvHR.
333. Law on the Election of the Saeima of 25 May 1995, Art. 9.

312. Latvia is divided into five constituencies for *Saeima* elections: Riga, Vidzeme, Latgale, Kurzeme, and Zemgale.[334]

313. The *Satversme* stipulates that elections for the *Saeima* are to be held on the first Saturday in October.[335]

314. In order for a party or an association of parties to be represented in the *Saeima*, it must receive at least 5% of the total number of votes cast in all five constituencies.

315. The Constitutional Court has reviewed the compliance of both the norms that apply to parliamentary elections,[336] and to the elections of regional representative institutions (local government elections) with the norms of the *Satversme*.[337]

316. The Constitutional Court has examined a number of issues linked to the exercise of election rights: issues of exercising active election rights (e.g., the right to participate in elections by persons who in prison),[338] as well as those pertaining to the exercise of passive election rights (e.g., the regulations applying to the former salaried employees of the Committee for State Security and a judge, registered as candidates for elections).[339]

317. Regulations regarding the system and organization of elections was reviewed by the Constitutional Court in two cases. The first concerned whether the *Saeima* had the right to set the percentage threshold to be reached in order for a person to be elected an MP of the *Saeima*. The second examined the compatibility of various restrictions to pre-election campaigns before local government elections with freedom of speech.[340]

318. The Constitutional Court has reviewed all restrictions imposed upon the right to vote in the light of ECtHR judgments. When examining restrictions the Court applied methodology used by the ECtHR.

319. The *Saeima* elects the Mandate, Ethics and Submissions Committee, whose MPs verify election documents and investigate complaints about elections if such complaints have been submitted to the Central Election Commission not later than four days after the official election results have been announced as prescribed by law.[341]

334. Article 7 of the *Satversme*.
335. *Ibid.*, Art. 11.
336. Constitutional Court, Case No. 2000-03-01, 30 Aug. 2000.
337. Constitutional Court, Case No. 2009-45-01, 22 Feb. 2010.
338. Constitutional Court, Case No. 2002-18-01, 5 Mar. 2003.
339. Constitutional Court, Case No. 2005-13-0106, 15 Jun. 2006.
340. Constitutional Court, Case No. 2002-08-01, 23 Sep. 2002 and Constitutional Court, Case No. 2009-45-01, 22 Feb. 2010.
341. Rules of Procedure of the *Saeima* of 27 Jul. 1994, Art. 2.

VI. Composition of the *Saeima*

320. According to Article 5 of the *Satversme*, 'The *Saeima* shall be composed of one hundred representatives of the people.'

321. The 100 representatives are the MPs of the *Saeima*, whose mandates have been approved by the *Saeima*.[342]

322. Article 18 of the *Satversme* provides:

> The *Saeima* itself shall review the qualifications of its MPs. A person elected to the *Saeima* shall acquire the mandate of an MP of the *Saeima* if such person gives the following solemn promise: 'I, upon assuming the duties of an MP of the *Saeima*, before the people of Latvia, do swear (solemnly promise) to be loyal to Latvia, to strengthen its sovereignty and the Latvian language as the only official language, to defend Latvia as an independent and democratic State, and to fulfil my duties honestly and conscientiously. I undertake to observe the Constitution and laws of Latvia.'

323. An MP must take the oath in Latvian language and must confirm it under signature. MPs must take the solemn oath at the rostrum. If an MP is a person with a physical disability preventing them from reaching the rostrum, the MP may take the solemn oath while remaining in their seat in the Plenary Chamber.[343]

324. The approval of an MP's mandate is a very important prerequisite, since an MP of the *Saeima* is so authorized only after its conferral. It is another manifestation of the *Saeima* as a permanent legislative institution. The approval of mandates comprises both the verification of the legality and accuracy of the election results and taking of the solemn oath, and the decision on confirming authorization. It is important to note that the Parliament does not have a broad discretion to decide which of the MPs will or will not have their mandate approved. It is a constitutional obligation, not a political decision. Moreover, the possibility not to approve an MP's mandate must be expressly included in law and must follow from the relevant norms of the *Satversme*.[344]

VII. The Members of Parliament

325. An MP enjoys all the rights of a *Saeima* MP until the expiry of their mandate. The mandate of an MP expires as of the moment:

342. *Ibid.*, Art. 1.
343. *Ibid.*, Art. 3.
344. Pleps, J., Pastars, E., Plakane, I. *Konstitucionālās tiesības. Papildinātais un pārstrādātais izdevums.* (Rīga, Latvijas Vēstnesis, 2014), p. 250.

(1) a newly elected *Saeima* has been convened;
(2) the MP has given notice of resignation, and the mandate of another MP has been approved to replace him/her;
(3) the MP has been expelled from the *Saeima*;
(4) the MP has died.

326. Article 14 of the *Satversme* states that 'electors may not recall an individual MP of the *Saeima*'.

327. If a person holding a position incompatible with the position of an MP is elected to the *Saeima*, that person must either leave that position or resign their mandate as a *Saeima* MP within one month from approval of their mandate.[345]

328. An MP has the right to terminate their mandate during their term of office as Prime Minister, Deputy Prime Minister, Minister, or during maternity and childbirth leave, child adoption leave, as well as childcare leave. Upon receiving notice of resignation from a mandate, the Presidium of the *Saeima* invites the next candidate from the parties' list for elections to become an MP and notifies the Mandate, Ethics and Submissions Committee thereof. The Mandate, Ethics and Submissions Committee verifies the election documents and notifies the *Saeima* of the results of this verification. The *Saeima*, by its decision, approves the mandate of the said candidate.[346]

329. Article 7 of the *Saeima* Rules of Procedure provides that every MP is obliged 'to participate in the work of the *Saeima*.'

330. An MP is permitted to be absent from the work of the *Saeima* for no longer than one week, provided that they have informed the Presidium and have requested leave in advance. This right must not be used more than once during each session. This leave is unpaid and is granted for a specific period of time.[347]

331. Restrictions and obligations of *Saeima* MPs concerning their business activities, income, and work outside the *Saeima* are prescribed by the Law on Prevention of Conflict of Interests in Activities of Public Officials.[348]

332. Article 33 of the *Satversme* stipulates that the remuneration of MPs is paid from State funds. While in office, in accordance with the procedure and schedule set out by the Presidium, an MP receives a monthly salary set by the Law on Remuneration of Officials and Employees of State and Local Government Authorities. The monthly salary is paid from the *Saeima* budget.[349]

345. Rules of Procedure of the Saeima of 27 Jul. 1994, Art. 11.
346. *Ibid.*, Art. 5.
347. *Ibid.*, Art. 8.
348. Rules of Procedure of the Saeima of 27 Jul. 1994, Art. 10.
349. Rules of Procedure of the Saeima of 27 Jul. 1994, Art. 12.

333. Article 32 of the *Satversme* provides that MPs of the *Saeima* may not, either personally or in the name of another person, receive government contracts or concessions. The provisions of this article apply to Ministers even if they are not MPs of the *Saeima*.

334. MPs of the *Saeima* may not be held liable in any judicial, administrative, or disciplinary process in connection with their voting or their views expressed when performing their duties. Court proceedings may be brought against MPs of the *Saeima* if, albeit in the course of performing parliamentary duties, they disseminate:

(1) defamatory statements which they know to be false; or
(2) defamatory statements about an individual's private or family life.[350]

335. Article 29 of the *Satversme* reads:

> MPs of the *Saeima* shall not be arrested, nor shall their premises be searched, nor shall their personal liberty be restricted in any way without the consent of the *Saeima*. MPs of the *Saeima* may be arrested if apprehended in the act of committing a crime. The Presidium shall be notified within twenty-four hours of the arrest of any MP of the *Saeima*; the Presidium shall raise the matter at the next sitting of the *Saeima* for decision as to whether the MP shall continue to be held in detention or be released. When the *Saeima* is not in session, pending the opening of a sitting, the Presidium shall decide whether the MP of the *Saeima* shall remain in detention.

336. If the *Saeima* agrees that a criminal prosecution of a *Saeima* MP be initiated, the respective *Saeima* MP loses the right to participate in the sittings of the *Saeima*, meetings of its committees, and other institutions to which this MP has been elected or appointed by the *Saeima* until the dismissal of the charges or earlier. During this time, the Prosecutor's Office and the court have the right to apply any coercive measures applicable under the criminal procedure laws.[351]

337. Article 30 of the *Satversme* provides that a criminal prosecution may not be commenced and administrative fines may not be levied against its MPs without the consent of the *Saeima*. Article 31 of the *Satversme* sets out that MPs of the *Saeima* have the right to refuse to give evidence:

(1) concerning persons who have entrusted to them, as representatives of the people, certain facts or information;
(2) concerning persons to whom they, as representatives of the people, have entrusted certain facts or information; or
(3) concerning such facts or information itself.

350. Article 28 of the *Satversme*.
351. Rules of Procedure of the Saeima of 27 Jul. 1994, Art. 17.

338. An MP who has been convicted of a criminal offence is deemed expelled from the *Saeima* as of the date when the sentence comes into force.[352]

339. An MP may be expelled from the *Saeima* by a decision of the *Saeima* if, upon approval of his or her mandate, it is established that he or she:

(1) has been elected in violation of the provisions of the *Saeima* Election Law;
(2) lacks command of the official language at the level necessary for the performance of his/her professional duties;
(3) holds a position which is incompatible with the mandate of a *Saeima* MP;
(4) has been absent during the period of a current sitting for more than half of all *Saeima* sittings without a valid excuse;
(5) has committed a crime in a state of diminished responsibility or, after committing the crime, has become mentally ill rendering them incapable of self-aware, conscious action.[353]

VIII. Recall and Dissolution of the *Saeima*

340. Pursuant to Article 14 of the *Satversme:*

> Not less than one tenth of voters have the right to initiate a national referendum to recall the *Saeima*. If the majority of voters and at least two thirds of the number of the voters who participated in the last elections of the *Saeima* vote in favour, the *Saeima* should be deemed recalled. The right to initiate a national referendum to dissolve the *Saeima* may not be exercised one year after the convening of the *Saeima* and one year before the end of the term of office of the *Saeima*, during the last six months of the term of office of the President, as well as earlier than six months after the previous national referendum regarding recalling of the *Saeima*.

This article establishes the mechanism for recalling the *Saeima*.

341. Article 48 of the *Satversme* divides the right to dissolve the *Saeima* between the President of the State and the totality of citizens. The first sentence in Article 48 of the *Satversme* provides that the President shall be entitled to propose the dissolution of the *Saeima*. Under the second part of this article, a national referendum must be held following the President's proposal, putting the decision to dissolve the *Saeima* for adoption by the totality of citizens. This construction thus avoids a casuistic enumeration of the cases where the *Saeima* may or may not be dissolved, since this is decided by the people.[354] In Latvian constitutional law, Article 48 has been applied only once. Until Valdis Zatlers' decision to initiate the

352. *Ibid.*, Art. 18.
353. *Ibid.*, Art. 18.
354. Pleps, J., Pastars, E., Plakane, I. *Konstitucionālās tiesības. Papildinātais un pārstrādātais izdevums*, (Rīga, Latvijas Vēstnesis, 2014), p. 263.

procedure for dissolving the *Saeima*, the procedure envisaged in the *Satversme* was considered to be ineffective and in need of major alterations.

342. Article 49 of the *Satversme* envisages that if the *Saeima* has been dissolved or recalled, the mandates of the MPs of the *Saeima* continue to be effective until the newly elected *Saeima* is convened. During this time, the former *Saeima* may only hold sittings upon the request of the President. The President determines the agenda of such sittings of the *Saeima*. New elections must take place not earlier than one month and not later than two months after the recall of the *Saeima*.

343. Following the dissolution of the tenth *Saeima* in 2011, the President of the State made public the procedure for organizing the convening of the *Saeima* for sittings, to clarify the organization of the work done by the *Saeima* until the new *Saeima* was convened. The Chancellery of the President announced that each issue on the agenda of the *Saeima* sitting would not be included automatically, but only after additional information had been requested and consultations and meetings had been held. This was intended to ensure the control of the President of the State over the issues placed on the agenda of the *Saeima*. The Chancellery of the President of the State also noted that, depending upon the number of issues, the sittings of the *Saeima* could be convened less frequently than every week as usual.[355]

Selected Further Reading

Auers, D. 'Referendums and Initiatives in the Baltic States'. In *Financing Referendum Campaigns*, edited by Simon Hug & Karin Gilland Lutz. London: Palgrave MacMillan, 2009.

Balodis, R. & J. Pleps. *Financial Crisis and the Constitution in Latvia. Constitution in the Global Financial Crisis. A Comparative Analysis* edited by Xenophon Contiades. Centre for European Constitutional Law. Greece, ASHGATE 2013, p. 115–140.

Kārkliņa, A. 'Dissolution of Parliament in Latvia: Legal Regulation and Practice'. *Jurisprudence Lithuania* 20(3): 2013.

Mits M. 'Legal Benchmarks for Lowering Social Protection in Times of Austerity. Lessons from Latvia', (ΔΙΚΑΙ'ΩΜΑΤΑ ΤΟΥ ΑΝΘΡ'ΩΠΟΥ:Επιθεώρηση ατομικών και κοινωνικών δικαιωμάτων [Human Rights: Theory of Civic and Social Rights] No. 57, 2013).

355. *Ibid.*, p. 265.

Chapter 4. The Executive

§1. Introduction

344. The Constitutional Court has recognized that executive activity is that activity of the State which is neither legislation nor the administration of justice.[356]

345. The *Satversme* has entrusted the Cabinet of Ministers to perform the executive function, even though some activities of executive power, with the aim of ensuring the separation of powers, have been also granted to other constitutional institutions.[357]

346. The Constitutional Court has also noted that, in Latvia, the bearer of constitutional executive power is the Cabinet of Ministers. The constitutional basis for its activities is the *Saeima*'s confidence. The *Satversme* grants some functions of executive power to the President of the State, who carries no political responsibility.[358] However, pursuant to the second sentence of Article 53 of the *Satversme*, the approval by the members of the Cabinet is needed to fulfil these functions.[359] Those actions of executive power, which have not been transferred to other constitutional institutions, fall within the competence of the Cabinet of Ministers, and the Cabinet is responsible for performing them.

347. The main task of the Cabinet of Ministers is to fulfil the functions of the executive power. The *Satversme* provides that the Cabinet of Ministers may establish institutions of public administration and delegate to them part of its competences. The Cabinet retains control over and responsibility for the performance of delegated tasks. Institutions of public administration fulfil the administrative functions of executive power (public administration) together with the political functions of executive power fulfilled by the Cabinet of Ministers.[360]

348. Until 1934, the activities by the Cabinet of Ministers was regulated by the 1925 Law on the Structure of the Cabinet of Ministers. It provided that nine ministries functioned in Latvia: Foreign Affairs, Finance, Interior, Education,

356. Constitutional Court, Case No. 2006-05-01, 16 Oct. 2006, para. 10.2.
357. Constitutional Court, Case No. 2006-05-01, 16 Oct. 2006, para. 10.4.
358. The President has the right, at his request, to receive information that is at the disposal of government institutions and offices, taking into account the regulations on the use of information that are stated in the law. Upon the proclamation of war against the state or a military invasion, the President must immediately act in accordance with the regulations of the National Defence Plan, issue instructions and orders to the National Armed Forces, as well as to state and local government institutions and the people of Latvia, summon a meeting of Parliament to take a decision on the proclamation and launching of war, and appoint the senior commander of the National Armed Forces. See The Law on the National Armed Forces of 14 Dec. 2000, Arts 8 and 24.2.
359. Constitutional Court, Case No. 2006-05-01, 16 Oct. 2006, para. 15.3.
360. *Ibid.*, para. 11.

Agriculture, Transport, National Welfare and Justice.[361] Until 15 May 1934, eighteen Cabinets of Ministers succeeded each other in Latvia.

349. After 15 May 1934, when the coup d'état lead by Kārlis Ulmanis took place, the Cabinet of Ministers fulfilled not only the functions of the executive power, but also turned into the legislator, assuming the functions of the *Saeima*.[362]

350. Following the occupation by the Soviet Union, on 24 August 1940, the Constitution of the Latvian Social Soviet Republic was adopted. This Constitution regulated the operation of executive power.[363]

351. Following the restoration of Latvia's independence, on 16 July 1993, the Law On Reinstating the Law of 1 April 1925 on the Structure of the Cabinet of Ministers was adopted. On 15 May 2008, the *Saeima* replaced this with the Law on the Structure of the Cabinet of Ministers, which currently regulates the work of the Cabinet.

§2. Establishment

352. Article 55 of the *Satversme* provides, 'The Cabinet shall be composed of the Prime Minister and the Ministers chosen by the Prime Minister.' Article 56 of the *Satversme* provides that the Cabinet is formed by the person who has been invited by the President to do so.

353. Article 59 of the *Satversme* provides that in order to fulfil their duties, the Prime Minister and other Ministers must have the confidence of the *Saeima* and that they are accountable to the *Saeima* for their actions. If the *Saeima* expresses no confidence in the Prime Minister, the entire Cabinet must resign. If there is an expression of no confidence in an individual Minister, then the Minister must resign and another person should be invited to replace him or her by the Prime Minister.

354. The Constitutional Court has noted that the confidence of the *Saeima* is the sole constitutional basis for the actions of the Cabinet of Ministers. If it is lost, then the President of the State has the right to invite either the former Prime Minister or another person to form a new government.[364]

355. The legislator has prescribed in more detail the formation of the Cabinet of Ministers in the Law on the Structure of the Cabinet of Ministers. According to this, the person, who has been invited by the President of the State to form the Cabinet is to be regarded as the candidate for the Prime Minister's office. The Chancellery

361. Lēbers, D.A. *Ministru kabinets: komentārs Latvijas Republikas Satversmes IV nodaļai 'Ministru kabinets'. (*Rīga, Tiesiskās informācijas centrs, 1998), p. 13.
362. *Ibid.*
363. Lēbers, D.A. *Ministru kabinets: komentārs Latvijas Republikas Satversmes IV nodaļai 'Ministru kabinets'. (*Rīga, Tiesiskās informācijas centrs, 1998), p. 11.
364. Constitutional Court, Case No. 03-04-(98), 13 Jul. 1998, para. 2.

of the President notifies in writing the State Chancellery about a candidate's invitation for the office of Prime Minister.[365]

356. A person who, in accordance with Law on Electing the *Saeima*, cannot be registered as a candidate for and elected to the *Saeima*, in turn cannot be proposed and approved as a member of the Cabinet of Ministers.[366]

357. Political parties are important in the process of choosing the candidate for the Prime Ministers' office,[367] because the President of the State holds consultations with those political parties which have been elected to the *Saeima* on the possible composition of the Cabinet of Ministers and the candidate for the Prime Minister's office as suggested by those parties. However, the President of the State has the discretion to choose the candidate for the Prime Minister's office without consulting political parties, since the *Satversme* does not impose an obligation to consult.

358. The candidate for the Prime Minister's office submits a Declaration, signed by the candidate and the ministers invited by him or her, and a draft decision of the *Saeima* on reposing confidence in the Cabinet of Ministers, to the President of the State and the Speaker of the *Saeima*. The draft decision on giving a vote of confidence to the Cabinet of Ministers is included in the agenda of the *Saeima* in accordance with the *Saeima* Rules of Procedure.[368]

359. This Declaration (on the policy agenda of the Cabinet of Ministers) is a political document, a guide, which outlines long-term and shorter-term policy plans, including those addressing national security. It is intended to serve for the term of office of the Cabinet, and sets forth the priorities of the Cabinet, the aims and objectives to be reached.[369]

360. The *Saeima* votes its confidence in the Cabinet of Ministers after the candidate for the Prime Minister's office has reported on the possible composition of the Cabinet of Ministers and the Declaration of the Cabinet.[370]

361. The Cabinet of Ministers is recognized as formed when the *Saeima*, rendering its vote of confidence on the Cabinet of Ministers, has expressed its confidence in all Cabinet members.[371]

362. If the Prime Minister invites a person to become a Minister after the *Saeima* has given a vote of confidence in the Cabinet of Ministers, this person must receive an individual vote of confidence from the *Saeima*. Members of the Cabinet

365. Law on the Structure of the Cabinet of Ministers of 15 May 2008, Art. 13(1).
366. *Ibid.*, Art. 12.
367. Lēbers, D.A. *Ministru kabinets: komentārs Latvijas Republikas Satversmes IV nodaļai 'Ministru kabinets'.* (Rīga, Tiesiskās informācijas centrs, 1998), p. 49.
368. Law on the Structure of the Cabinet of Ministers of 15 May 2008, Art. 14(1) and Art. 14(2).
369. *Ibid.*, Art. 15.
370. *Ibid.*, Art. 14(3).
371. *Ibid.*, Art. 14(4).

commence their duties of office immediately after the *Saeima* has given them a vote of confidence.[372]

363. The Constitutional Court has concluded that inviting a person to become a minister to replace another minister who has resigned from office does not create a change in the Cabinet of Ministers.[373]

364. If the Prime Minister determines that the Cabinet needs a fresh vote of confidence from the *Saeima* in order to continue its work, the Prime Minister will submit to the *Saeima* Presidium a draft decision on a fresh vote of confidence by the *Saeima* or a written application linking a fresh vote of confidence with another matter on which the *Saeima* is to vote. The procedure for a new vote of confidence in the Cabinet of Ministers or in the Prime Minister is set out in the *Saeima* Rules of Procedure.[374]

365. The Constitutional Court has explained that the decision to seek a fresh vote of confidence to the Cabinet of Ministers or a member thereof is the Government's initiative, whereas a vote of no confidence in the Cabinet of Ministers or a member thereof is the initiative of the *Saeima*. These are two separate matters which establish whether the Cabinet of Ministers and ministers enjoy the confidence of the *Saeima*. In both cases it is possible to establish with precision whether the required confidence does or does not exist. Thus pursuant to Article 59 of the *Satversme*, the *Saeima* has the right to examine the decision for a fresh vote of confidence in the Cabinet of Ministers. The adoption or rejection of this decision has concrete legal consequences: if a vote of confidence is given, then the Government has the right to continue its work; if no confidence is voted, the President of the State has the right to invite either the former Prime Minister or another person to form a new Cabinet of Ministers.[375]

§3. Composition

366. The legislator has defined the Cabinet of Ministers in Article 1 of Law on the Structure of the Cabinet of Ministers. 'The Cabinet of Ministers is a collegial body, which through the institutions of public administration subject to it, exercises executive power.'[376] This means that the effectiveness of the Cabinet's work depends in numerous ways upon consensus among Ministers and the implementation of a government's policy.[377]

372. *Ibid.*, Art. 16 and Art. 17.
373. Constitutional Court, Case No. 03-04-(98), 13 Jul. 1998, para. 2.
374. Law on the Structure of the Cabinet of Ministers of 15 May 2008, Art. 18.
375. Constitutional Court, Case No. 03-04-(98), 13 Jul. 1998, para. 2.
376. Law on the Structure of the Cabinet of Ministers of 15 May 2008, Art. 1.
377. Pleps, J., Pastars, E., Plakane, I. *Konstitucionālās tiesības. Papildinātais un pārstrādātais izdevums*, (Rīga, Latvijas Vēstnesis, 2014), p. 335.

367. Article 57 of the *Satversme* provides that 'the number of Ministries and the scope of their responsibilities, as well as the relations between State institutions, shall be as provided for by law'.

368. Article 5 of Law on the Structure of the Cabinet of Ministers provides that the Cabinet of Ministers is composed of the Prime Minister and the following Ministers and their respective Ministries:

(1) Minister for Defence.
(2) Minister for Foreign Affairs.
(3) Minister for Economics.
(4) Minister for Finance.
(5) Minister for the Interior.
(6) Minister for Education and Science.
(7) Minister for Culture.
(8) Minister for Welfare.
(9) Minister for Transport.
(10) Minister of Justice.
(11) Minister for Health.
(12) Minister for Environmental Protection and Regional Development.
(13) Minister for Agriculture.

369. The Deputy Prime Minister performs the duties of the Prime Minister in the absence of the latter. If the Cabinet of Ministers has no Deputy Prime Minister, then the Prime Minister will set out a standing procedure for a substitute, designating the Minister who, during the absence of the Prime Minister, will perform the Prime Minister's duties.[378]

370. When substituting for the Prime Minister, a Minister has no right to adopt decisions which are not urgent and could have a significant impact on national developments. A Minister, while performing the duties of the Prime Minister, has no right to:

(1) set political guidelines for other Ministers;
(2) resign from office or announce the resignation of the Cabinet of Ministers;
(3) demand the resignation of a Minister;
(4) request from the *Saeima* a fresh vote of confidence in the Cabinet of Ministers or the Prime Minister;
(5) request from the *Saeima* a vote of confidence in a particular Minister.[379]

378. Law on the Structure of the Cabinet of Ministers of 15 May 2008, Art. 10.
379. Law on the Structure of the Cabinet of Ministers of 15 May 2008, Art. 10(3) and Art. 10(4).

§4. JURISDICTION

371. Article 61 of the *Satversme* reads, 'The Cabinet shall deliberate on draft laws prepared by individual Ministries as well as matters which pertain to the activities of more than one Ministry, and issues of State policy raised by individual members of the Cabinet.'

372. The legislator has particularized this norm further in the Law on the Structure of the Cabinet of Ministers. 'The Cabinet of Ministers shall discuss or decide on all issues that fall within its jurisdiction in accordance with the *Satversme* of the Republic of Latvia, provisions of international law and laws.'[380]

373. The Prime Minister heads up the work of the Cabinet and sets its main political guidelines, as well as ensures the drafting and implementation of the Declaration on intended activities by the Cabinet of Ministers. The Prime Minister, without special authorization, represents the Cabinet of Ministers, and may also assume permanently or temporarily a Minister's duties.[381]

374. A member of the Cabinet performs those tasks envisaged for him or her by way of normative acts and also the tasks which derive from duties in office. A member of the Cabinet, in exercising the competences defined for him or her, takes into consideration the Declaration and the main political guidelines defined by the Prime Minister.[382]

375. The Cabinet of Ministers is generally responsible for the policy implemented by the government. Each member of the Cabinet carries political responsibility for his or her actions. The Prime Minister carries political responsibility for the Cabinet's work in general. It follows from Article 59 of the *Satversme* that the Cabinet of Ministers is politically responsible to the *Saeima*.

376. By Article 58 of the *Satversme*, the administrative institutions of the State 'shall be under the authority of the Cabinet'.

377. For the Cabinet of Ministers to assume political responsibility for the realization of its entire jurisdiction in its assigned area of executive power, the State administration must necessarily be subject to the Cabinet of Ministers. The Cabinet of Ministers must have at its disposal such legal mechanisms which can ensure the requisite actions by the State administration.[383]

378. This control, in accordance with Article 57 of the *Satversme*, is determined by the State Administration Structure Law, and it is realized in the form of

380. *Ibid.*, Art. 3.
381. *Ibid.*, Art. 6.
382. *Ibid.*, Art. 9(1) and Art. 9(3).
383. Constitutional Court, Case No. 2006-05-01, 16 Oct. 2006, para. 11.

'subordination' and supervision. In accordance with Article 7(4) of the State Administration Structure Law, 'subordination' (or control) means the rights of higher institutions or officials to issue orders to lower institutions or officials, as well as to revoke the decisions of lower institutions or officials. Supervision, as defined in Article 7(5), means the rights of higher institutions or officials to examine the lawfulness of decisions taken by lower institutions or officials and to revoke unlawful decisions, as well as to compel decisions in cases of an unlawful failure to act.[384]

379. In accordance with Article 6 of the State Administration Structure Law, 'the State administration is organized in a united hierarchic system. No institution or official of the administration shall exist out of this system'.[385]

380. The Constitutional Court has noted, however, that 'subordination of the State administration institutions to the Cabinet of Ministers is not an end in itself for Article 58 of the *Satversme*. Historically Article 58 of the *Satversme* did not have the purpose of determining the unity of State administration'. The provision in Article 58 of the *Satversme* that State administration institutions should be subordinated to the Cabinet of Ministers means first and foremost that they are not, and may not be, subordinated to the President of the State.[386]

381. In accordance with Article 58 of the *Satversme*, executive power is exclusively delegated to the Cabinet of Ministers. Those aspects of executive power explicitly entrusted to the State President are connected effectively to the will of the Cabinet of Ministers, by way of the requirement for counter-signatures.[387]

382. The Constitutional Court has concluded that Articles 1 and 57 of the *Satversme* represent the constitutional norm which authorizes the *Saeima* in certain cases where it is impossible to ensure due governance otherwise, to establish independent State institutions – institutions which are not subject to the Cabinet of Ministers. In a democratic State under the rule of law, exempting some institutions of public administration from subordination to the Cabinet of Ministers ensures appropriate governance in those fields, which are linked to controlling the activities of other State institutions.[388]

383. The Constitutional Court has provided an explanation of this situation, noting that, in constitutional practice, particular deviations from the principle of the separation of powers may be regarded as admissible if they make the realization of the functions of the State power more efficient, strengthen the independence of a certain institution from another powers, or secure a system of mutual counterbalances among the three powers.[389]

384. Constitutional Court, Case No. 2006-05-01, 16 Oct. 2006.
385. *Ibid.*, para. 11.
386. *Ibid.*, para. 15 and 15.2.
387. *Ibid.*, para. 15.3.
388. *Ibid.*, para. 16.3.
389. Constitutional Court, Case No. 2005-03-0306, 21 Nov. 2005, para. 7.

384. The legislator has included this holding of the Constitutional Court in Article 2(2) of the Law on the Structure of the Cabinet of Ministers. 'The *Saeima* may transfer by law the exercise of executive power in some fields also to other institutions, which are not subject to the Cabinet of Ministers, but for the supervision of the activities thereof effective mechanisms have been established in law.'[390]

385. A member of the Cabinet of Ministers may submit an issue for examination by the Cabinet. The types of documents to be examined by the Cabinet, the procedure for submitting, approving, and transferring, the procedure for preparing sittings of the Cabinet and the course thereof, as well as other issues related to the internal procedures and activities of the Cabinet of Ministers, are regulated by the Rules of Procedure of the Cabinet of Ministers.[391]

386. The State Chancellery is a central public administration institution directly subject to the supervision of the Prime Minister. The State Chancellery comprises the Prime Minister's Office, departments, divisions, and individual units set up by the Director of the State Chancellery. The State Chancellery ensures and controls the compliance of policy documents and draft legal acts of the Cabinet with the legislative requirements; develops and implements policy action plans in various areas, and presents opinions on policy documents and legal acts, as well as arranges the practicalities of the activities of the Cabinet of Ministers.[392]

387. A sitting of the Cabinet of Ministers may be held, and a decision adopted, only if more than half of the members of the Cabinet participate. The Cabinet of Ministers adopts a decision by consensus, if none of the members of the Cabinet object to the adoption of the decision. If any of the Cabinet members present objects and demands a vote, then the decision is to be adopted through a vote. A decision is then adopted by a majority vote of those members of the Cabinet of Ministers present. In case of a tied vote, the vote of the Prime Minister is decisive. The members of the Cabinet vote in open procedure. The vote of each member of Cabinet is entered into the minutes.[393]

388. Article 62 of the *Satversme* provides:

> If the State is threatened by an external enemy, or if an internal insurrection which endangers the existing political system arises or threatens to arise in the State or in any part of the State, the Cabinet has the right to proclaim a state of emergency and shall inform the Presidium within twenty-four hours and the Presidium shall, without delay, present such decision of the Cabinet to the *Saeima*.

---

390. Law on the Structure of the Cabinet of Ministers of 15 May 2008, Art. 2(2).
391. *Ibid.*, Art. 27.
392. Regulation of State Chancellery of 20 May 2003.
393. Law on the Structure of the Cabinet of Ministers of 15 May 2008, Art. 30.

389. A state of emergency represents a special legal regime, during which the Cabinet has the right to restrict the rights and freedoms of State administrative and local government institutions and natural and legal persons, as well as to impose additional duties on them. A state of emergency may be declared in case of a threat to national security, one which may be related to a disaster or risk thereof, or of a threat to critical infrastructure, if the safety of the State, society, environment, economic activity, or human health and life are significantly endangered. A state of emergency is declared by the Cabinet for a definite time period, but for no more than three months.[394]

390. A state of exception represents a special legal regime to be declared if:

(1) the State is endangered by an external enemy;
(2) internal disturbances which endanger the democratic structure of the State have arisen or are imminent in the State or any part thereof.

391. A state of exception allows the restriction of rights and freedoms of natural persons and legal persons to the extent and in the way prescribed by law, as well as the imposition of additional obligations on them. A state of exception is declared by the Cabinet.[395] A state of exception may be declared over the whole State or any part thereof. It is declared for a definite time period, but one not exceeding six months.

392. By Article 63 of the *Satversme*, 'Ministers, even if they are not members of the *Saeima*, and responsible government officials authorised by a Minister, have the right to attend sittings of the *Saeima* and its committees and to submit additions and amendments to draft laws.'

§5. Resignation and Removal from Office

393. If the Prime Minister resigns, then it is understood that the whole Cabinet of Ministers has also resigned. The Cabinet of Ministers is understood to have resigned also upon the following events:

(1) when the newly elected *Saeima* convenes for its first sitting;
(2) when the *Saeima* has voted no confidence in the Cabinet of Ministers or the Prime Minister;
(3) if, for the requested fresh vote of confidence, the *Saeima* votes no confidence in the Cabinet of Ministers or the Prime Minister;
(4) if the *Saeima* votes to reject the draft State budget submitted by the Cabinet of Ministers in first or second reading;
(5) if the Prime Minister dies.[396]

394. Law on an Emergency Situation and State of Exception of 7 Mar. 2013, Art. 4 and Art. 5.
395. *Ibid.*, Art. 11 and Art. 12.
396. Law on the Structure of the Cabinet of Ministers of 15 May 2008, Art. 19.

394. The Prime Minister must immediately inform Ministers of his or her resignation or the resignation of the whole Cabinet, and must submit an appropriate declaration in writing to the President of the State and the Speaker of the *Saeima*.

395. A Minister may resign voluntarily by submitting an application to the Prime Minister. A Minister's resignation is expected if the *Saeima* has expressed no confidence in the Minister. The Prime Minister may also remove a Minister from office.[397]

396. After the Cabinet of Ministers has stepped down, the members of the Cabinet continue performing their duties until the *Saeima* has given a vote of confidence in a new Cabinet of Ministers. The *Saeima* can also decide otherwise, and appoint members of the Cabinet temporarily entrusted with those offices until a vote of confidence in a new Cabinet of Ministers has passed.[398]

397. If a Minister has resigned from office or has been removed from it, the Prime Minister and the respective Minister may agree that this Minister may continue to perform his or her duties over a further, certain period of time, unless the *Saeima* has ruled otherwise.[399]

398. The replacement of the Cabinet of Ministers or a member of it does not per se suspend the drafting of legal acts or decisions on other matters that have been initiated. It also does not influence the validity of planning documents.[400]

§6. The Right to Adopt Regulatory Enactments

399. The Cabinet of Ministers may adopt normative acts – regulations – only in the following cases:

(1) where a law has specifically authorized the Cabinet of Ministers to do so. That authorization will indicate the main lines of the regulation's content;
(2) in order to ratify an international agreement or a draft, to denounce an international agreement or to suspend it, unless the *Satversme* or law provides otherwise;
(3) if necessary to implement EU legal acts, the particular issue not yet being regulated by law. Such regulations may not affect the fundamental rights of private persons.[401]

400. The Constitutional Court has developed a line of case law addressing where the Cabinet of Ministers has a right to adopt normative acts and what principles it

397. *Ibid.*, Art. 20.
398. Law on the Structure of the Cabinet of Ministers of 15 May 2008, Art. 21(1).
399. *Ibid.*, 21(2).
400. *Ibid.*, Art., 23.
401. Law on the Structure of the Cabinet of Ministers of 15 May 2008, Art., 31.

has to abide by. This is referred to as the '*ultra vires* doctrine'. The *ultra vires* doctrine, developed thus by the Constitutional Court, is grounded on the principle of the separation of powers, which defines the division of competencies among the organs of state. To a large extent, the development of this doctrine in the case law of the Constitutional Court has been determined by the scope of constitutional review, which allows the Court to examine legal acts adopted both by the *Saeima* and the Cabinet of Ministers, as well as the jurisdictional boundaries between legislative and executive power.

401. Until 31 May 2007, Article 81 of the *Satversme* defined the right of the Cabinet of Ministers to adopt regulations that had the force of law. It read, 'In cases of urgent necessity between sessions of the *Saeima*, the Cabinet of Ministers shall have the right to issue regulations which shall have the force of law.' These regulations did not have the power to amend, *inter alia*, the budget and budget rights, and they could not be applied to public loans and the issue of Treasury bonds.

402. The purpose of Article 81 of the *Satversme* was not to establish an independent legislator alongside the subjects defined in its Article 64, but to establish a substitute for the legislator, able to respond rapidly and effectively in emergency situations. On the one hand, this jurisdiction granted to the Cabinet of Ministers allowed the executive power to perform its functions also under emergency conditions. On the other hand, however, a significant risk of distorting the balance of powers in favour of executive power also existed.[402]

403. In view of the fact that this right granted to the Cabinet of Ministers was an exception to the division of legislative rights established by Article 64 of the *Satversme*, the *Saeima* decided to exclude this norm from the *Satversme*: it is currently no longer in force.

404. The Constitutional Court has noted that the fact that Article 81 has been deleted from the *Satversme* does not provide grounds for concluding that the matters specified therein would now fall within the area of authority of the Cabinet of Ministers. That is, even after the *Satversme* had been amended and Article 81 deleted, the *Saeima* still has exclusive authority to decide on the matters pertaining to the areas specified in this article, and the Cabinet of Ministers has no right to decide the matters regulated therein.[403]

405. It follows from the case law of the Constitutional Court that the adoption of Cabinet regulations, as well as other external regulatory enactments which are adopted on the basis of a particular authorization by the legislator, represents an act of the executive power. Since the adoption of such regulatory enactments is the action of an executive power, the Cabinet of Ministers or other institution may specify the political will included in the laws and establish a procedure for enforcing those laws. Cabinet regulations adopted under this procedure may not constitute

402. Constitutional Court, Case No. 2005-12-0103, 16 Dec. 2005, para. 12.
403. Constitutional Court, Case No. 2009-43-01, 21 Dec. 2009, para. 30.1.

legal norms which, without the legislator's authorization, would establish new legal relationships and restrict fundamental rights.[404]

406. The legal norm, by which the legislator authorizes the Cabinet of Ministers to regulate the procedure for exercising a person's fundamental rights established in the *Satversme* or restrictions to exercise these rights, must be clear and accurate. A restriction of a person's fundamental rights by referring to an unclear or ambiguous authorization is inadmissible. If the scope of the legislator's authorization raises doubts, then the Cabinet of Ministers must, in implementing this authorization, avoid restricting a person's fundamental rights to the greatest extent possible.[405]

407. The Constitutional Court has noted that the Cabinet of Ministers, in adopting an act, should observe not only the laws, but also the *Satversme*.[406]

408. The Constitutional Court has held that the requirement for the legislator itself to regulate all issues of the State is difficult to implement in practice, taking into account the complexity of modern society. In order to ensure an effective implementation of State power, it is possible to deviate from the requirement that the legislator itself should regulate all issues. Such is attained when the legislator in the process of lawmaking regulates all the most important issues, but delegates drafting the more detailed legal particulars to the Cabinet of Ministers or other State organ.[407]

409. The executive power falls within the competence of the Cabinet of Ministers, also in the case where it is necessary to adopt an act when the legislator has particularly authorized an institution of executive power. The Cabinet of Ministers or any other institution can be entrusted with the task of developing procedures for implementing a law in order to specify the political will included in the law. Such normative acts may not include norms that cannot be regarded as objectives for implementation of a particular legal norm.[408]

410. The requirement that the law should contain a direct authorization to prescribe certain matters, and the main guidelines for stipulating those provisions, follows from the requirement that it is the legislator who should decide the most important issues of social life.[409]

---

404. Constitutional Court, Case No. 2007-04-03, 9 Oct. 2007, para. 14.
405. Constitutional Court, Case No. 2005-03-0306, 21 Nov. 2005, para. 10.
406. Constitutional Court, Case No. 2001-09-01, 21 Jan. 2001, para. 10.
407. Constitutional Court, Case No. 2007-04-03, 9 Oct. 2007, para. 15.
408. Constitutional Court, Case No. 2000-07-0409, 3 Apr. 2001, para. 5.
409. Constitutional Court, Case No. 2005-03-0306, 21 Nov. 2005, para. 10.

411. The Constitutional Court has recognized that decisions with respect to international borrowing and lending, and the terms, should be regarded as an important issue for the State and society, and one which, in compliance with the procedure established by the *Satversme*, had to be decided by the legislator itself.[410]

412. In developing the *ultra vires* doctrine, the Constitutional Court has emphasized the importance of parliamentary control. 'The legislator, via parliamentary control or other legal remedies at its disposal, must ensure that the authorization is implemented in compliance with the *Satversme*, as well as considerations of usefulness and reasonability.'[411] Thus, first of all it is for the legislator itself to monitor whether the Cabinet of Ministers has remained within the limits of its competences and has acted in conformity with any authorizations.

413. If a regulation adopted by the Cabinet of Ministers is incompatible with the *Satversme*, then it is to be recognized as being invalid as of the date of its adoption.

SELECTED FURTHER READING

Pleps, J. Organisation of Executive Power in a Democratic State. (Конституционное Правосудие, 2013), pp. 121–139.

410. Constitutional Court, Case No. 2009-43-01, 21 Dec. 2009, para. 30.1. In this case, Constitutional Court *inter alia* discussed the right of the Cabinet of Ministers to accept international loan on conditions which had not been confirmed by the Saeima. At the time when a budget had to be adopted Saeima was constrained by international commitments already made. Therefore, its legislative competence was limited. As a result of the Court's ruling the practice was changed and currently any decisions by the Cabinet of Ministers which substantially affect budget due to international agreements require to receive prior consent by the Saeima.
411. Constitutional Court, Case No. 2010-43-03, 11 Jan. 2011.

Chapter 5. The Judiciary

414. Until 18 November 1918, the judicial system in Latvia followed the Russian Law on Judicial Institutions of 20 November 1864. This Law laid the foundation for a modern judicial system according to the French model. It entered into force in the Baltic's after the court reforms of 1889.[412]

415. Latvia's own court system was introduced after of Latvia proclaimed its independence. On 6 December 1918, the People's Council adopted a provisional regulation 'On the Courts of Latvia and the Procedure of Litigation'. The provisional regulation stipulated that the court system in Latvia would consist of magistrates' courts, regional courts, the Court Chamber, and the Senate, and that these courts would operate in accordance with local and Russian laws in force until 24 October 1917.[413]

416. After the 1922 adoption of the *Satversme*, the court system in Latvia remained basically the same as defined by that provisional regulation, 'On the Courts of Latvia and the Procedure of Litigation'. From the coup d'état of 15 May 1934 until occupation in 1940, the court system did not undergo any significant changes.[414] During the authoritarian regime, the functioning of the *Satversme* was suspended and the principle of the division of powers was not observed.[415] During the occupation period, the Soviet court system was introduced. After the restoration of Latvia's independence in 1990, the court system was introduced based on the rule of law. This was seen as one of the most important tasks for the functioning of Latvia as a democratic State.[416]

417. During the debates on the draft *Satversme* in 1922, the drafting commission's expert, Jānis Purgalis, underscored that the constitutional regulation on the judicial power had been developed to implement the requirement that 'the courts, as the guardians of law in the State, should be independent', because 'the court is the mechanism by which we maintain the validity of our legal order'.[417] Thus, the regulation by the *Satversme* of the judicial power is to guarantee the principle of the independence of the judiciary and judges.

---

412. *Latvijas Republikas Satversmes komentāri. VI nodaļa. Tiesa. VII nodaļa. Valsts kontrole.* Autoru kolektīvs prof. R. Baloža zinātniskā vadībā (Rīga, Latvijas Vēstnesis, 2013), p. 11.

413. On the Courts of Latvia and the Procedure of Litigation. Provisional Regulation of the People's Council.

414. Lēbers, D. A. (ed.), *Latvijas tiesību vēsture (1914-2000)*, (Rīga, Fonds Latvijas Vēsture, 2000), p. 279.

415. Osipova, S, Strupišs, A., Rieba, A. *Tiesu varas neatkarības un efektivitātes palielināšanas un nostiprināšanas rezerves.* (Jurista Vārds, 9 Mar. 2010, No. 10).

416. *Latvijas Republikas Satversmes komentāri. VI nodaļa. Tiesa. VII nodaļa. Valsts kontrole.* Autoru kolektīvs prof. R. Baloža zinātniskā vadībā. (Rīga, Latvijas Vēstnesis, 2013), p. 15.

417. *Latvijas Satversmes Sapulces stenogrammu izvilkums (1920–1922). Latvijas Republikas Satversmes projekta apspriešana un apstiprināšana.* (Rīga, Tiesu namu aģentūra), p. 489.

418. The fundamental principles for the operation of the judicial power and the courts are included in Chapter VI of the *Satversme*. The articles of the *Satversme* providing for the independence of the judiciary can be amended only by the *Saeima* or the people. In 1990, a new law regulating the court system was drafted. This new Law on Judicial Power entered into force on 1 January 1993.

419. The Constitutional Court, when examining cases pertaining to issues of judicial power, has highlighted the importance of other general principles of law. The Constitutional Court noted that 'one of the most important prerequisites for the division of powers is the institutional and functional separation of the judicial power from the legislative power and the executive power'.[418]

420. The Constitutional Court has provided the following explanation of the functions of the judicial power. 'The judicial power has the task to ensure that in the administration of justice the *Satversme*, laws and other regulatory enactments are complied with, as well human rights and freedoms are protected.'[419]

421. From 1922 until 1996, the *Satversme* provided for jury trials in Latvia. However, such trials were never introduced. Therefore, the constitutional legislator has abandoned the idea of establishing jury trials in Latvia.

422. On 29 January 1997, Chapter 16.1 'Persons Belonging to the Court System' was added to the Law on Judicial Power. Prosecutors, sworn advocates and sworn notaries, as well as sworn bailiffs are all considered officers of the court.

§1. Judicial Organization

I. The Courts of Ordinary Jurisdiction

423. Article 82 of the *Satversme* currently reads, 'In Latvia, court cases shall be heard by district (city) courts, regional courts and the Supreme Court, but in the event of war or a state of emergency, also by military courts.' This constitutional norm reflects the structure of the court system. The Latvian court system, as currently reflected in Article 82 of the *Satversme*, is the result of Latvia's historical development.

424. Article 82 of the *Satversme* had provided that all citizens were equal before the law and the courts. Two basic principles of Latvia's court system were enshrined in this norm: equal treatment as regards legal protection and equal treatment as regards protection by the courts. In 1996, a proposal was made to add to the *Satversme* a separate Part II which would codify fundamental human rights. Consequently the wording of Article 82 of the *Satversme* was amended.

418. Constitutional Court, Case No. 2006-12-01, 20 Dec. 2006, para. 7.
419. Constitutional Court, Case No. 2007-03-01, 18 Oct. 2007, para. 26.

425. Article 82 of the *Satversme* defines the court system as one of the constitutional institutions of the Republic of Latvia. Essentially, this article defines the institutional organization of the administration of justice, enumerating all those institutions administering justice. However, the Constitutional Court held that this enumeration of institutions in Article 82 of the *Satversme* is not exhaustive.[420] This is so because justice is administered also by the Constitutional Court (Article 85 of the *Satversme*). It follows from the system of *Satversme* that the EU Court of Justice also has the right to administer justice (the second part of Article 68 of the *Satversme*, Article 19 of the Treaty on EU).

426. Article 82 of the *Satversme* has three aims:

(1) to separate functionally and institutionally judicial power from legislative power and executive power;
(2) to constitute the court system in Latvia and the fundamental principles for its functioning;
(3) to define the functional essence of courts: the administration of justice.[421]

427. Article 82 of the *Satversme* consolidates the principle of the division of powers, since this norm clearly separates the administration of justice from legislative functions and executive (public administration) actions. At the same time, Article 82 of the *Satversme* is an essential element of a State based on the rule of law.[422]

428. Article 82 of the *Satversme* is linked with Article 86 of the *Satversme* and the right to a fair trial included in the first sentence of Article 92. Functionally, Chapter 6 ensures the right defined in the first sentence of Article 92 to a fair trial by an institution established by law.[423] The first sentence of Article 92 of the *Satversme*, in turn, ensures that the courts referred to in Article 82 are directly linked to fundamental rights. The binding nature of fundamental rights manifests itself not only in the procedure of administering justice and in the application of substantive law, but also in the institutional operation of the courts.[424]

429. The Constitutional Court has underlined that the concept of 'a fair court' includes two aspects: an institution of an independent judicial power, and due process, as is compatible with a State based on the rule of law.[425] Likewise, the

420. Constitutional Court, Case No. 2006-12-01, 20 Dec. 2006, para. 9.2.
421. *Latvijas Republikas Satversmes komentāri. VI nodaļa. Tiesa. VII nodaļa. Valsts kontrole.* Autoru kolektīvs prof. R. Baloža zinātniskā vadībā. (Rīga, Latvijas Vēstnesis, 2013), p. 39.
422. *Latvijas Republikas Satversmes komentāri. VI nodaļa. Tiesa. VII nodaļa. Valsts kontrole.* Autoru kolektīvs prof. R. Baloža zinātniskā vadībā. (Rīga, Latvijas Vēstnesis, 2013), p. 41.
423. Constitutional Court, Case No. 2001-10-01, 5 Mar. 2002, para. 2.
424. *Latvijas Republikas Satversmes komentāri. VI nodaļa. Tiesa. VII nodaļa. Valsts kontrole.* Autoru kolektīvs prof. R. Baloža zinātniskā vadībā. (Rīga, Latvijas Vēstnesis, 2013), p. 41.
425. Constitutional Court, Case No. 2001-10-01, 5 Mar. 2002, para. 2.

Constitutional Court has noted that the right to a fair trial, guaranteed in Article 92 of the *Satversme*, comprises also the right to the impartiality of the court.[426]

430. The court system in Latvia is comprised of district courts, administrative district courts, regional courts, administrative regional courts, and the Supreme Court. Initially, the legislator had intended the district courts and administrative district courts to be courts of first instance; the regional courts and administrative regional courts to be appellate courts only, with the Supreme Court as the highest instance. But over time the legislator has introduced various exemptions, for example in some types of cases regional courts and administrative regional courts may be the courts of first instance.

431. The Constitutional Court has noted that the breakdown in Article 82 of the *Satversme* of the court order may not be used as the basis for broader conclusions on the functional activities of courts, such as regional courts being appellate courts, or the Senate as a cassation court, or the legislator being obliged to ensure access in all cases to the particular institutions referred to in this Article (to ensure appellate or cassation procedures).[427]

432. The content of the abstract concepts used in Article 82 of the *Satversme* may be specified by another law, for example, the Law on Judicial Power, or in procedural laws. This requirement follows from the fact that the organization of the courts and their jurisdiction should be established by law.

433. Article 30 of the Law on Judicial Power provides that 'a district (city) court is the court of first instance for civil matters, criminal matters, and administrative matters, unless it has been laid down otherwise in the law'. That in most cases justice at first instance is administered by one judge, is the outcome of historical development.[428] It is within the discretion of the President of the Court, particularly in complicated cases, to have a panel of judges hear cases, a panel composed of three judges.[429]

434. Article 36 of the Law on Judicial Power provides that a 'regional court is a court of appellate instance for civil matters, criminal matters, and administrative matters, unless it has been laid down otherwise in the law'. That in appellate proceedings justice is administered in a collegial fashion, is the outcome of historical development.[430] Six regional courts are established in the Republic of Latvia: the Rīga Regional Court, the Kurzeme Regional Court, the Latgale Regional Court, the

426. Constitutional Court, Case No. 2004-19-01, 15 Feb. 2005, para. 6.3.
427. Constitutional Court, Case No. 2009-93-01, 17 May 2010, para. 13.1.
428. *Latvijas Republikas Satversmes komentāri. VI nodaļa. Tiesa. VII nodaļa. Valsts kontrole.* Autoru kolektīvs prof. R. Baloža zinātniskā vadībā (Rīga, Latvijas Vēstnesis, 2013), p. 47.
429. Law 'On Judicial Power' of 15 Dec. 1992, Art. 31.
430. *Latvijas Republikas Satversmes komentāri. VI nodaļa. Tiesa. VII nodaļa. Valsts kontrole.* Autoru kolektīvs prof. R. Baloža zinātniskā vadībā. (Rīga: Latvijas Vēstnesis, 2013), p. 48.

Vidzeme Regional Court, the Zemgale Regional Court, and the Administrative Regional Court.[431]

435. Article 43 of the Law on Judicial Power stipulates that the Supreme Court consists of the Department of Administrative Cases, the Department of Civil Cases, and the Department of Criminal Cases. The Supreme Court is the highest, cassation, instance (unless otherwise prescribed by law).

436. The Constitutional Court differentiates institutions for the administration of justice from institutions of the judicial power, recognizing that the latter have a broader content, including also the prosecutor's office.[432]

437. On 29 January 1997, amendments were introduced to the Law on Judicial Power, which provided that Land Register Offices were too established at the regional courts and that these too were court institutions. The inclusion into the court system of 'judges of the Land Register Offices' as an institution of that system was debated, starting with the establishment of the Land Registry. These are officials who deal with the public registration of real estate work at Land Registry Offices, and thus do not administer justice. Nevertheless they have been made judges.

438. On 21 July 2011, important amendments were introduced into the Law on Judicial Power. The institutional affiliation of the Land Registry Office judges was reviewed, establishing that that Land Registry Offices belonged to the district (city) court. The jurisdiction of the judges of the Land Registry Offices was also expanded, providing that Land Registry Office judges oversaw the Land Registers, as well as examined applications for undisputed expropriation, the procedure for warning of an undisputed compulsory execution of obligations, and the confirmation of statements of auction.

439. On 1 October 2005, the provisions of the Criminal Procedure Law entered into force. The Criminal Procedure Law provided that investigating magistrates were one of the officials who had been granted certain authority in particular criminal proceedings. An investigating magistrate is the judge whom the Chairperson of the District (city) Court has assigned, for a specific term in the cases and in accordance with the procedures laid down in the law, to ensure observance of human rights in criminal proceedings.[433]

440. Article 82 of the *Satversme* establishes the obligation of the State to set up military courts in the event of a war or a state of emergency, when cases need to be adjudicated rapidly. The beginning and the end of a state of war should be established in accordance with Article 44 of the *Satversme* and the provisions of

431. Law 'On Judicial Power' of 15 Dec. 1992, Art. 35.
432. Constitutional Court, Case No. 2006-12-01, 20 Dec. 2006, para. 14.
433. Criminal Procedure Law of 21 Apr. 2005, Art. 40.

international law. The beginning and the end of a state of emergency must be established in accordance with Article 62 of the *Satversme* and the Law on the State of Emergency.

441. A court functions permanently in a location established for it. The legislator has the right to define the territorial jurisdiction wherein courts operate, or to delegate this task to the executive power. The State finances the functioning of courts from the State budget. Court operations are also funded through obligations on parties to pay the commission of state fees.[434]

II. The Administrative Courts

442. Initially the Law on Judicial Power envisaged that there would be administrative judges in the district courts who would hear administrative law matters and other cases assigned to them for review. However, on 15 October 1998, amendments were adopted and this provision was deleted from the Law on Judicial Power.

443. On 25 October 2001, the Law on Administrative Procedure was adopted. One of the purposes of this Law was defined as subjecting to judicial review those actions of executive power pertaining to concrete public law relationships between the State and private persons.[435] To ensure that administrative cases were examined in compliance with the new law, it was decided to establish separate administrative courts.[436]

444. On 4 December 2003, amendments to the Law on Judicial Power were adopted (which entered into force on 18 December 2003) that established an Administrative District Court, and Administrative Regional Court of Latvia, and a Department of Administrative Cases of the Supreme Court. These courts commenced their activities on 2 February 2004.

III. Legal Status of Judges

445. Article 83 of the *Satversme* provides that judges 'shall be independent and subject only to the law'.

446. Article 83 of the *Satversme* means that a judge must comply with the principle of the rule of law and justice, as well as that he or she has the obligation to provide reasoned decisions using legal methods.

434. *Latvijas Republikas Satversmes komentāri. VI nodaļa. Tiesa. VII nodaļa. Valsts kontrole.* Autoru kolektīvs prof. R. Baloža zinātniskā vadībā. (Rīga, Latvijas Vēstnesis, 2013), p. 43.
435. Administrative Procedure Law of 25 Oct. 2001, Art. 2.
436. See Part I Ch. 6.

447. If a court considers that a legal provision included in a law is incompatible with the *Satversme*, it must suspend legal proceedings and submit an application to the Constitutional Court.[437] If a court considers that a legal provision does not correspond to EU law, it should submit a preliminary ruling to the EU Court of Justice. Being 'subject to the law' does not mean that a judge may refuse to adjudicate a case if a legal lacuna exists or if the text of the law is difficult to understand. Instead it means filling in the legal lacunae.[438]

448. The principle of the institutional independence of the courts as a branch of power and the principle of the independence and impartiality of judges follow from Article 83 of the *Satversme*. Even though the text of the article mentions only judges, this text must be unequivocally understood more broadly, as applying also to the independence of the courts.[439]

449. The Constitutional Court has noted that the independence of judges is linked to a number of following guarantees: guarantees for attaining the office of judge (the procedure for appointing or confirmation of judges, the qualifications necessary for appointment to office); guarantees for holding the office (rules on promotion and transfer, rules on suspending the mandate of a judge, and rules on removal from the office); guarantees of social and material nature (inviolability of a judge, financial security), of an institutional nature (administrative independence of a judge), and the actual independence of the judicial power from the executive and legislative powers. All these guarantees are closely interconnected, and if incommensurate restrictions are placed upon even one of them, then the principle of judicial independence is breached, thus bringing under threat the fulfilment of the basic functions of a court and the ensuring of human rights and fundamental freedoms.[440] Hence Article 83 of the *Satversme* is closely linked with Article 84 of the *Satversme*, which regulates judicial appointment and removal from the office, as well as sanctions against judges.

450. Article 84 of the *Satversme* provides:

> Judicial appointments shall be confirmed by the *Saeima* and they shall be irrevocable. The *Saeima* may remove judges from office against their will only in the cases provided for by law, based upon a decision of the Judicial Disciplinary Board or a judgment of the court in a criminal case. The age of retirement from office for judges may be determined by law.

Thus Article 84 of the *Satversme* envisages guarantees for holding judicial office, providing explicitly for the appointment of a judge, the principle of the

437. Constitutional Court Law of 5 Jun. 1996, Art. 17.

438. *Latvijas Republikas Satversmes komentāri. VI nodaļa. Tiesa. VII nodaļa. Valsts kontrole.* Autoru kolektīvs prof. R. Baloža zinātniskā vadībā. (Rīga, Latvijas Vēstnesis, 2013), p. 66.

439. *Ibid.*, p. 70.

440. Constitutional Court, Case No. 2009-11-01, 18 Jan. 2010, para. 8.2.

irrevocability of judicial office, and the exceptions to this principle: removal from office and retirement age.[441]

451. In connection with the aims of some guarantees included in Article 84 of the *Satversme*, the Constitutional Court has held that:

> in regulating the procedure for appointing judges to office, Article 84 of the *Satversme* has the aim to implement the principle of the division of powers and thus to ensure the existence of an independent judicial power;[442] the irrevocability of judges is essential for ensuring the independence of judges and the terms for the holding the office are important for ensuring the independence of judges in the meaning of Article 83 of the *Satversme.*[443]

452. With regard to appointment to judicial office, Article 84 defines only the form of confirming judges. That is, it provides that the *Saeima* decides on electing judges to office. However, the issues of selecting candidates for the office and the procedures for confirmation and career development are not regulated by the *Satversme*. The legal regulation of these issues is included in the Law on Judicial Power and Cabinet Regulations adopted on the basis of this Law.

453. The Minister for Justice nominates candidates to be appointed or confirmed to the office of a judge of the district (city) courts, or of a judge of a regional court, on the basis of an opinion from the Judicial Qualification Board. A candidate for confirmation to the office of a Judge of the Supreme Court is nominated by the Chief Justice of the Supreme Court, on the basis of an opinion from the Judicial Qualification Board.[444]

454. The issues linked to nominating a candidate for or appointment to judicial office, as well as the legal status of these decisions, have been examined by administrative court a number of times. The Department of Administrative Cases of the Supreme Court has held that the Judicial Qualification Board, in assessing the suitability of candidates for judicial office and by setting a qualification exam, fulfils the function of judicial power in creating the corpus of judges. The Judicial Qualification Board fulfils this function permanently: it is not subordinated to other institutions and no intervention in its activities is provided for. The Judicial Qualification Board has not been granted authorization in the field of public administration, and cannot be recognized as being an institution in the procedure for selecting candidates for judicial office. Its findings regarding a candidate for such office are not administrative acts and are not subject to review by an administrative court.[445] It

441. *Latvijas Republikas Satversmes komentāri. VI nodaļa. Tiesa. VII nodaļa. Valsts kontrole.* Autoru kolektīvs prof. R. Baloža zinātniskā vadībā. (Rīga, Latvijas Vēstnesis, 2013), p. 51.
442. Constitutional Court, Case No. 2004-04-01, 5 Nov. 2004, para. 10.
443. Constitutional Court, Case No. 2007-03-01, 18 Oct. 2007, para. 31.
444. Law on the Judicial Power of 15 Dec. 1992, Arts 57 and 59.
445. Department of Administrative Cases of the Supreme Court, Senate, Case No. SKA-528/2009. 29 Jun. 2009, para. 12.

should be noted that the opinion of the Judicial Qualification Board is not binding on the Minister for Justice.

455. The Judicial Qualification Board shall be composed of one judge from the Department of Administrative Cases of the Supreme Court, one judge from the Department of Civil Cases of the Supreme Court, one judge from the Department of Criminal Cases of the Supreme Court, one judge from the Civil Matters Board of the Regional Court, one judge from the Criminal Matters Board of the Regional Court, one judge from the Administrative Matters Board of the Regional Court, two judges from district (city) courts and one judge from the Land Registry Office. The Judicial Qualification Board shall elect by secret ballot the Conference of Judges.

456. The Decision of 12 October 2010 by the Senate Department of Administrative Cases, No. SKA-589/2010, includes an analysis of the legal status of each decision connected with the advancement of a candidate for judicial office:

> In view of the fact that the conclusion by the Judicial Qualification Board is not a decision, but an opinion regarding the compatibility with the office of a judge, whereas the decision by the *Saeima* is a political decision, of all the stages in the procedure only the decision by the Minister for Justice on not promoting a judge can be considered to be an administrative act. This decision prohibits further promotion of a person for appointment, repeated appointment or confirmation to an office of a judge. The review of this decision by an administrative court in an independent and impartial procedure gives the possibility to avoid losing the status of a judge because of political reasons and is one of the guarantees for ensuring the independence of the judicial power.[446]

457. Article 51 of the Law on Judicial Power provides that:

> in selecting a candidate for the office of a judge, the principle shall be observed that only Latvian citizens, who are highly qualified and honest lawyers, may work as judges. In the selection of judges, no discrimination based on origin, social and financial status, race or nationality, sex, attitude towards religion, type and nature of occupation, or political or other beliefs is permitted. The requirement that a judge must be a Latvian citizen shall not be considered as discriminatory. The selection of candidates for the office of a judge shall take place in an open competition. Pursuant to the recommendation of the Minister for Justice and the Chief Justice of the Supreme Court, the Board of Justice shall announce the competition by law.

458. Neither Article 84 nor any other articles of the *Satversme* define the procedure for confirming judges of the general jurisdiction courts. The *Satversme* does not stipulate whether a vote on confirming judges should be open or closed. Likewise, the *Satversme* does not stipulate the number of votes needed to confirm a

446. Department of Administrative Cases of the Supreme Court, Senate, Case No. SKA-589/2010, 12 Oct. 2010, para. 11.

judge. The procedure is defined by the Rules of Procedure of the *Saeima*. Pursuant to those Rules, decisions on confirming judges are adopted by open vote.[447] The decision by the *Saeima* on appointing a judge is a political decision.[448]

459. The concept 'confirmation' is used in the *Satversme* to characterize the way in which a judge comes into office. Chapter 9 of the Law on Judicial Power prescribes the 'Procedures for the Appointment and Confirmation of Judges and their Term in Office'. Article 60 of the Law on Judicial Power provides:

> Judges of a district (city) court shall be appointed to office by the *Saeima*, upon the recommendation of the Minister for Justice, for three years. On the basis of the decision by the *Saeima* regarding the appointment of a judge to the office as a judge of a district (city) court, the Board of Justice shall determine the specific district (city) court or the courthouse in which the duties of a judge shall be performed. After a judge of a district (city) court has held office for three years, the *Saeima*, upon the proposal of the Minister for Justice, and on the basis of the opinion of the Judicial Qualification Board in the evaluation of the professional work of the judge, shall confirm him or her in office, for an unlimited term of office, or shall re-appoint him or her to office for a period of up to two years.

Obviously, the term 'appoints' is consistently used in Article 60 of the Law on Judicial Power, if a judge of a district court comes into the office only for a limited term.

460. Judges of a regional court shall be confirmed by the *Saeima*, upon a proposal of the Minister of Justice, for an unlimited term of office. On the basis of the decision by the *Saeima* regarding the confirmation of a judge in the office of a judge of a regional court, the Board of Justice shall determine the specific regional court or courthouse in which the duties of that judge are to be performed.[449]

461. Judges of the Supreme Court, upon the proposal of the Chief Justice of the Supreme Court, are confirmed in office by the *Saeima* for an unlimited term of office.[450]

462. If a judge has been appointed or confirmed in office, he or she must give an oath (or solemn promise). This is a prerequisite for commencing a judge's duties in office.

463. Article 84 of the *Satversme* does not envisage a limited term for the mandate of a judge. However, the third sentence of this article authorizes the legislator

447. Rules of Procedure of the Saeima of 27 Jul. 1994, Arts 31 and 139.
448. Department of Administrative Cases of the Supreme Court, Senate, Case No. SKA-32/2009, 23 Mar. 2009, para. 32.
449. Law 'On the Judicial Power' of 15 Dec. 1992, Art. 61. On composition of the Board of Justice s. IV of this part.
450. Law 'On Judicial Power', 15 Dec. 1992, Art. 62.

to define the age upon which a judge is to leave his or her office. The maximum age for holding judicial office is 70 years.[451]

464. The independence of judges is consolidated in a number of regulatory enactments. The most important among these is the Law on Judicial Power and its Chapter 2, 'Principles and Guarantees for the Independence of the Judiciary'. It is stipulated in this chapter that 'State institutions, public and political organisations and other legal and natural persons have the duty to respect and observe the independence of a court and the immunity of judges.'

465. Article 11(2) of the Law on Judicial Power provides that no restrictions, pressure, influence, direct or indirect threats, or other unlawful interference in the adjudication of a court are allowed. Demonstrations and picketing at the premises of a court building are prohibited. Any attempt to influence judges or interference with adjudication by a court is to be punished in accordance with the law.

466. The Constitutional Court has noted that the obligation not to interfere with the administration of justice applies not only to the legislator and the executive power, but also to the court itself and the officials connected to exercising judicial power. Therefore the Constitutional Court has recognized that a legal norm which authorized the Plenary Session of the Supreme Court to adopt decisions binding upon the courts on the application of laws, is incompatible with the principle of the division of powers since it would restrict the independence of judges and courts.[452]

467. No one has the right to require from a judge an account or explanation concerning how a particular matter was adjudicated, or to disclose the views expressed during court deliberations.[453]

468. A judge may not participate in the adjudication of any matter in which he or she is personally, directly or indirectly, interested in the outcome, or if there are other circumstances which may raise doubts regarding his or her impartiality, as well as in those cases provided for in the Law on Prevention of Conflict of Interest in the Activities of Public Officials. In such cases, judges must withdraw from the proceedings. If a judge does not do so, any party to the case may apply for the recusal of the judge. The grounds for the recusal of a judge and the procedure for its adjudication is stipulated by law.[454] The basis for withdrawal or recusal, as well as the procedure for reviewing a withdrawal or recusal is defined by Articles 116–118 of the Administrative Procedure Law, and Articles 18–22 and Article 160 of the Civil Procedure Law, as well as Articles 55–58 of the Criminal Procedure Law.

451. Law 'On Judicial Power' of 15 Dec. 1992, Art. 63.
452. Constitutional Court, Case No. 2002-06-01, 4 Feb. 2003, para. 2.4.
453. Law 'On Judicial Power' of 15 Dec. 1992, Art. 11.
454. *Ibid.*, Art. 14.

469. A judge is not financially liable for the damages incurred by a participant in a case as a result of an unlawful or unfounded court judgment. As prescribed by law, the State may be liable for damages. A person who considers that a judgment of a court is unlawful or unfounded may appeal it as provided by law, but has no claim against the judge who adjudicated the matter.[455]

470. According to the Article 13(1) and 13(2) of the Law on Judicial Power, a judge has immunity during the time he or she fulfils his or her adjudicatory duties. A criminal case against a judge may be brought only by the Prosecutor General of the Republic of Latvia. A judge may not be detained nor be subjected to criminal liability without the consent of the *Saeima*. A Supreme Court Judge specially authorized for that purpose must render the decisions concerning detention, forcible conveyance, arrest, or search warrants. If a judge is apprehended committing a serious or especially serious criminal offence, a decision concerning the forcible conveyance, arrest, or search and seizure is not necessary, but a Supreme Court judge specially authorized and the Prosecutor General must be informed thereof within twenty-four hours.

471. An administrative sanction may not be applied to a judge and he or she shall not be arrested under administrative procedures. A judge is subject to disciplinary sanction for administrative offences in accordance with the provisions of Chapter 14 of the Law.[456]

472. Judges are in public service.[457] According to Article 7(3) of the Law On Prevention of Conflict of Interest in the Activities of Public Officials, judges are permitted to combine the status of a public official only with the office that they hold in accordance with law or international treaties ratified by the *Saeima*, and Cabinet regulations and orders, as well as with the work of a teacher, scientist, professional athlete, or with creative work. The Constitutional Court has held that the prohibition on combining offices has been established due to the special legal status of a judge and the judiciary as one of the branches of power.

473. In 2010, the Constitutional Court rendered three judgments in connection with judges' 'remuneration for work', holding some provisions of the Law on Judicial Power as being incompatible with the *Satversme*.[458]

474. The Constitutional Court has noted that Article 83 of the *Satversme*, in principle, contains a prohibition on reducing judges' remuneration defined by law during their term in office. However, under special economic circumstances – in a situation of economic recession, when the State had to decrease the remuneration in

455. Law 'On Judicial Power' of 15 Dec. 1992, Art. 13(5) and Art. 13(6).
456. *Ibid.*, Art. 13(4).
457. *Latvijas Republikas Satversmes komentāri. VI nodaļa. Tiesa. VII nodaļa. Valsts kontrole.* Autoru kolektīvs prof. R. Baloža zinātniskā vadībā. (Rīga, Latvijas Vēstnesis, 2013), p. 42.
458. Constitutional Court, Case No. 2009-11-01, 18 Jan. 2010.

institutions funded from the State budget in general – a deviation from this prohibition on reduction was permissible. Likewise, the fact that the legislator decides on the budget of the courts and the remuneration of officials does not mean that the independence required for those respective functions was infringed upon. However, also under conditions of economic recession, funding can be decreased only and solely by abiding with constitutional principles and constitutional procedures, namely respecting fundamental rights and freedoms, in particular, the constitutional principle of equality.[459]

475. The amendments of 16 December 2010 to the Law introduced a new system of judges' remuneration, which provides that a salary of a judge is calculated by equalling it to the maximum amount of monthly salary received by the head of the legal structural unit at an institution of direct public administration. Judicial remuneration levels differ according to different levels of court.

476. A judge by consent and with the permission of the Chief Justice may be assigned for specific time to work in another court (also higher instance courts), the Ministry of Justice, the Court Administration, or an international organization. Assigning a judge ad hoc to a higher instance court does not require an opinion from the Judicial Qualification Board.[460]

477. Article 86(3) of the Law on Judicial Power stipulates that the office of judge may not be combined with membership in a party or other political organization. The Constitutional Court has held that this restriction is compatible with the *Satversme*.[461]

478. Article 84 of the *Satversme* expressly refers to the principle of the irrevocability of judicial appointment.[462] The principle of irrevocability, included in the first sentence of Article 84 of the *Satversme*, is linked to the second and the third sentences of this article, which partially reveal the content of the principle. Article 84 of the *Satversme* directly contemplates two exceptions. First are the exceptional cases, based on decisions of the Judicial Disciplinary Board or a criminal case judgment, where the *Saeima* may remove a judge from the office against his or her will. Second, a judge must leave the office upon reaching retirement age.

479. Article 84 of the *Satversme* provides that in order to remove a judge from office against his or her will in the cases provided for by law, a decision by the Judicial Disciplinary Board or a criminal court judgment is necessary. Such a judgment regarding a judge or a decision by the Judicial Disciplinary Board, as the basis for removing a judge from office, may be adopted only in cases provided for by law.

459. Constitutional Court, Case No. 2009-11-01, 18 Jan. 2010.
460. Law 'On Judicial Power' of 15 Dec. 1992, Art. 86.1.
461. Constitutional Court, Case No. 2012-16-01, 10 May 2013.
462. *Latvijas Republikas Satversmes komentāri. VI nodaļa. Tiesa. VII nodaļa. Valsts kontrole.* Autoru kolektīvs prof. R. Baloža zinātniskā vadībā. (Rīga, Latvijas Vēstnesis, 2013), p. 26.

480. The powers of a judge expire in the following cases:

(1) pursuant his own request;
(2) in the case of the death of the judge;
(3) upon expiry of the term of powers, if such has been established;
(4) if the judge is not advanced for, or is not confirmed in, office for an unlimited term after having served any prescribed probationary period;
(5) upon reaching the maximum age for serving in office set by law;
(6) upon removal from office against his or her will.[463]

IV. Judges' Institutions of Self-governance

481. The initial wording of the Law on Judicial Power envisaged only two institutions of self-governance: the Conference of Judges and the Judicial Qualification Boards of three different levels. Later the Judicial Disciplinary Board, the Judicial Ethics Committee, and the Judicial Disciplinary Court were established. Amendments were introduced to the 15 October 1998 Law on the Judicial Power to create one Judicial Qualification Board.

482. On 20 April 1995, the Conference of Judges of the Republic of Latvia adopted the Judicial Code of Ethics. For a long time, however, no institution was tasked with implementing or enforcing it. Only on 3 April 2008 were amendments to the Law on Judicial Power adopted to provide that judges should establish a Judicial Ethics Committee.

483. The amendments of 3 June 2010 to the Law on Judicial Power established a new judicial institution of self-governance: the Board of Justice, which is an advisory and coordinating institution, and which participates in the development of the policy and strategy of the court system and in improving the functioning of the courts.

484. Initially the Board of Justice was intended as a judicial institution of self-governance, the status of which would be consolidated in the *Satversme*. But the legislator decided to regulate the status and the jurisdiction of the Board of Justice in the Law on Judicial Power.[464]

485. The Law on Judicial Power defines the Board of Justice as composed of the following permanent members:

(1) the Chief Justice of the Supreme Court;
(2) the Chief Justice of the Constitutional Court;
(3) the Minister of Justice;

---

463. *Latvijas Republikas Satversmes komentāri. VI nodaļa. Tiesa. VII nodaļa. Valsts kontrole.* Autoru kolektīvs prof. R. Baloža zinātniskā vadībā. (Rīga, Latvijas Vēstnesis, 2013), p. 103.

464. *Ibid.*, p. 26.

(4) the Chairperson of the Judicial Committee of the *Saeima*;
(5) the Prosecutor General;
(6) the Chairman of the Latvian Council of Sworn Advocates;
(7) the Chairman of the Latvian Council of Sworn Notaries;
(8) the Chairman of the Latvian Council of Sworn Bailiffs.

486. The Board of Justice has the following elected members:

(1) a judge elected by the Plenary Session of the Supreme Court;
(2) six judges elected by a conference of judges.

A conference of judges also elects one member of the Board of Justice from among the Land Registry Office judges, three from among the district (city) court judges and two from among the regional court judges.[465]

487. The term of office of an elected member of the Board of Justice is four years. Members of the Board of Justice may be re-elected, but for not more than two successive terms.[466]

488. The Chief Justice of the Supreme Court is the Chair of the Board of Justice.[467] The Board of Justice provides opinions regarding the territories of operation of courts and courthouses and the location thereof, as well as regarding budget requests from the various courts. Following the appointment or confirmation of a judge, the Board of Justice determines the specific court, courthouse, or Land Registry Office to which the judge is assigned, and it decides on transfers of judge within a court of the same instance. The Board of Justice hears the candidates for Constitutional Court office and provides an opinion to the *Saeima* regarding them. The Board of Justice hears the candidates for the office of the Chief Justice of the Supreme Court and provides an opinion to the Plenary Session of the Supreme Court regarding them. The Board of Justice approves the rules of association for the Conference of Judges, as well as convening the Conference of Judges, determining the matters to be considered there. The Board of Justice approves the basic principles for the specialization of judges and the procedure for determining the case workload, and develops guidelines in other work organization matters in the courts and Land Registry Offices. The Board of Justice hears the annual report of the Court Administration. In the cases and procedures laid down by the Law on the Constitutional Court, the Board of Justice may submit an application to the Constitutional Court. The Board of Justice determines the content and procedures by which judges take the qualification examination and approves the document samples necessary for the qualification examination of judges. The Board of Justice performs any other functions specified by law.[468]

465. Law 'On Judicial Power' of 15 Dec. 1992, Art. 892.
466. *Ibid.*, 893.
467. *Ibid.*, 897.
468. Law 'On Judicial Power' of 15 Dec. 1992, Art. 8911.

§2. CONSTITUTIONAL COURT

I. Establishment

489. Since the establishment of Latvia and up to its occupation in 1940, the idea of a need to introduce constitutional review was not recognized. Therefore at the time, no special institution of constitutional review was established.[469]

490. Even though a specialized constitutional court was not established until 1940, it could be observed that constitutional review as a method was used in the case law of the Latvian Senate (Supreme Court), which, *inter alia*, ruled on the validity of legal acts by the executive power, namely, on their compliance with the *Satversme*.[470]

491. On 4 May 1990, the Supreme Council of the LSSR adopted the Declaration on the Restoration of Independence of the Republic of Latvia. The second sentence of Article 6 of Declaration provides that '[i]n case of disputes, the issue regarding the application of legal acts shall be adjudicated by the Constitutional Court of the Republic of Latvia'.

492. The Law on Judicial Power of 15 December 1992 contemplated entrusting the function of constitutional supervision to the Supreme Court. However, soon afterwards, the legislator gave up this idea of conferring the right to constitutional supervision on the Supreme Court, and work to establish a separate judicial institution – Constitutional Court – was commenced. This led to amendments being introduced to Article 85 of the *Satversme*, defining the jurisdiction of the Constitutional Court.

493. Article 85 of the *Satversme* provides:

> In Latvia, there shall be a Constitutional Court, which, within its jurisdiction as provided for by law, shall review cases concerning the conformity of laws with the Constitution, as well as other cases conferred within the jurisdiction thereof by law. The Constitutional Court is entitled to declare laws or other enactments or parts thereof invalid. The *Saeima* shall confirm the appointment of judges to the Constitutional Court for the term provided for by law, with a majority of the votes of not less than fifty-one members of the *Saeima*.

This norm comprises three sentences that contain the basic rules regarding the functioning of the Constitutional Court.

494. The interpretation of Article 85 should be considered in the context of other norms of the *Satversme*, in particular Article 92. The right to a fair trial includes the

469. *Latvijas Republikas Satversmes komentāri. VI nodaļa. Tiesa. VII nodaļa. Valsts kontrole.* Autoru kolektīvs prof. R. Baloža zinātniskā vadībā. (Rīga, Latvijas Vēstnesis, 2013), p. 124.
470. Pleps, J. *Satversmes iztulkošana.* (Rīga, Latvijas Vēstnesis, 2012), pp. 119–121.

right of a person to submit a constitutional complaint to the Constitutional Court. If 'a person's fundamental rights established in the *Satversme* are breached by a legal norm, which is incompatible with a norm of higher legal rank, the Constitutional Court is the institution of judicial power, where a person may protect his or her rights and lawful interests'.[471]

II. Jurisdiction

495. In accordance with the principle of the division of powers, the Constitutional Court is an institution of judicial power implementing that power. Even though the *Satversme* does not provide that the Constitutional Court implements judicial power or that it is a judicial institution, this nevertheless follows from the structure of the *Satversme*, because the provisions regarding the Constitutional Court are included in Chapter VI, 'Courts'.

496. The legislator underscores in Article 1 of the Constitutional Court Law:

> The Constitutional Court shall be an independent judicial authority, which within the jurisdiction specified in the *Satversme* of the Republic of Latvia and in this Law, shall adjudicate cases regarding the conformity of laws and other regulatory enactments with the *Satversme*, as well as other cases regarding which jurisdiction is conferred upon it by this Law.

497. The Constitutional Court as an institution of judicial power fulfils its functions by administering justice, thus ensuring control over two other branches of power.[472] The independence of the Constitutional Court as an institution of judicial power is the basis for its activities. Only an independent Constitutional Court is able to fulfil the functions defined for it in the *Satversme*.

498. In contrast to the courts of ordinary jurisdiction, the essence of the administration of justice by the Constitutional Court is to resolve specific disputes on the compliance of legal norms with norms of higher legal rank.[473] In proceedings before the Constitutional Court, a dispute will be resolved either if the contested norm is recognized as being incompatible or as being compatible with a legal norm of higher legal rank.[474]

499. The Constitutional Court adjudicates cases regarding:

(1) the conformity of laws with the *Satversme*;
(2) the conformity of international agreements signed or entered into by Latvia (also until the ratification of the relevant agreements in the *Saeima*) with the *Satversme*;

---

471. Constitutional Court, Case No. 2005-12-0103, 16 Oct. 2006, para. 16.2.
472. Constitutional Court, Case No. 2001-06-03, 22 Feb. 2002, para. 1.2.
473. Constitutional Court, Case No. 2011-11-01, 3 Feb. 2012, para. 11.1.
474. *Ibid.*

(3) the conformity of other laws and regulations or parts thereof with the norms (acts) of a higher legal rank;
(4) the conformity of other acts of the *Saeima*, the Cabinet, the President, the Speaker of the *Saeima*, and the Prime Minster, except for administrative acts, with the law;
(5) the conformity with law of such an order with which a Minister authorized by the Cabinet has suspended a decision taken by a local government council;
(6) the conformity of Latvian national legal norms with those international agreements which are entered into by Latvia and which are not in conflict with the *Satversme*.[475]

500. The Constitutional Court examines only legal issues – the compliance of legal norms with the norms of higher legal force. The Constitutional Court has recognized that the Constitutional Court Law 'does not grant to the Constitutional Court the right to examine the political expedience of the actions taken by other constitutional institutions'. Likewise, it has also noted that the Constitutional Court has the right to examine cases:

> only insofar law (legal) arguments can be applied to it, separating these from law policy arguments. Where sufficiently strict legal standards have not been set for deciding on some issues and where the findings predominantly depend upon political expediency, decisions should be taken by political bodies of State power, which have been democratically legitimised, first of all – by the legislator.[476]

501. The procedural order for adjudicating cases is established by the Constitutional Court Law and the Rules of Procedure of the Constitutional Court.[477] Thus, regulation of the proceedings before the Constitutional Court, insofar it is not regulated by Constitutional Court Law, has been transferred to the Constitutional Court itself. The proceedings before the Constitutional Court take place according to the procedural order adopted by an absolute majority vote of all its justices.

502. The Constitutional Court decides on procedural issues that are not regulated in the Constitutional Court Law and the Rules of Procedure of the Constitutional Court.[478] In view of the fact that the legislator, upon adopting the Constitutional Court Law, has defined the limits to the discretion of the Constitutional Court in deciding on procedural issues, this regulation should be interpreted systemically in connection with other provisions of the Constitutional Court Law, the fundamental principles of proceedings before the Constitutional Court, and the principle of proportionality.[479]

475. Constitutional Court Law of 5 Jun. 1996, Art. 16.
476. Constitutional Court, Case No. 2011-11-01, 3 Feb. 201, para. 11.2.
477. Constitutional Court Law of 5 Jun. 1996, Art. 14.
478. *Ibid.*, Art. 26.
479. Constitutional Court, Decision on the Applicant's Request in Case No. 2007-10-0102, 10 May 2007, para. 3.

503. The second sentence of Article 85 of the *Satversme* grants to the Constitutional Court the exclusive jurisdiction to recognize 'laws and other acts or parts thereof' as being invalid. Essentially, these are all legal acts or parts thereof over which the Constitutional Court has the right to conduct constitutional review. Upon establishing an incompatibility between the contested norm (acts) and a legal norm of higher legal rank, the Constitutional Court simultaneously recognizes the contested norm (act) as being invalid.

504. The procedure for examining a case by the Constitutional Court can be broken down into successive stages and begins with the initiation of the case, followed by preparing the case, adjudicating the case, passing judgment, and enforcing the judgment. Since legal proceedings can commence only after the initiation of a case, the initiation of a case is a mandatory part of the legal proceedings before the Constitutional Court. An application shall be reviewed and the initiation of a case or a refusal to initiate a case shall be decided by a panel comprising three Justices.[480]

505. The right to submit an application is given to:

(1) the President;
(2) the *Saeima*;
(3) not less than twenty members of the *Saeima*;
(4) the Cabinet;
(5) the Prosecutor General;
(6) the Council of the State Audit Office;
(7) a local government council;
(8) the Ombudsman,[481] if the authority or official who has issued the contested act has not rectified the identified deficiencies within the time period specified by the Ombudsman;
(9) a court adjudicating a civil, criminal, or administrative case;
(10) a Land Registry Office judge performing an entry of immovable property or associated corroboration of rights thereof in the Land Register;
(11) a person in the case of an infringement of the fundamental rights defined in the *Satversme*;
(12) the Judicial Council within the scope of the competences stipulated in law.[482]

506. An individual review, where a person may submit an application to the Constitutional Court, is implemented in Latvia when the fundamental rights enshrined in the *Satversme* are alleged to have been breached. This right is also granted to a court of ordinary jurisdiction in adjudicating a specific case. The Constitutional Court also implements abstract review: the examination of the constitutional compliance of legal norms not related to the protection of the subjective rights of a specific person. There is no 'full' constitutional complaint procedure in Latvia: the Constitutional Court does not act as the court of 'fourth' instance.

480. Constitutional Court Law of 5 Jun. 1996, Art. 20.
481. See Part IV Ch. 5.
482. Constitutional Court Law of 5 Jun. 1996, Art. 17.

507. The Constitutional Court may exercise its right to recognize laws and other acts 'as being invalid' only in one procedural form: by rendering judgment.

508. Pursuant to Article 32(3) of the Constitutional Court Law, a legal norm (act) which the Constitutional Court has declared as non-compliant with the norm of higher legal force, shall be regarded as not in effect from the day of publication of the Constitutional Court judgment, unless the Constitutional Court determines otherwise. If the voiding of the contested provision from the date of passing or coming into force could cause, for instance, a considerable violation of or threat to the State (society) interests, then the usefulness of continuing legal proceedings must be assessed during preparation of the decision by the Constitutional Court.[483]

509. Should the contested norms be recognized as non-constitutional, the task of the Constitutional Court is to prevent such a situation where the retroactive force of the present judgment would considerably infringe on the rights of other persons. Namely, the task of the Court is to balance the different interests of persons as far as possible.[484] The Constitutional Court Law authorizes the Constitutional Court to decide the important legal consequences of its judgments by itself. Namely, the Law not only authorizes the Constitutional Court to render, but also charges it with responsibility for, its judgments so as to ensure legal stability, clarity, and peace in the public sphere.[485]

III. The Composition of the Court

510. Article 85 of the *Satversme* does not define a number of the Justices of Constitutional Court.

511. The Constitutional Court Law provides, 'The Constitutional Court shall be composed of seven Justices'.[486]

512. The entire bench of Constitutional Court Justices shall adjudicate cases regarding:

(1) the conformity of laws with the *Satversme*;
(2) the conformity of other acts of the *Saeima*, the Cabinet, the President, the Speaker of the *Saeima* and the Prime Minster, except for administrative acts, with the law;
(3) the conformity of Latvian national legal norms with those international agreements entered into by Latvia that are not in conflict with the *Satversme*;
(4) the conformity of regulatory enactments of the Cabinet with the *Satversme*;

483. Constitutional Court, Case No. 2007-23-01, 3 Apr. 2008, para. 6.
484. Constitutional Court, Case No. 2010-22-01, 27 Apr. 2011, para. 15.
485. Judgment of the 21 Dec. 2009 the Constitutional Court in Case No. 2009-43-01, para. 35.1.
486. Constitutional Court Law of 5 Jun. 1996, Art. 3.

(5) the conformity of international agreements signed or entered into by Latvia (also until the confirmation of the relevant agreements in the *Saeima*) with the *Satversme*; and
(6) the conformity of other laws and regulations or their parts with the *Satversme*.[487]

513. If the Constitutional Court is to adjudicate a case en banc, it must include all the Justices whose health or other objective circumstances do not prevent them from taking part in the hearing. There should be not be less than five Justices of the Constitutional Court on a full panel. The hearing must be chaired by the President or the Vice-President of the Constitutional Court. No recusal issues may be raised with Constitutional Court Justices.[488]

514. Other cases, which are not specified by law, are heard by panels of three Justices unless the Constitutional Court provided otherwise.

515. The Constitutional Court Justices elect from among the corpus of Justices, by secret ballot and with an absolute majority of votes by all Justices, the President and Vice-President of the Constitutional Court for a term of three years.[489]

516. The President of the Constitutional Court chairs sittings of the Constitutional Court, organizes the work of the Court, and represents the Court. The Vice-President of the Constitutional Court shall assist the President in fulfilling the duties of President specified in Article 13 of Constitutional Court Law and replace the President when absent. Specific duties of the President of the Constitutional Court may be fulfilled by a designated Justice.[490]

IV. The Status of a Judge

517. The third sentence of Article 85 of the *Satversme* includes the rules for confirming Justices of the Constitutional Court in office. The Constitutional Court Law contains more detailed rules on forming the corpus of Court Justices.

518. The Constitutional Court has established a different procedure for filling its bench than that of confirming in office judges of the ordinary court system (Article 84 of the *Satversme*).

519. Three Constitutional Court Justices are confirmed following a proposal by not less than ten members of the *Saeima*; two are proposed by the Cabinet, and two

487. Constitutional Court Law of 5 Jun. 1996, Art. 16.
488. *Ibid.*, Art. 25.
489. *Ibid.*, Art. 12.
490. *Ibid.*, Art. 13.

others, by the Supreme Court in plenary session. The Supreme Court in plenary session selects candidates for the position of Constitutional Court Justice from among the judges of the Republic of Latvia.[491]

520. A person may be confirmed as a Justice of the Constitutional Court who:

(1) is a citizen of the Republic of Latvia;
(2) has an unimpeachable reputation;
(3) has reached 40 years of age on the day when the proposal regarding confirmation as a Justice of the Constitutional Court was submitted to the Presidium of the *Saeima*;
(4) has acquired a higher professional or academic education (except the first level professional education) in legal science and also a master's degree (including a higher legal education, which in regard to rights is equal to a master's degree), or a doctoral degree;
(5) has at least ten years of service in a legal speciality, in a judicial speciality, or in scientific educational work at a scientific or higher educational establishment after acquiring a higher professional or academic education (except the first level professional education) in legal science.

521. Candidates for the position of a Constitutional Court Justice are assessed by the Council for the Judiciary, which provides its opinion on them.[492]

522. The formation of Latvian institutions of judicial power is based upon the principle that all judges, including the Justices of the Constitutional Court, are confirmed in office by the *Saeima*. This means that the corpus of Constitutional Court Justices is formed in accordance with a system of voting where the parliament has the final say. A Constitutional Court Justice is elected by an open vote, with the absolute majority votes of the *Saeima* Members present. At least fifty-one MPs have to vote for a Constitutional Court Justice, just like for the President of the State.

523. A Constitutional Court Justice commences office only after giving the oath (solemn promise) to the President of the State, as provided in the Law on Judicial Power. Those persons who have already taken judge's office and have given the oath (solemn promise) of a judge are exempt from this. Such persons do not give the oath (solemn promise) repeatedly, as the need for repeated oath (solemn promise) is excluded.

524. Constitutional Court Justices are confirmed in office 'for the term envisaged in law'. Thus the *Satversme* contemplates that, firstly, in contrast to the judges of the court system who are confirmed in office during tenure (Article 84), the Justices of the Constitutional Court are confirmed in office for a set term. The term of office for a Constitutional Court Justice is ten years.[493]

491. Constitutional Court Law of 5 Jun. 1996, Art. 4.
492. See Part II Ch. 6 s. D.
493. Constitutional Court Law of 5 Jun. 1996, Art. 7.

525. A Constitutional Court Justice is irremovable during his or her term of office. The principle that all issues regarding loss of office as a Constitutional Court Justice is decided by the Constitutional Court itself, not the *Saeima*, is enshrined in the Constitutional Court Law.

526. The Constitutional Court Law provides an exhaustive list of reasons for losing office as a Constitutional Court Justice (dismissal, removal, loss of office, resignation). The Constitutional Court Law also envisages suspending the mandate of a Constitutional Court Justice if circumstances have arisen that demand additional clarification or investigation, but at the same time are not so serious as to be incompatible with the office of a Justice.

527. If a Constitutional Court Justice is unable to continue work because of health reasons, he or she is removed from office upon the decision of the Constitutional Court. For this decision to be taken, an absolute majority vote of all the Justices is necessary.[494]

528. Commencement of criminal prosecution against a Constitutional Court Justice, as well as being taking into custody, is not permissible without the agreement of the Constitutional Court. For this decision to be taken, an absolute majority vote of all the court's members is necessary. A Constitutional Court Justice may be subject to disciplinary liability for any administrative violations committed.[495]

529. A Constitutional Court Justice may be subject to disciplinary liability regarding:

(1) a breach of the restrictions specified in Article 34 of the Law;
(2) a failure to fulfil the duties of office;
(3) reprehensible conduct;
(4) an administrative violation.

530. A disciplinary case may be initiated by the President or the Vice-President of the Constitutional Court, or not less than three Constitutional Court Justices. Disciplinary fines, which the Constitutional Court may impose on a Justice, shall be as follows:

(1) a reproof;
(2) a reprimand;
(3) a reduction of the monthly wage for a period of up to one year, withholding up to 20% of the monthly wage;
(4) dismissal from office according law.[496]

494. Constitutional Court Law of 5 Jun. 1996, Art. 10.
495. *Ibid.*, Art. 35.
496. *Ibid.*, Art. 36.

531. A Constitutional Court Justice loses office if he or she is convicted of a criminal offence and the judgment has come into effect.

532. A Constitutional Court Justice may leave his or her position of his or her own accord prior to expiration of the term of office, informing the Constitutional Court thereof in writing.[497]

533. Whatever term remains a Constitutional Court Justice, a Justice must leave office when he or she has reached 70 years of age.[498]

534. A Constitutional Court Justice has to fulfil his or her professional duties during court sittings attired in his or her judicial robes and wearing his or her insignia of office.[499]

535. If a Justice of the Constitutional Court combines the office of Justice with other offices or activities, he or she must ensure that the dignity and honour of a Justice, and the impartiality and independence of the Court are preserved.[500] Usually the Justices of the Constitutional Court combine their offices with scientific and research work.

Selected Further Reading

Rodiņa A. *Liability of judges in Latvia - Problematical Aspects. Liability of public officers*. Selected issues. (Plock: Szkola Wyzsza im.Pawla Wlodkowica, 2013), pp. 133–148.

497. Constitutional Court Law of 5 Jun. 1996, Art. 8.
498. *Ibid.*
499. Constitutional Court Law of 5 Jun. 1996, Art. 6.
500. *Ibid.*, Art. 34.

Chapter 6. State Audit Office

536. The State Audit Office is an independent collegial institution. According to Article 88 of the *Satversme* Auditors General are appointed following the same procedure as for judges. However, they are appointed for a fixed period.

537. Detailed rules on the competences of the State Audit Office are set out in the Law on the State Audit Office.[501] According to the Law, the main task of the Office is to perform audits of and examine transactions from the State and local budgets. The Office also controls expenditures from the EU and other international organizations which have been included in the State and local budgets. Expenditures are checked for legality, correctness, and economic efficiency. On the basis of these audits, the Office also provides recommendations

538. The State Audit Office reports to the *Saeima* and the Ministry of Finance on an annual basis. They should also cooperate with other institutions and international organizations. Article 4 entitles the Office to receive draft legislative acts on which to provide its opinion. Relevant internal procedures should be established by the Office itself.

539. The Office consists of the Auditor General, the Council of the Office, audit departments, and the Secretariat. The main tasks of representation, internal organization, and audit standards are allocated to the Auditor General according to Article 8 of the Law. The Auditor General is elected by the *Saeima* for four years and can hold office for maximum two consecutive terms. The Council of the State Audit Office consists of the Auditor General and six members of the Council of the State Audit Office. They are confirmed by the *Saeima* upon recommendation of the Auditor General. The tasks for the Council are enumerated in Article 11 and, *inter alia*, include the approval of annual audit plans, a division of labour among departments, passing decisions on applications to the Constitutional Court. Departments perform audits in accordance with their annual plan approved by the Council. The Directors of departments are appointed by the Auditor General. Departments consist of sectors.

540. The conditions and restrictions to hold the office of Auditor General and the Council are set out in Article 30 of the Law. For instance, they should be citizens with the required professional and work experience; have not reached retirement age; have not been elected to offices of political organizations during the previous three years; have not been convicted of any international criminal offence or criminal offence with intent, nor have not been employed by the USSR or Latvian SSR intelligence services, and such like.

501. See, http://www.lrvk.gov.lv/en/about-the-state-audit-office/regulatory-acts/law-state-audit-office/, accessed 6 Apr. 2015.

541. According to Article 61, audited entities have the right to become acquainted with the task of the audit and to express their views on the draft. Complaints about the decisions of the audit department can be submitted to the Council. In cases where the rights and legal interests of a person or an audited entity are affected, the person or the audited entity have the right to appeal the decision of the Council to the Senate of the Supreme Court. Audited entities must submit a report on their rectification of deficiencies mentioned in the recommendations of the Audit Office.

542. Audited entities should provide appropriate working conditions for employees of the State Audit Office, as well as the books and documents related to the audit. They should also provide information and explanations as required (Article 67).

Chapter 7. Local Government

§1. Introduction

543. According to Article 3 of the *Satversme*, the Republic of Latvia is a unitary state. As is common for a unitary state, its administrative territorial units, their status, powers, and structure are all determined by the central state power. However, the central power cannot fully administer the state without the participation of local government. Therefore some of the functions of public administration are decentralized by transferring their implementation to democratically legitimized local governments.[502]

544. The *Saeima* adopted the main law on local governments in 1994. In the history of Latvia this is the first law binding on all local governments – on all levels and for all types (municipal, rural).

545. A local government is a local administration which, through bodies of elected representatives – city or municipal councils – and the authorities and institutions established by them, ensures the performance of the functions prescribed by law. These are also charged with the performance of tasks assigned by the Cabinet of Ministers. Local governments can undertake other initiatives, observing the interests of the State and the residents of the relevant administrative territory.[503]

546. In implementing local territorial administration, local governments, within the scope specified in the Law on Local Governments, are subject to public law. In the field of private law, however, local governments have a capacity equivalent to a private legal person.[504]

547. The restored independent Republic of Latvia inherited from previous periods an administrative territorial division which consisted of twenty-six regions and more than 500 local level administrative territorial units: seven cities directly under national government control, cities under regional control, and townships and village where power was exercised by councils of people's representatives and executive committees.

548. In 1992, discussions started regarding the necessity for reform of this territorial arrangement. In 1993, the Concept Document of Local Government Reform was adopted by the Government. One chapter was dedicated to the reform of territorial divisions. It envisaged that reforms would be implemented during the term of the local governments elected at the next elections. However, the administrative territorial reform was completed only in 2009.[505]

---

502. Constitutional Court, Terminating Judicial Proceedings in Case No. 2008-08-0306, 20 Jan. 2009, para. 16.
503. Law 'On Local Governments' of 19 May 1994, Art. 3.
504. *Ibid.*, Art. 4.
505. Vilka I. *Administratīvi teritoriālais iedalījums un pašvadības. 'Latvieši un Latvija', III sējums 'Atjaunotā Latvijas valsts'*. (Rīga, Latvijas Zinātņu akadēmija, 2013), 217.

549. After this administrative territorial reform, Latvia's administrative territorial structure now comprises 119 units, administered by local governments or local powers, within the limits of their jurisdiction. There are nine 'major cities' and 111 municipalities. The nine Republic cities of Latvia are Rīga, Daugavpils, Jelgava, Jēkabpils, Jūrmala, Liepāja, Rēzekne, Valmiera and Ventspils.

550. Article 101 of the *Satversme* provides that every citizen of Latvia has the right, as provided for by law, to participate in the work of the State and of local government, and to hold a position in the civil service. Local governments are elected by Latvian citizens and citizens of the EU who permanently reside in Latvia. Every citizen of the EU who permanently resides in Latvia has the right, as provided by law, to participate in the work of local governments.[506]

551. The Law on Local Elections was amended on 11 November 2004 to implement Directive 1994/80/EC, which entered into force on 26 November 2004. In addition, the Law on the Register of Voters entered into force on 5 February 2004.

552. The Constitutional Court has noted that the legislator, in guaranteeing the exercise of that right found in the first sentence of Article 101 of the *Satversme*, has a broad discretion in regulating the procedure for electing local governments, *inter alia*, defining which individuals have the right to submit lists of candidates for local government elections and the procedure therefore. However, the legislator does not have an obligation to establish such regulations on local government elections that would allow every citizen to choose an own way of exercising passive election rights apart from the one established by law. Thus the State has an obligation to establish those procedures according to which every citizen may exercise passive election rights and which would comply with the norms and principles of the *Satversme*.[507]

553. The Constitutional Court has also underscored the general status of a local government as an elected institution of self-governance and is therefore enshrined in Article 101 of the *Satversme*.[508]

554. City or municipality councils are composed of elected representatives.[509]

555. The number of representatives to be elected to city or municipality councils is determined by the Law on City and Municipal Council Elections. That Law provides that a Republic city council and a municipal council are elected for a

506. See EUDO Citizenship Observatory, *Access to Electoral Rights*, Latvia, Kristine Kruma, European University Institute, Florence Robert Schuman Centre for Advanced Studies EUDO Citizenship Observatory, June 2013, available at http://cadmus.eui.eu/bitstream/handle/1814/29816/ER_2013_14-Latvia-FRACIT.pdf?sequence=1, accessed 14 Aug. 2014.
507. Constitutional Court, Case No. 2014-03-01, 5 Feb. 2015.
508. Constitutional Court, Terminating Judicial Proceedings in Case No. 2007-21, 16 Apr. 2008, para. 8.
509. Law 'On Local Governments' of 19 May 1994, Art. 18.

period of four years in equal, direct, secret, and proportional elections. Elections for a city or municipal council take place on the first Saturday of June.[510]

556. An electoral association is composed of persons who have signed the relevant list of candidates, as well as those persons who have been nominated to this list. Those submitting a list of candidates are responsible for the lawfulness of the electoral association's actions.

557. The number of representatives to be elected to a municipal council is determined in compliance with the number of inhabitants registered in the Population Register of the administrative territory of the relevant local government on the day elections are announced. Thus:

(1) for up to 5,000 inhabitants: thirteen representatives;
(2) from 5,001 to 20,000 inhabitants: fifteen representatives;
(3) from 20,001 to 50,000 inhabitants: seventeen representatives; and
(4) for more than 50,000 inhabitants: nineteen representatives.[511]

558. The number of representatives to be elected to a Republic city council, except Rīga City Council, is determined according to the number of inhabitants registered in the Population Register of the administrative territory of the relevant local government on the day elections are announced. Thus:

(1) for up to 50,000 inhabitants: thirteen representatives;
(2) more than 50,000 inhabitants: fifteen representatives.[512]

Rīga City Council, however, contains sixty representatives.[513]

559. In municipalities where the number of inhabitants exceeds 5,000 on the day elections are announced and in Republic cities, the following are eligible to submit lists of candidates:

(1) a registered political party;
(2) a registered union of registered political parties; or
(3) two or more registered political parties who have not joined in a registered union of political parties.[514]

560. In municipalities, where the number of inhabitants is less than 5,000 on the day elections are announced, the following are eligible to submit lists of candidates:

---

510. Law on Elections of the Republic City Council and Municipality Council of 13 Jan. 1994, Art. 1.
511. Law on Elections of the Republic City Council and Municipality Council of 13 Jan. 1994, Art. 2(1).
512. *Ibid.*, Art. 2(2).
513. *Ibid.*, Art. 2(3).
514. *Ibid.*, Art. 15(1).

(1) a registered political party;
(2) a registered union of registered political parties;
(3) two or more registered political parties who have not joined in a registered union of political parties; or
(4) electoral associations.[515]

561. In the Republic of Latvia, the following persons have the right to elect a city or municipal council:

(1) a citizen of Latvia; and
(2) a citizen of the EU, other than a citizen of Latvia, who has been registered in the relevant Population Register.[516]

562. A person who has reached the age of 18 on the day of the elections, is registered in the Voters' Register according to place of residence in that administrative territory. The length of residence must be for at least ninety days prior to the day of the elections, or a person shoud have real estate there.[517]

563. If absent during local elections, a voter can vote three days before the election day in the district of the local government where registered. Article 26 of the Law on Local Elections sets the opening hours for polling stations during those days.[518]

564. The Constitutional Court, in Case No. 2014-03-01, has considered the validity of those provisions for Republic cities and municipalities (where the number of residents exceeded 5,000) restricting the lists of candidates for municipal councils election to political parties only, thus excluding electoral associations.

565. The Constitutional Court held that whereas in the smaller municipalities citizens had the right to run for election based on the lists of candidates submitted by electoral associations, the case of the Republic cities and larger municipalities situation was different. The legitimate aim of such differential treatment was to strengthen the system of political parties. The legislator has tried to provide incentives to persons to found political parties, to become members thereof, or to participate in the activities of political parties in other ways. This would allow achieving a more extensive involvement of people in the political process and strengthening the system of political parties.

566. At the same time, the Constitutional Court recognized that by granting every citizen the right to run for election to any municipal council from a list of an electoral association, a more extensive representation of the inhabitants' interests at the municipal council level could possibly be ensured. However, such a procedure

515. *Ibid.*, Art. 15(2).
516. *Ibid.*, Art. 5(1).
517. *Ibid.*, Art. 5(2).
518. Wednesdays, 5 p.m.–8 p.m.; Thursdays, 9 a.m.–12 a.m.; Fridays, 10 a.m.–4 p.m.

would not facilitate the strengthening of the system of political parties at the national level. Moreover, this differential treatment did not prohibit any citizen from exercising his or her passive election rights. Therefore the contested norm did not violate the principle of legal equality.

567. Elections to a city or municipal council are conducted under the supervision of the Central Election Commission in accordance with the procedures specified by law.

568. Lists of candidates are submitted to the Central Election Committee forty to fifty days before elections (Article 15(4) of the Law on Local Elections). Information and documents to be attached are enumerated in the law (Articles 16–17 of the Law on Local Elections). Candidates are also requested to give a self-assessment on their knowledge of Latvian. Lists of candidates must also pay a deposit, which varies in proportion to the number of voters within the constituency of a particular local government (EUR 130–EUR 210). The biggest deposit is payable in the case of Riga (EUR 860) (Article 18 of the Law on Local Elections). If at least one candidate from the list is elected, the deposit is reimbursed.

569. The lists of candidates, as well as nominated candidates, have the right to contest a decision of the Election Commission regarding the approval of election results within three working days after the Central Election Commission has rendered such a decision. The Central Election Commission must decide on the contested results within three days. This decision of the Central Election Commission may in turn be appealed to the court within three working days.[519]

570. If the court examining the complaint determines that a breach of the law has occurred in the organization of the elections, the counting of the votes, or the calculation of the election results, which have affected the distribution of council seats to representatives among political parties, unions of political parties, or associations of voters, it repeals the decision approving the Republic city or municipal election results and issues one of the following orders:

(1) the Central Election Commission must ensure the recounting of votes;
(2) the Central Election Commission must announce repeated voting; or
(3) the Central Election Commission must announce repeated elections.[520]

571. In the Republic of Latvia, the following persons may be disenfranchised from council elections:

(1) those declared by law to be incapacitated;[521]
(2) those serving sentences in centres of detention or prison; and

519. Law on Elections of the Republic City Council and Municipality Council of 13 Jan. 1994, Arts 451 and 452.
520. Law on Elections of the Republic City Council and Municipality Council of 13 Jan. 1994, Art. 453.
521. The procedure is set in Civil Law and requires a decision of the court (Art. 358 of the Civil Law).

(3) those who do not have the right to vote in a Member State of the EU of which they are citizens.[522]

572. In the Republic of Latvia the following persons have the right to stand as candidates in council elections:

(1) citizens of Latvia; and
(2) citizens of the EU (other than a citizen of Latvia) registered in the Population Register.[523]

573. The following persons may not be nominated as candidates for council elections and cannot be elected to a council:

(1) those serving custodial sentences;
(2) those declared by law as not having the capacity to act;
(3) those with a criminal record for serious or especially serious crime, unless formally rehabilitated or having it otherwise expunged or set aside;
(4) those held by law to be mentally ill or in a state of reduced mental capacity, at the time of committing an offence or becoming so thereafter, and to whom compulsory measures of a medical nature have been applied (or where the matter has been terminated without the application of such a compulsory measures);
(5) those having worked after 13 January 1991 in the C.P.S.U. (L.C.P.), the Working People's International Front of the Latvian S.S.R., the United Council of Labour Collectives, the Organisation of War and Labour Veterans, or the All-Latvia Salvation of Society Committee or regional Committees thereof;
(6) those holding, or having held, staff positions in the State security service, intelligence or counter-intelligence service of the U.S.S.R., the Latvian S.S.R. or some foreign state;
(7) those penalized by a prohibition from standing as a candidate in elections for the *Saeima*, the EU Parliament, a Republic city council or municipal council, excepting where formally rehabilitated or where the criminal record has been expunged or set aside; and
(8) a citizen of the EU deprived by judgment of a court in his EU Member State of the right to be nominated as a candidate and be elected.[524]

574. The President, MPs, members of the government, prosecutors, judges, the State auditor, members of the Board of the State Audit Office, members of the panels of Audit Departments of the State Audit Office, and soldiers may be nominated

522. Law on Elections of the Republic City Council and Municipality Council of 13 Jan. 1994 Art. 6.
523. *Ibid.*, Art. 8.
524. Law on Elections of the Republic City Council and Municipality Council of 13 Jan. 1994, Art. 9. *For details* See EUDO Citizenship Observatory, *Access to Electoral Rights*, Latvia, Kristine Kruma, European University Institute, Florence Robert Schuman Centre for Advanced Studies EUDO Citizenship Observatory, June 2013, available at http://cadmus.eui.eu/bitstream/handle/1814/29816/ER_2013_14-Latvia-FRACIT.pdf?sequence=1, accessed 14 Aug. 2014, pp. 4–8.

as deputy candidates to a city or municipal council. When elected, however, a member of the *Saeima* lose their mandate and any position therein, and soldiers must retire from military service.[525]

§2. JURISDICTION

575. Local governments act independently, within the scope of their competences and the law.[526]

576. State administrative institutions may authorize local governments to perform additional functions, if provided by law or Cabinet regulation. Such delegations should specify the procedures for the performance of such functions and monitor their performance.[527] Local government may implement the functions delegated, but the State institution transferring the functions remains liable for performance. State institutions delegate those functions and tasks to local governments for whose performance no financial allocation is provided.[528]

577. Local governments, in the interests of residents of the relevant administrative territory, may voluntarily carry out their initiatives with respect to any matter if it is not within the competence of the *Saeima*, the Cabinet, Ministries, other State administrative institutions, the courts, or other local governments, and if such activity is not prohibited by law.[529]

578. In carrying out their functions, local governments have the right to do the following, in accordance with procedures laid down by law:

(1) to establish local government institutions, founding societies, or foundations and capital companies, as well as invest their own resources in capital companies;
(2) to acquire and dispose of movable and immovable property; privatize facilities owned by local governments; conclude transactions and perform other activities of a private law nature;
(3) to introduce local fees and determine their amounts; decide on tax rates, rebates and exemptions;
(4) to launch court proceedings and complaints under administrative law; and
(5) to receive information from State institutions.[530]

579. In order to perform their functions, local governments have the following duties (in accordance with procedures laid down by law):

525. Law on Elections of the Republic City Council and Municipality Council of 13 Jan. 1994, Art. 10.
526. Law 'On Local Governments' of 19 May 1994, Art. 5(1).
527. *Ibid.*, Art. 9.
528. *Ibid.*, Arts 9 and 13.
529. Law 'On Local Governments' of 19 May 1994, Art. 12.
530. Law 'On Local Governments' of 19 May 1994, Art. 14(1).

(1) preparation of development programmes for the territory of the relevant local government; ensuring the implementation of territorial development plans, and the administrative supervision of territorial planning;
(2) preparing and approving the local government budget;
(3) due and appropriate management of the local government's movable and immovable property;
(4) collecting taxes and fees;
(5) carrying out projects included in the State investment programme in conformity with expected obligations;
(6) due and appropriate use of local government financial resources in conformity with the approved local government budget;
(7) providing information to the Cabinet and Ministers on issues related to the activities of the relevant local government;
(8) accumulating, utilizing, and preserving documents created in the course of local government activities, until their transfer to the State Archives.[531]

580. To ensure the performance of their functions, local governments issue binding regulations as prescribed by law.[532]

A city or municipality council passes:

(1) external laws and regulations (binding regulations);
(2) internal laws and regulations (regulations, by-laws, instructions);
(3) individual acts (administrative acts and other administrative decisions);
(4) other decisions.[533]

581. The operation of an unlawful binding regulation or other regulatory act or parts of it as adopted by a city or municipal council, may be suspended by an order (with reasons given) of the Minister for Environmental Protection and Regional Development. The order must indicate the paragraphs of the regulation that are to be revoked as unlawful, or must indicate what actions are to be revoked in their entirety. The suspension order must be published in *Latvijas Vēstnesis* within three days of issue and be sent to the chairperson of the relevant city or municipal council.

Upon receiving the suspension order, the chairperson of the city or municipal council should convene an extraordinary meeting of the council within two weeks. The meeting should examine revocation of the relevant act or parts of it. The Minister for Environmental Protection and Regional Development must have timely notice of the time and place of this extraordinary meeting.

If the city or municipal council fails to take a decision revoking the relevant act or parts of it, the council is to submit within three months an application to the Constitutional Court requesting a repeal of the Minister's order. The suspension order

531. *Ibid.*, Art. 14(2).
532. *Ibid.*, Art. 14(3).
533. *Ibid.*, Art. 41.

of the Minister for Environmental Protection and Regional Development, remains in force until the Constitutional Court rules on the matter.[534]

582. A local government adopts and implements the local government budget. Binding regulations regarding the approval of local government budgets and amendments to the budget come into force the next day after signing. Another times can also be indicated. The regulations should be freely accessible at the city or municipal council building and rural territory ('*pagasts*') or city administration and they must be published on the Internet home page of the local government.[535]

§3. Organization and Workings

583. The Constitutional Court has noted that the principle of self-governance, which includes minimum requirements with regard to the organization of local self-governance in a democratic state based on the rule of law, derives from the first sentence of Article 101(2) of the *Satversme* read in the context of Article 1 of the *Satversme*.[536] The detailed regulation on the organization of the work of local governments is provided for in the Law on Local Governments.

584. The Constitutional Court has also emphasized that the principle of self-governance includes the existence of local self-government and its democratic legitimation. In establishing the content of the principle of self-governance, policy principles should be taken into consideration, for example, the principle of subsidiarity, the principle of a socially responsible state, as well as considerations of public benefit. Moreover, the understanding of these principles may change over time.[537]

585. The representative institution which exercises the decision-taking power of the local government is elected by the voters. In Latvia, the decision-making body is the council, which consists of elected representatives. The council has broad competences. It may examine any issue within the competence of the local government. Moreover, there are a series of issues in which a decision can be taken only by the council. For example, only the council may approve the by-laws of the local government and the budget of the local government; approve the development programme for the territory of the local government and its local planning; establish, reorganize, or liquidate municipal institutions and capital companies.

586. The first meeting of a newly elected council must be convened by the chairperson of the city or municipal electoral commission within the time period laid down in the Law on Elections of the Republic City Council and Municipal Council.

534. Law 'On Local Governments' of 19 May 1994, Art. 49.
535. *Ibid.*, Art. 46.
536. Constitutional Court, Terminating Judicial Proceedings in Case No. 2007-21-01, 16 Apr. 2008.
537. Decision of 20 Jan. 2009 by the Constitutional Court on Terminating Judicial Proceedings in Case No. 2008-08-0306, para. 13.1.

The term of office of the previous city or municipal council terminates on this first meeting of the newly elected city or municipal council.[538]

587. The Chairperson of a city or municipal council and the Vice-Chairperson of a city or municipal are elected from among the representatives of the relevant city or municipal council. Any representatives of a city or municipal council have the right to nominate a candidate for the position of chairperson of the council. The Chairperson of a city or municipal council is elected if the candidate has received more than half of the votes of the elected representatives of the council. If none of the candidates receives the necessary majority in the first round, a vote is held again for those two candidates who had received the most votes. The candidate who receives the necessary majority is elected. If in the second round neither of the candidates receives the necessary majority, a vote is held for the candidate who had received in the second round more votes. If no candidate in the third round receives the necessary number of votes for election, a new election is held for Chairperson of the council.[539]

588. The mandate of the Chairperson and Vice-Chairperson of a city or municipal council enters in effect from the moment of election.

The Chairperson of a council:

(1) manages the work of the council and coordinates work in the committees;
(2) represents the local government in relations with the State and other local governments;
(3) represents the city or municipal council in court proceedings without special authorization;
(4) issues powers of attorney, signs contracts and other legal documents in the name of the city or municipal council;
(5) manages the work of the finance committee;
(6) issues binding instructions to local government administrative employees;
(7) recommends the examination of issues in the council and committees;
(8) prepares submissions from officials of State institutions for examination at meetings of the council;
(9) is responsible for the execution of court judgments in which one of the parties is the city or municipal council;
(10) may recommend the dismissal of the local heads of State administrative institutions or officials from such institutions within the relevant administrative territory;
(11) performs other duties provided for by law, Cabinet decision, by-laws of the relevant local government, and decisions of the city or municipal council.[540]

589. The Constitutional Court has noted that the Chairperson of the council is the highest official of local government who, in cases of necessity and on the basis

538. Law 'On Local Governments' of 19 May 1994, Art. 19.
539. Law 'On Local Governments' of 19 May 1994, Art. 19.
540. *Ibid.*, Art. 62.

of guidelines prescribed by the local government council, should assume responsibility for the presentation of the local government's position in a particular discussion or with regard to a particular issue, or looking for compromise solutions, if such are needed.[541]

590. The Chairperson of a local government city or municipal council may be removed from office, if requested by at least one-third of the representatives of the council. If the Chairperson of a city or municipal council fails to fulfil the duties stipulated by law or the by-laws of the relevant local government; fails to execute decisions of the city or municipality council and court decisions, or fails to observe the law or Cabinet regulations, the Minister for Environmental Protection and Regional Development has the right to request the removal from office of the Chairperson of a city or municipal council. The Chairperson is to be considered removed from office where more than one-half the total number of elected representatives of the city or municipal council have voted for removal.[542]

591. City or municipal councils select, from among the representatives in the council, standing committees which:

(1) prepare issues for examination at meetings of the city or municipal council;
(2) provide opinions on questions within the competence of the committee;
(3) monitor the work of the local government institutions, in accordance with local government by-laws;
(4) examine draft budgets of local government institutions, and submit them to the finance committee;
(5) approve and monitor expenditure estimates of local government institutions; and
(6) perform other duties in conformity with the local government by-laws.[543]

592. The local government sets up a finance committee and committees on social, educational, and cultural issues. The local government of a municipality may establish a territorial committee. If at least one-quarter of the residents registered in the relevant local government administrative territory are aliens or stateless persons, the city or municipal council may establish an aliens and stateless persons affairs committee.[544]

593. Each council representative must be a member of at least one city or municipal council committee. A committee member may terminate his or her activities in a committee only if the council, after receiving a written submission from the committee member, has decided to approve the release of the member from their duties.

---

541. Constitutional Court, Case No. 2009-04-06, 30 Oct. 2009, para. 12.3.1.
542. Law 'On Local Governments' of 19 May 1994, Art. 65.
543. *Ibid.*, Art. 50.
544. *Ibid.*, Arts 51 and 52.

594. The work of a city or municipal council is managed by its Chairperson. The Vice-Chairperson of the council acts for the chairperson during absence, and performs any duties assigned by the chairperson or specified in local government by-laws.[545]

595. Decisions of city or municipal councils must be taken at meetings. Meetings of the councils must be public, unless otherwise provided by law. Decisions of the councils and the minutes of council meetings must be publicly accessible. Decisions of city or municipal councils must be published on the Internet home page of the local government not later than the third working day following the signing thereof. The accessibility to council decisions and minutes of council meetings must be ensured, taking into account any restrictions on access to information prescribed by law and regulation.[546]

596. The chairperson must convene regular meetings of the city or municipal council not less than once a month, specifying the time and location of meetings and announcing the agenda. Extraordinary meetings of city or municipal councils are convened by the Chairperson on his or her own initiative. The Chairperson of a city or municipal council has the duty to convene an extraordinary meeting if such is requested by:

(1) at least one-third of the representatives;
(2) the Minister for Environmental Protection and Regional Development; or
(3) the Cabinet.[547]

597. City or municipal councils may examine any issue under the supervision of the relevant local government. In addition, only city or municipal councils may:

(1) approve local government by-laws;
(2) approve the local government budget, budget amendments and reports of the implementation of the budget, as well as economic and annual public reports;
(3) approve the local government territorial development programme and territorial planning;
(4) decide on the liquidation of the relevant administrative territory, any modification of its boundaries or change of name;
(5) approve the local government economic and social development and the environmental protection long-term programmes;
(6) approve the local government territorial divisions and their administration structure;
(7) specify the official symbols of the city, municipality or rural territory (or *pagasts*), and coordinate such with the Latvian State Heraldry Commission;

545. *Ibid.*, Art. 25.
546. Law 'On Local Governments' of 19 May 1994, Art. 26.
547. *Ibid.*, Art. 27 and 28.

(8) establish, reorganize, or liquidate local government institutions, local government capital companies, societies and foundations and approve the by-laws of local government institutions;
(9) appoint to and remove from office the heads of local government institutions and other officials in cases provided for by law and local government by-laws;
(10) elect to and discharge from office the Chairperson of the city or municipal council, the Vice-Chairperson, members of standing committees, and members of the audit commission;
(11) appoint to and remove from office the executive director;
(12) determine the amount and method of remuneration of a councillor, and the reimbursement of work-related expenditures;
(13) determine the remuneration of the chairperson of the council, his or her vice-chairperson, local government administrative employees, heads of local government institutions and other local government officials and employees;
(14) determine (unless otherwise prohibited or prescribed by law or Cabinet regulation) the fees and charges for:
   (a) use of (lease) of local government land and other immovable or movable property;
   (b) renting/leasing local government residential and non-residential property;
   (c) use of the local government water supply and sewerage;
   (d) heating provided by the local government;
   (e) collection of municipal waste;
   (f) issuance of licences (permits); and
   (g) other services;
(15) adopt binding regulations with respect to implementing local government fees and, in cases prescribed by law, determine tax rates;
(16) approve binding regulations and determine administrative liability for the violation of such;
(17) take decisions with respect to the disposition, pledging, or privatization of local government immovable property, as well as local government ownership and acquisition of immovable property;
(18) determine the procedures for transactions with local government movable property, as well as the procedures for accepting and managing gifts and bequests, and for public borrowing, the acceptance of loans and other economic obligations in the name of the local government;
(19) grant or change the names to streets, parks, and public squares;
(20) suspend and revoke decisions of the heads of local government institutions;
(21) revoke orders of the chairperson of the city or municipal council;
(22) elect local government representatives and members to local government or State committees, commissions, boards of directors, and working groups;
(23) take decisions with respect to organizing elections and referendums, in accordance with procedures laid down by the Central Electoral Commission;
(24) elect and remove chief judges and members of the Orphans' Court; and
(25) take decisions in other cases provided for by law.

598. City or municipal council meetings must examine draft decisions submitted by:

(1) the Chairperson of a city or municipal council;
(2) committees of a city or municipal council;
(3) representatives of a city or municipal council; or
(4) the initiator of an extraordinary meeting.

599. Draft decisions of a city or municipal council, opinions regarding them, and information materials must be made available to all representatives of the city or municipal council not later than three working days prior to regular meetings and not later than three hours prior to extraordinary meetings.[548]

600. City or municipal councils may discuss only such matters as are included in the announced agenda of the meeting. Exceptions may be made only if not less than two-thirds of the council representatives present consent to them.[549]

601. Meetings of city or municipal councils may take place if more than half the representatives of the council participate. A decision is considered taken if more than half of the council representatives present vote for it, and if the law does not provide otherwise. If the necessary number of votes in favour of a draft decision is not received, the draft decision is considered rejected. In such cases, the draft decision may be submitted to the city or municipal council for re-examination, as prescribed by law.[550]

602. The organization of the work of a city or municipal council is determined by the by-laws of the relevant local government, as prescribed by law. The by-laws of a local government are binding regulations, which determine the administrative organization of the local government, the decision-making procedures, the rights and duties of residents in the territorial administration, as well as other organizational issues regarding the activities of the local government.[551]

603. The implementation of a city or municipal council decision must be ensured by officials elected or appointed by the city or municipal council, and by local government institutions, as well as capital companies.

604. Upon the proposal of the Chairperson of the council, a council appoints an executive director who is responsible for the work of municipal institutions and capital companies. The executive director may not be a deputy of the Council, except for municipalities where the number of inhabitants does not exceed 5,000. In those cases the chairperson of the council may perform the functions of executive director.

548. Law on Local Governments of 19 May 1994, Art. 30.
549. *Ibid.*, Art. 31.
550. *Ibid.*, Art. 34.
551. Law on Local Governments of 19 May 1994, Arts 23 and 24.

605. Municipal budget revenues consist of tax revenues which are deducted from state taxes, non-tax revenues, including municipal fees, received payments, paid services, and other revenue of the municipality.

606. In Latvia, municipalities differ significantly in their financial capacity. Therefore, since 1995, local government finances are being equalized. The different tax revenue in the local government budgets and the different expenditure needs (predominantly defined by the age structure of inhabitants) are taken into account. The system for equalizing local government finances is regulated by the Law on the Equalisation of Local Government Finances, adopted in 1998 and amended in 2009 to adapt the system of financial equalization with the reformed system of local governments. The equalization of the local government finances is implemented by using the Local Government Equalisation Fund, the resources of which consist of local government contributions and a State budget subsidy.

Part III. Citizenship

Chapter 1. Rules concerning Nationality

§1. General Approach and Reforms

607. The concept of Latvian citizenship is embedded in the historical context of Latvia, but adjusted to deal with post-occupation consequences. After regaining its independence, Latvia had to take into account the political situation and requirements stemming from human rights law by adopting certain political compromises.[552]

608. An important step in the process of consolidating its new statehood proclaimed on 18 November 1918 was the adoption of the Law on Citizenship in 1919. This Law was not repealed subsequent to the occupation of Latvia by the Soviet Union in 1940. During the occupation, Latvian citizens also became citizens of the USSR by way of automatic imposition of the latter's citizenship.[553]

609. Latvian citizenship policy is based on the principle of State continuity: the *ex iniuria ius non oritur* principle. According to this approach only those who were Latvian citizens and their descendants could restore their citizenship de facto.

610. According to the Declaration of Independence the Supreme Council was entrusted to re-establish the aggregate body of Latvian citizens in accordance with the 1919 Law on Citizenship, as amended in 1927. It was considered applicable with the adoption of the 15 October 1991 Resolution on the Renewal of the Republic of Latvia's Citizens' Rights and Fundamental Principles of Naturalisation by the Supreme Council.[554] Another decision regulating the renewal of citizenship rights was adopted by the Supreme Council on 27 November 1991, entitled 'On the application of the Supreme Council decision "On renewal of the Republic of Latvia's citizens rights and fundamental principles of naturalisation in relation to citizens of

552. Kruma, K., *EU citizenship, Nationality and Migrant Status. An Ongoing challenge* 325–339 (Leiden: Martinus Nijhoff Publishers 2014).
553. Kruma, K., *Country Report: Latvia* (European University Institute 2013), available at http://eudo-citizenship.eu/admin/?p=file&appl=countryProfiles&f=Latvia.pdf, accessed 5 Nov. 2014. See also Ziemele, I., *State Continuity and Nationality: The Baltic States and Russia. Past, Present and Future as Defined by International Law* (Leiden: Martinus Nijhoff Publishers, 2005).
554. Constitutional Court, Case No. 2009-94-01, 13 May 2010, paras 14–16.

the Republic of Latvia residing abroad".' The decision provided that upon registration, citizens residing abroad are entitled to preserve their other citizenship. Soviet nationality was thus declared null and void *ab initio*. Latvian citizens recovered their de facto rights and obligations deriving from their Latvian citizenship.

611. According to the Resolution on the Renewal of the Republic of Latvia's Citizens' Rights and Fundamental Principles of Naturalisation the following groups of individuals were recognized as citizens: (1) those who were Latvian citizens on 17 June 1940 and their descendants if they had lived in the country and had registered by 1 July 1992; (2) persons who were Latvian citizens on 17 June 1940 and their descendants if they did not reside in Latvia or were citizens of another State and had submitted an expatriation permit; and (3) persons born and residing in Latvia if their parents were unknown. The process of naturalization was also made easy for persons who were living in Latvia on 17 June 1940 without Latvian citizenship.

612. The new Law on Citizenship was adopted on 22 July 1994. Slightly amended in 1995, it followed the *ius sanguinis* principle. In addition, several other groups could qualify for citizenship, such as Latvians and Livs residing in Latvia and not holding other citizenship; women who had lost citizenship upon marriage; orphans, and persons who had completed education in schools with Latvian as a language of instruction.[555] The right of a child to acquire Latvian citizenship was ensured by providing that if at least one parent was a Latvian citizen the child would acquire Latvian citizenship, subject to mutual agreement by the parents.

613. Those who did not belong to the above-mentioned groups had to seek naturalization according to the procedures set out by law and the regulations of the Cabinet of Ministers. The Law provided for gradual naturalization, the so-called window-system. It provided that persons would be naturalised in stages starting in 1996. After 2003, all persons would have the right to apply.

614. Over the years Latvia has liberalized its citizenship policies in relation to naturalization.[556] Latvia amended its Citizenship Law in 1998. The amendments were confirmed in a referendum and became effective in November 1998.[557] These amendments abolished the 'window-system' and provided citizenship to children

555. *For details* see Kruma, K., *Country Report: Latvia* (European University Institute 2013), available at http://eudo-citizenship.eu/admin/?p=file&appl=countryProfiles&f=Latvia.pdf, accessed 5 Nov. 2014, p. 5.

556. On naturalization requirements See: Strik, T. et al., The INTEC Project: Synthesis Report. *Integration and Naturalisation Tests: The New Way to European Citizenship*, in *Which Integration Policies for Migrants? Interaction between the EU and its Member States* 285–405 (Pascouau Y. & Strik T. eds, The Netherlands: Wolf Legal Publishers 2012). Kruma, K., *Latvian Integration Policy: Lost in Translation* in *A Re-definition of Belonging? Language and Integration Tests in Europe* 142–270 (van Oers Ricky, Ersbøll Eva & Kostakopoulou Dora eds, Leiden: Martinus Nijhoff Publishers 2010).

557. The amendments were adopted on 22 Jun. 1998. The referendum was held on 3 Oct. 1998 and about 53% of the electorate voted for the adoption of the amendments.

born in Latvia after 21 August 1991, and to stateless persons or non-citizens. Several classes of individuals were exempted from the naturalization process or did not have to pass naturalization exams.

615. Comprehensive amendments to Citizenship Law were adopted in 2013. After these amendments, the Citizenship Law has become more complex.[558] The amendments re-defined the groups of persons to be considered Latvian citizens; further liberalized the registration of children of non-citizens and stateless persons as citizens, and made more stringent the regulations on deprivation of citizenship. According to the amendments, Latvia accepts dual citizenship in relation to several countries, and in relation to Latvian citizens who had left Latvia during the occupation.

§2. Main Principles of Latvian Citizenship

616. According to Article 1 of the Citizenship Law, as amended in 2013, it is based on the Law on Nationality of 23 August 1919, the continuity doctrine, and the interests of Latvia. Therefore, the primary principles of the citizenship policy are defined as follows:

(1) to determine the persons to be deemed citizens of Latvia and to guarantee the existence and continuity of Latvian citizenship;
(2) to guarantee the right to register as citizens of Latvia for the constituent nation (Latvians) and the autochthonous population (Livs);
(3) to provide an opportunity for exiles from Latvia and their descendants to register as citizens of Latvia;
(4) to promote the development of a united society of Latvia on the basis of the common values of the people of Latvia;
(5) to recognize dual citizenship in compliance with the political objectives and interests of the State of Latvia and to retain the aggregate of the citizens of Latvia under increased mobility conditions.

558. On history of amendments See: http://eudo-citizenship.eu/news/citizenshipnews/700-latvia-comprehensive-citizenship-reform-on-the-agenda-in-parliament-and-in-a-referendumcampaign-, accessed 9 Dec. 2014.

Chapter 2. Acquisition and Loss of Citizenship

§1. Acquisition of Latvian Citizenship

617. Article 2 of the Citizenship Law defines the groups of persons to be considered citizens of Latvia:

(1) persons who were citizens on the date of occupation and their descendants if they register as citizens by 1 October 2013 or if they had right to register according to the Law in force before 1 October 2013;
(2) persons born to parents (one or both) who are Latvian citizens;
(3) Latvians and Livs whose ancestors in 1881 or later have permanently resided in Latvia as it existed until 17 June 1940. In addition, they must prove knowledge of Latvian. They have to submit documentary evidence on belonging to the constituent national or autochthonous population or to provide reasons why such evidence cannot be submitted;
(4) women who permanently reside in Latvia and who had lost their citizenship according to the Law on Citizenship of 1919 as well as their descendants;
(5) children who are found in the territory of Latvia whose parents are unknown or children left without parental care, except for those children for whose parents custody rights have been suspended; and
(6) orphans under extra-familial care in Latvia.

618. The general rule in Article 2(2) provides that children of Latvian citizens are citizens if they comply with the provisions on dual citizenship. The will to register a child as Latvian citizen should be expressed by a lawful representative of a child if the child has not reached the age of 15, or by the child itself if between the ages 15 and 18.

619. The 1998 amendments provided for citizenship for children born in Latvia to stateless persons or non-citizens after 21 August 1991.[559] Thus, a conditional *ius soli* acquisition of citizenship was created. After the 2013 amendments, the Citizenship Law now provides that at least one parent should express a wish to register the child as a Latvian citizen upon registration of birth or until the child reaches the age of 15. In order to apply for citizenship according to Article $3^1(1)$, a parent should possess a permanent residence in Latvia. A child should be recognized as a Latvian citizen if the mother of the child is a non-citizen or stateless person and the father is unknown; or if one of parents is a non-citizen or stateless person and the status of another parent is unknown; or if one parent is non-citizen or stateless person and the other parent is deceased.

620. In cases when a stateless child or a child of non-citizen parents applies for citizenship when aged between 15–18, he or she should present a Latvian language certificate. There are also requirements that the child has not been sentenced for the

559. On the concept of non-citizens Part III.

commission of a serious crime and has not been involved in activities threatening security, society, democratic constitutional order, independence, and territorial integrity. When children reach 18 years of age, the general naturalization procedures apply.

621. Pursuant to the 2013 amendments, dual citizenship is now permitted in Latvia. Dual citizenship is accepted in cases when a Latvian citizen has acquired citizenship of the EU, EFTA, NATO countries, Australia, Brazil, New Zealand, or the citizenship of a state with whom Latvia has concluded an international agreement. The Cabinet of Ministers has a discretion to allow a person to retain the other citizenship if this is in compliance with important State interests. The decision is to be taken by the Cabinet of Ministers within a year and is not subject to appeal. Furthermore, dual citizenship is allowed if a person acquired another citizenship by marriage (*ex lege*) or as a result of adoption.

622. Furthermore, dual citizenship is allowed in cases where a person acquires citizenship after 1 October 2013 according to Article 2; in cases when citizenship is acquired by Latvians and Livs after 1 October 2013, as well as in cases of naturalization and children.

623. There is a specific article regulating dual citizenship and the acquisition of citizenship for persons who had left Latvia during the time of the Soviet occupation. The Transitional Regulations of the Citizenship Law before amendment provided that those Latvian citizens and their descendants who, during the period from 17 June 1940 until 4 May 1990, left Latvia as refugees or were deported could register as Latvian citizens until 1 July 1995.[560] The Citizenship Law in Article 8^1 provides that if a person who was a Latvian citizen on 17 June 1940, or a descendant of such person, submits a certification of the fact that, from 17 June 1940 until 4 May 1990, he or she had left Latvia to escape from the USSR or German occupation regime or had been deported, and due to those reasons had not returned to Latvia for permanent residence until 4 May 1990, such a person and the descendants thereof shall retain the right to register as Latvian citizens. The same applies in cases of descendants born up to 1 October 2014. These persons can become dual citizens.

624. Individuals who have registered with the Residents' Register are considered to reside lawfully in Latvia and are entitled to acquire citizenship through naturalization if they have received a permanent residence permit. The naturalization requirements are the following: (1) permanent residence in Latvia for five years;[561]

560. The compliance of this norm with the principle of state continuity and with the *Satversme* was contested in the Constitutional Court. The Court declared that this norm does comply with the Constitution, and with the doctrine of state continuity derived from the *Satversme* and the Declaration of Independence. See: Constitutional Court, Case No. 2009-94-01, 13 May 2010.

561. There is a possibility that a person has not lived in Latvia for one year which cannot be a year before submission of naturalization application. According to Art. 24 of the Immigration Law, permanent residence can be acquired after five years of residence in Latvia with a temporary residence

(2) knowledge of the Latvian language, the Constitution, the anthem, and the history of Latvia; (3) a loyalty oath to the Republic of Latvia; (4) a legal source of income, and (5) acknowledging renunciation of previous citizenship or testimony that a person does not have other citizenship (except refugees) (Article 12). The requirement to renounce citizenship is not applicable in cases of citizens of the EU, EFTA, NATO countries, as well as citizens of Australia, Brazil, New Zealand, and those citizens of a State with whom Latvia has concluded an agreement on recognition of dual citizenship. Moreover, these persons can serve in the military in those countries to qualify for Latvian citizenship. Otherwise the statement on renunciation of other citizenship should be submitted when all other requirements for citizenship are met.[562]

625. Article 4 of the Citizenship Law states that Latvian citizens have equal rights and obligations irrespective of the manner in which citizenship has been acquired. Marriage or residence outside Latvia should also not affect Latvian citizenship (Articles 5 and 6).

§2. Loss of Latvian Citizenship

626. Latvian citizenship is lost in cases of renunciation or revocation. The main grounds are stated in Articles 23–25 of the Citizenship Law, but detailed procedures are set out in the 24 September 2013 Regulation No. 975 on the procedures regarding loss and renewal of Latvian citizenship.

627. Renunciation can take place if a person has been guaranteed the citizenship of another State except where he or she has unfulfilled fiscal obligations towards the State. Application for renunciation of Latvian citizenship should be submitted within thirty days after acquiring the citizenship of another State. In cases where a child has acquired dual nationality, an application for renunciation of Latvian citizenship should be submitted between the ages of 18–25. These requirements do not apply in cases of dual citizenship in countries where dual citizenship is permitted. If a person has renounced Latvian citizenship, it can be re-acquired only by naturalization.

628. Citizenship can be revoked by a decision of the Office of Citizenship and Migration Affairs (OCMA). It is subject to appeal according to the procedures set out in the Law on Administrative Procedure. Citizenship is revoked in cases where a person (1) has acquired the citizenship of another State without renouncing

permit. This means that a person shall reside five years in Latvia in order to obtain permanent residence and a further five years with permanent residence to acquire the right to apply for citizenship. Exceptional cases provide for a shorter residence requirement as permanent residence permits can be issued in certain cases immediately after arrival (for instance, family reunification, former citizens and non-citizens alike).

562. See: Kruma, K., *Country report: Latvia* (EUDO citizenship observatory, RSCAS/EUDO-CIT-CR 2013/13), available at http://eudo-citizenship.eu/admin/?p=file&appl=countryProfiles&f=Latvia.pdf, accessed 25 Jan. 2015. See also s. 3 below.

Latvian citizenship; (2) continues to serve in foreign armed forces or similar organizations without permission from the Cabinet of Ministers (except in those cases where such is allowed in the countries where dual citizenship is permitted); or (3) has committed acts promoting the violent overthrow of the government of Latvia; has incited publicly the violent overthrow of public authorities established in the *Satversme* or the political system; or has publicly incited or has undertaken steps for the abrogation of the independence of Latvia, all of which has been proven to the satisfaction of the court. In none of these cases can revocation of citizenship lead to statelessness. The only exception is the case where the person has acquired citizenship by fraud. In such cases revocation is allowed within a ten-year term. Yet this term is not applicable in two cases only: (1) if person has been convicted of a crime mentioned in Article 5 of the Statute of International Criminal Court; and (2) if person holds citizenship in another country with which dual nationality is not allowed. Family members are not affected by such proceedings. A former citizen can re-apply for citizenship after five years of residence after the date of revocation of citizenship.

629. When dealing with cases of deprivation of citizenship, Latvian courts apply the principle of proportionality.

§3. Conditions for Naturalization

630. Upon application, a person shall declare that none of the restrictions apply as specified in Article 11 of the Citizenship Law. Article 11 establishes restrictions on naturalization where:

(1) a person has threatened the security of Latvia, its society, the democratic constitutional order, or the independence and territorial integrity of Latvia;[563]
(2) a person has served in the military organization or the armed forces of another State without governmental permission;
(3) a person has served in the USSR army and was called-up from outside Latvia;[564]
(4) a person has been employed by the KGB, the security or intelligence services, or a similar service of another State;
(5) a person has been sentenced in Latvia or another State for a crime which is also a crime in Latvia, except where the Cabinet of Ministers acknowledges that the judgment violated fair trial rights and proportionality;

563. The Law also mentions examples, e.g., acted against the independence of Latvia, democratic parliamentary structure, have propagated fascist, chauvinist, national-socialist, communist or other an ideas after 4 May 1990, incited ethnic or racial hatred, is related to terrorism or is member of criminal organization, is related to legalization of the proceeds from crime.

564. This is not applicable in cases when a person has lived for at least ten years in marriage with Latvian citizen or has been citizen of Lithuania or Estonia before occupation.

(6) a person has, after 13 January 1991, worked against Latvia in a number of specified organizations;[565]
(7) a person has not fulfilled tax or other financial obligations to Latvia.

Children up to the age of 15 acquire citizenship together with the naturalized parent.

631. The Naturalisation Board is part of the OCMA, working under the auspices of the Ministry of Interior. It is responsible for the examination of naturalization applications. The procedure for naturalization is set out in detail in a number of regulations of the Cabinet of Ministers. Regulation No. 1001 on the Procedure for Acceptance and Review of Naturalisation Applications includes model application forms and specifies the procedure for submission of applications including the accompanying documents.[566]

632. The naturalization procedure is to take no more than six months from the date of application. The fee has been set at EUR 28.46 and EUR 4.27 for certain groups of applicants.[567]

633. The requirements for the naturalization examinations are set out in detail in Regulation No. 973 on the Examination of Proficiency in the Latvian Language and the Examination of Knowledge of the Basic Principles of the Constitution, the Text of the National Anthem and the History of Latvia in accordance with the Citizenship Law adopted on 24 September 2013.[568] The regulations provide that knowledge of the language, of the Constitution, the anthem, and history shall be tested by an examination commission established by the OCMA.

634. Decisions of the OCMA can be contested pursuant to the provisions of the Law on Administrative Procedure. In cases where naturalization has been refused

565. These include the Communist Party of the Soviet Union, the Latvian Communist Party, the Working People's International Front of the Latvian SSR, the United Council of Labour Collectives, the Organisation of War and Labour Veterans, the All-Latvia Salvation of Society Committee or their regional Committees or the Union of Communists of Latvia.
566. A special procedure is provided by the Regulation No. 976 on the Procedure for Submission and the Review of Application for Recognition of a Child being a Citizen of Latvia adopted on 24 Sep. 2013.
567. Regulations on the State Duty Payable for Submission of a Naturalisation Application, Regulation No. 849, 17 Sep. 2013. The rate is lowered for: (1) members of poor families or poor persons; (2) unemployed; (3) members of families with at least three under age children; (4) persons receiving old age pension; (5) disabled persons with a certain degree of disability; (6) pupils and students; (7) full-time students of tertiary education establishments. Persons exempted are: (1) politically repressed; (2) severely disabled persons; (3) orphans and children who are not under their parents' charge; (4) persons sheltered by social care institutions of the state or self-government. The fees were changed in 1997, 2001 and 2002.
568. There are certain groups exempted from the language and knowledge exam. *For details* See Kruma, K., *Country report: Latvia*, (EUDO citizenship observatory, RSCAS/EUDO-CIT-CR 2013/13), available at http://eudo-citizenship.eu/admin/?p=file&appl=countryProfiles&f=Latvia.pdf, accessed 25 Jan. 2015.

on the basis of information obtained as a result of intelligence or counter-intelligence, the refusal may be appealed to the Prosecutor General whose decision shall not be subject to appeal. The final decision on naturalization is taken by the Cabinet of Ministers. The Cabinet may take a decision on a refusal to admit a person to citizenship if his or her behaviour or actions threaten security and the public order, the democratic constitutional order, or independence and territorial integrity. This decision is without appeal.[569]

569. This approach is in line with the practice of the Administrative Cases Department of the Supreme Court's Senate. See case No. SKA 221, 11 Apr. 2006. This has also been confirmed by the European Court of Human Rights in Case *Petropavlovskis v. Latvia*, Application No. 44230/06, 13 Jan. 2015.

Chapter 3. Rules concerning Non-citizens

635. Latvia inherited large Russian-speaking communities who had arrived from the ex-USSR. The Soviet central authorities had encouraged the large-scale immigration of the labour force to meet the local demands of Soviet industrialization and ethnic politics. There were also Russian military personnel (50,000–80,000 military personnel with more than 22,000 retired Soviet military officers) who remained in Latvia pending an interstate withdrawal agreement.[570]

636. The Law on the Entrance and Residence of Foreigners and Stateless Persons entered into force on 2 July 1992. It determined the procedures for applying and receiving residence permits. The Law was unclear and the status of individuals who entered Latvia between 4 May and 2 July 1992 was even more uncertain.[571] Settlers had an option to register as Russian citizens or citizens of other states of the Commonwealth of Independent States (CIS), which they did not use for various reasons.

637. Persons with undetermined status could not be extradited as settlers from an occupying State because this would be contrary to human rights law which prohibits the expulsion of aliens en masse due to a lack of an interstate agreement requiring the occupying power to observe the Geneva Convention. Nor could those persons be classified as stateless because that would be against the principle of reduction of statelessness.[572]

638. In an attempt to strike a balance between State continuity and the obligation to avoid statelessness, Latvia introduced the special temporary status of 'non-citizen' in 1995 by adopting the Law on the Status of Former Soviet Citizens who are not Citizens of Latvia or any Other State. According to the Law:

> The persons governed by this Act – 'non-citizens' – shall be those citizens of the former USSR who reside in the Republic of Latvia as well as those who are temporarily absent, and their children, who simultaneously comply with the following conditions:
>
> 1) on 1 July 1992 they were registered as being resident within the territory of Latvia, regardless of the status of their residence; or their last registered place of residence by 1 July 1992 was in the Republic of Latvia; or a court

570. *For details* see Muižnieks, N., *Government Policy and the Russian Minority, Latvian-Russian Relations: Domestic and International Dimensions* (Rīga: LU Apgāds and Baltijas Sociālo zinātņu institūts 2006). Muižnieks, N., *Russian Foreign Policy Towards 'Compatriots' in Latvia*, in *Latvian-Russian Relations: Domestic and International Dimensions* (Muižnieks, N. ed., Rīga: LU Apgāds 2006).
571. See Ziemele, I., *State Continuity and Nationality: The Baltic States and Russia. Past, Present and Future as Defined by International Law* 160–161 (Leiden: Martinus Nijhoff Publishers 2005).
572. Krūma, K., *An Ongoing Challenge. EU Citizenship, Migrant Status and Nationality. Focus on Latvia* 348 (Lund: Media Tryck, 2012). Ronen, Y., *Status of Settlers Implanted by Illegal Territorial Rigimes*, 79/1 British Y.B. Intl. L. 94–263 (2009).

has established that before the above-mentioned date they had been resident within the territory of Latvia for not less than ten years;[573]

2) they do not hold Latvian citizenship;
3) they are not and have not been citizens of any other State.

639. Persons excluded from the scope of the Law are those who have been affiliated with the Soviet military and their family members if they arrived in Latvia in connection with the service of a member of those armed forces, as well as persons who were reimbursed for departure to or with a registered residence in the CIS after 1 July 1992.

640. Non-citizens are given a special passport. The passport grants them the special status of belonging to the State, thus giving them the constitutional right to return. Article 98 of the *Satversme* states, 'Everyone having a Latvian passport shall be protected by the State when abroad and has the right to freely return to Latvia.' Non-citizens enjoy the diplomatic protection of Latvia. Non-citizens also enjoy those human rights granted to nationals. This has been submitted by Latvia to and accepted by a number of international treaty monitoring bodies. Non-citizens, however, are not granted political rights and they are barred from practicing certain professions related to civil service jobs and the judiciary. There are also restrictions on owning land.

641. The Constitutional Court reviewed the amendments made to the Former USSR Citizens Law which provided for the revocation of the status of non-citizen for persons who acquired the status of permanent resident in another country after 1 June 2004. Until these amendments, the status could only be renounced on condition that a nationality had been acquired. The Court regarded the amendments as unconstitutional.[574]

642. The Court acknowledged that the introduction of the status of non-citizen was a complicated political compromise as a result of which a category unknown in international law had been created. The Court noted that Latvia has consistently defended its position that non-citizens cannot be qualified as stateless persons and this view has been accepted by the international monitoring bodies.

643. The Court defined the status of non-citizen in the following way:

> The status of non-citizens is not and cannot be considered as a mode of Latvian citizenship. However, the rights given to non-citizens and the international

573. In 1998, the Former USSR Citizens Law was amended to normalize the situation of those persons who had entered Latvia but who did not have 'unlimited propyska' in their passports. The Law now reads that nationals of the former USSR who had been 'registered' as living in Latvia on 1 Jul. 1992 or who could prove with a court verdict, at least, a ten year long residence in Latvia are subjects of the Law. Ziemele, I., *State Continuity and Nationality: The Baltic States and Russia. Past, Present and Future as Defined by International Law* 162 (Leiden: Martinus Nijhoff Publishers 2005).

574. Constitutional Court, Case No. 2004-15-0106, 7 Mar. 2005.

obligations which Latvia has undertaken in relation to these persons signify that the legal link of non-citizens to Latvia is recognised to a certain extent and based on it mutual obligations and rights have emerged. This is derived from Article 98 of the *Satversme* which *inter alia* states that anyone who possesses a Latvian passport has a right to protection by the State and the right to freely return to Latvia.[575]

644. Thus, non-citizens are a special category whose legal status in some areas provides them with more rights and guarantees than, for example, permanent residents. However, non-citizens are not yet nationals of Latvia.

645. Over the years the status of non-citizens in Latvia has been strengthened and is no longer treated as temporary. The main agents contributing to this phenomenon have been the national administrative courts and the EU.[576] This concerns access to and loss of the status of non-citizen, the right to reside (private life), and equality of treatment.

646. In relation to the access and loss of the status of non-citizen, the approach of the administrative courts resembles the approach in citizenship cases. For instance, in cases of revocation of non-citizen status it has been stated that 'although there is no time limit for revocation of the status of non-citizen, it would not be fair to consider that the term for revocation is unlimited. In this case general principles of law should be applied'.[577]

647. In another case the court stated that the:

> connection of a non-citizen with the Republic of Latvia is closer than that of a stateless person or a foreign national. Therefore, withdrawal of the status of non-citizen is an important infringement of personal rights and cannot be based on external causes and facts that have not been fully established.[578]

648. In the EU non-citizens enjoy visa-free travel. Non-citizens can apply for the status of long-term resident third-country nationals within the EU framework in accordance with the provisions of Directive 2003/109/EC. They have to pass a Latvian language exam. Moreover, Russia has decided to open to holders of non-citizen passports visa-free travel to Russia.

---

575. *Ibid.*, para. 19.
576. For details on the practice of administrative courts, ECtHR and the EU See Kruma, K., *EU citizenship, Nationality and Migrant Status. An Ongoing challenge* 367–398 (Leiden: Martinus Nijhoff Publishers 2014). See also *Kaftailova v. Latvia* (App No. 59643/00) ECHR 22 Jun. 2006, 7 Dec. 2007 and *Slivenko v. Latvia* (App. No. 48321/99) ECHR 9 Oct. 2003, *Andrejeva v. Latvia* (App. No. 55707/00) Grand Chamber Judgment 18 Feb. 2009.
577. Judgment of the Regional Court of administrative cases in Case No. A42051204 (AA43-1868-07/9), 28 Apr. 2008.
578. Judgment of the Department of Administrative Cases, the Senate of the Supreme Court in Case No. SKA – 89 (C27261801). 24 Aug. 2004.

SELECTED FURTHER READING

Brasington, C.E. *After Alyosha: Baltic Citizenship Requirements Twenty Years After the Fall of Soviet Communism,* TLCP No. 20 2011, 197–238.

Kalvaitis R.M. 'Citizenship and national identity in the Baltic States'. *Boston University International Law Journal* 16 (1998): 231–271.

Kruma, K. *EU citizenship, Nationality and Migrant Status. An Ongoing challenge.* Leiden, Martinus Nijhoff Publishers, 2014.

Kruma, K. Latvian Integration Policy: Lost in Translation. In *A Re-definition of Belonging?,* edited by van Oers, R., E. Ersbøll & D. Kostakopoulou. Martinus Nijhoff Publishers: Leiden Boston, 2010, pp. 241–269.

Kruma, K. *Chapter 2: Checks and balances in Latvian nationality policies: National Agendas and International Frameworks.* In *Citizenship Policies in the New Europe*, edited by Bauböck, R., B. Perchinig & W. Sievers. 2nd ed., IMI-SCOE Research, Amsterdam University Press, 2009, pp. 67–96.

Kruma, K. *Country Report on Latvia, EUDO Citizenship Observatory.* European University Institute, Country Report, RSCAS/EUDO-CIT-CR 2015/6, 2015, available at http://cadmus.eui.eu/bitstream/handle/1814/34481/EUDO_CIT_2015_06-Latvia.pdf?sequence=1.

Kruma, K. *Report on Naturalisation Procedures for Immigrants. Latvia (EUDO Citizenship Observatory Migration Policy Group in collaboration with Robert Schuman Centre for Advanced Studies Naturalisation Procedures Report,* RSCAS/EUDO-CIT-NP 2013/20 2013, available at http://cadmus.eui.eu/bitstream/handle/1814/29788/NPR_2013_20-Latvia.pdf?sequence=1.

Kruma, K. *Country Report: Latvia, The Intec project: Integration and Naturalisation tests: the new way to European Citizenship, European Integration Fund.* Centre of Migration Law, Radboud University Nijmegen: The Netherlands, November, 2010, available via http://www.ru.nl/law/cmr/projects/intec/.

Rozenvalds, J. 'The Soviet Heritage and Integration Policy Development since the Restoration of Independence'. In *How Integrated Is Latvian Society? An Audit of Achievements, Failures and Challenges*, edited by Muižnieks Nils. Riga: University of Latvia Press, 2010, pp. 33–60.

Ziemele, I. 'State Continuity, Human Rights and Nationality in the Baltic States'. In *The Baltic States at Historical Crossroads*, edited by Jundzis Tālavs. Riga, Academy of Sciences of Latvia, 2001, pp. 224–248.

Ziemele, I. *State Continuity and Nationality: The Baltic States and Russia. Past, Present and Future as Defined by International Law.* Leiden, Martinus Nijhoff Publishers, 2005.

Part IV. Fundamental Rights and Liberties

Chapter 1. General

649. The National Council's Political Platform of 1918 considered in a general way the issues of fundamental rights, with its Chapter IV, 'Aliens' Rights' and Chapter V, 'Political Freedoms'.[579]

650. Article 9 of the 1920 Provisional Rules of the Regime of the State of Latvia provided, 'Inviolability of persons and lodging, freedom of press, speech, conscience, strike, meeting and association, inviolability of correspondence exist in Latvia and shall be ensured and established by the respective laws.'

651. On 15 February 1922, the draft of the second part of the *Satversme* 'Fundamental Rules on Citizens' Rights and Obligations' did not pass final reading. Thus, only the concept of fundamental rights was included in the *Satversme*, without any catalogue of rights.[580]

652. Professor Kārlis Dišlers noted in 1930 that the absence of any guarantees of a citizen's rights (inviolability of a person, freedom of speech, freedom of assembly, and so on) did not mean that these freedoms and rights would not be recognized or would otherwise be under threat in Latvia.[581] Civil rights were ensured by laws, and thus, in the interwar period, parliamentary regulation replaced a catalogue of fundamental rights of constitutional rank.

653. Article 4 of the Declaration on the Restoration of the Independence of the Republic of Latvia stated:

> To guarantee to the citizens of the Republic of Latvia and of other states, permanently residing on the territory of Latvia, social, economic and cultural rights, as well as political freedoms, which comply with universally recognised international human rights. This fully applies also to those citizens of the USSR, who will express a wish to live in Latvia, without taking its citizenship.

579. *Latvijas Republikas Satversmes komentāri. VIII nodaļa. Cilvēka pamattiesības.* Autoru kolektīvs prof. R. Baloža zinātniskā vadībā. (Rīga, Latvijas Vēstnesis, 2011), p. 6.
580. *Ibid.*, p. 8.
581. Dišlers, K. *Ievads Latvijas valststiesību zinātnē.* (Rīga, A. Gulbis, 1930), p. 75.

Simultaneously with the adopting of the Declaration of Independence, the Republic of Latvia acceded to a number of international human rights instruments.[582]

654. On 10 December 1991, the *Saeima* adopted the constitutional law, 'Human and Citizen's Rights and Obligations'. The provisions of the Law resembled the main provisions of various international human rights instruments.

655. On 27 June 1997, Latvia ratified the EConvHR. Latvia also has ratified the Protocols Nos 1,[583] 2, 4, 6, 7, 11, 13, 14.

582. This is still debated in among scholars how to classify this document and what are its legal consequences. Since internationally Latvia did not submit letters of ratification, it can be assumed that certain legal importance this act could have had only at the national level.

583. Reservation contained in a Note Verbale from the Minister of Foreign Affairs of Latvia, dated 25 Jun. 1997, handed over to the Secretary General at the time of deposit of the instrument of ratification, on 27 Jun. 1997. In accordance with Art. 64 of the Convention for the Protection of Human Rights and Fundamental Freedoms of 1950, the Republic of Latvia declares that the provisions of Art. 1 of the First Protocol shall not apply to the laws on property reform which regulate the restoration or compensation to the former owners or their legal heirs of property nationalized, confiscated, collectivized or otherwise unlawfully expropriated during the period of Soviet annexation; and privatization of collectivized agricultural enterprises, collective fisheries and of State and local self-government owned property. The reservation concerns the Law On Land Reform in the Republic of Latvia Rural Regions (published in *Zinotajs [The Bulletin]* 1990, No. 49; 1991, No. 41; 1992, No. 6/7; 1992, No. 11/12; 1993, No. 18/19; *Latvijas Vestnesis [The Latvian Herald]* 1994, No. 137), Law On Privatisation of Agricultural Enterprises and Collective Fisheries (*Zinotajs* 1991, No. 31; 1992, No. 40/41; 1993, No. 5/6; *Latvijas Vestnesis* 1995, No. 90; 1996, No. 177), Law On Land Reform in the Republic of Latvia Cities (*Zinotajs* 1991, No. 49/50; *Latvijas Vestnesis* 1994, No. 47; 1994, No. 145; 1995, No. 169; 1997, No. 126/127), Law On Land Privatisation in Rural Regions (*Zinotajs* 1992, No. 32; 1993, No. 18/19; *Latvijas Vestnesis* 1993, No. 130; 1994, No. 148; 1995, No. 162; 1996, No. 111; 1996, No. 225), Law On Privatisation of Property in Agroservice Enterprises (*Zinotajs* 1993, No. 14), Law On Privatisation Certificates (*Latvijas Vestnesis* 1995, No. 52), Law On the Privatisation of Objects of State and Municipal Property (*Latvijas Vestnesis* 1994, No. 27; 1994, No. 77; 1996, No. 192; 1997, No. 16/17/18/19/20/21), Law On Privatisation of Co-operative Apartments (*Zinotajs* 1991, No. 51; *Latvijas Vestnesis* 1995, No. 135), Law On the Privatisation of State and Local Self-Government Apartment Houses (*Latvijas Vestnesis* 1995, No. 103; 1996, No. 149; 1996, No. 223), Law On Denationalisation of Real Estate in the Republic of Latvia (1991, No. 46; *Latvijas Vestnesis* 1994, No. 42; 1994, No. 90; 1995, No. 137; 1996, No. 219/220), Law On the Return of Real Estate to the Legitimate Owners (*Zinotajs* 1991, No. 46; *Latvijas Vestnesis* 1994, No. 42; 1996, No. 97) and their wording being in force at the moment the Law On Ratification entered into force. Annex to the reservation contained in a Note Verbale from the Minister of Foreign Affairs of Latvia, dated 25 Jun. 1997, handed over to the Secretary General at the time of deposit of the instrument of ratification, on 27 Jun. 1997. In addition to the reservation to Art. 1 of the First Protocol, made in accordance with Art. 64 of the Convention, the Republic of Latvia hereby gives a brief summary of the laws concerned. The goal of the Law On Land Reform in the Republic of Latvia Rural Regions is to allocate the land for paying use to natural persons and legal persons and to renew to the Republic of Latvia citizens, who desire so, the land ownership rights in the procedure stipulated by law or to deliver the land into ownership without compensation or for pay. The Law On Privatisation of Agricultural Enterprises and Collective Fisheries regulates privatization of agricultural enterprises and collective fisheries. The objective of the Law is to decrease sequels of unlawful methods of collectivization changing the forms of property in agricultural enterprises and collective fisheries as well as to promote the process of privatization in agriculture and development of private entrepreneurial activity. The aim of the Law On

656. On 15 October 1998, amendments were introduced to the *Satversme*, adding a new chapter, 'Chapter VIII Fundamental Human Rights'. With these amendments the regulation of fundamental rights was introduced into hierarchically the highest legislative act, the constitution.

657. Chapter VIII 'Fundamental Human Rights' of the *Satversme* starts with Article 89, which reads, 'The State shall recognise and protect fundamental human rights in accordance with this *Satversme*, laws and international agreements binding upon Latvia.'

658. The text of Article 89 of the *Satversme* refers to three sources of fundamental rights:

Land Reform in the Republic of Latvia Cities, during the gradual process of State property denationalization, conversion, privatization and the return of unlawfully expropriated land, is to restructure the legal, social and economic relations between city land owners and users in order to promote the respective city's construction, land protection and its rational utilization in accordance with the interests of society. The main objectives of the Law On Land Privatisation in Rural Regions are: (1) to create a basis and guarantees for agricultural development; (2) to renew land ownership rights to the former landowners who owned the land on 21 Jul. 1940 or their heirs; and

(3) to give the land into ownership of the Republic of Latvia citizens for compensation. The Law On Privatisation of Property in Agroservice Enterprises regulates the change of ownership rights on property under the use and disposal of agroservice enterprises. The main objective of the Law is to promote the development of entrepreneurial activity in this branch by property privatization, and to create conditions for organization of the system for protection of the interests of agricultural producers on the basis of cooperation and competition. The Law establishes the rights of the State and local self-governments, agricultural producers and employees of an enterprise, as well as of other natural persons and legal persons, and the procedure by which the ownership rights on the property under use and disposal of agroservice enterprise shall be obtained or specified. The goal of the Law On Privatisation Certificates is to establish a legal basis for most of Latvia's residents to participate in the process of privatization of State and local self-government owned property, using privatization certificates as form of payment. Certificates are issued to Latvia's residents according to the years of residence in Latvia. Additional certificates can be issued to former owners or their heirs, as compensation for illegally nationalized real estate which cannot be returned; politically repressed persons who are recognized as such, according to the Republic of Latvia Law of 13 May 1992 'On the Determination of the Status of a Politically Repressed Person', corresponding to time of imprisonment, deportation or time of settling. The Law On the Privatisation of Objects of State and Municipal Property determines the procedure for privatization of objects of State and local self-government property, as far as it is not regulated by other laws, as well as the establishment and operational principles of the Latvian Privatisation Agency. The Law On Privatisation of Co-operative Apartments establishes the legal basis for the privatization of the cooperative dwelling fund of house-building cooperatives in the territory of the Republic of Latvia. Apartments in large dwelling houses owned by house-building cooperatives shall be considered as the object of privatization. The Law On the Privatisation of State and Local Self-Governments Apartment Houses establishes the procedure for privatizing State and local self-government apartment houses, and the goal is to develop the real estate market and stimulate the upkeep of apartment houses, while protecting the interests of residents. The Law On Denationalisation of Real Estate defines the real estate which can be denationalized, fixes the terms and procedure of denationalization, the form of compensation and social guarantees of present tenants. The Law On the Return of Real Estate to the Legitimate Owners guarantees that the real estate which has been expropriated by the State in the 1940s–1980s without compensation will be returned to the former owners or their legal heirs.

(a) the *Satversme*;
(b) laws; and
(c) international agreements binding upon Latvia.[584]

659. The list of fundamental rights included in Chapter VIII of the *Satversme* is not exhaustive. It also includes rights provided for in international agreements binding upon Latvia. In accordance with the doctrine of monism prevailing in Latvia, the provisions of international agreements concluded and ratified by Latvia are part of the national legal system.[585] Moreover, the provisions of international agreements ratified by the *Saeima* are of higher legal force than the norms of Latvian law, and in case of conflict, provisions of international law have precedence.[586]

660. With regard to the scope of Article 89 of the *Satversme*, the Constitutional Court has noted, 'In cases, when there is doubt about the contents of the human rights included in the *Satversme*, they should be interpreted in compliance with the case law of international norms on human rights.'[587]

661. International obligations of Latvia in the field of human rights influence the interpretation of fundamental rights and the principle of a rule of law. International norms of human rights and their application in practice serve as means of interpretation of constitutional law, to determine the contents and scope of fundamental rights and the principle of the rule of law, insofar as it does not lead to any decrease or limitation of the fundamental rights included in the *Satversme*.[588]

662. Thus, Article 89 is to be understood in such a way that the fundamental rights are guaranteed in principle not only to individuals, but also to legal persons.[589] Whether, indeed, this is so in each particular Article of Chapter VIII depends upon the essence of the respective human right.[590] Chapter VIII of the *Satversme* protects only the rights of private persons (a natural person and a person in private law), but not the rights of public persons and their institutions.

584. *Latvijas Republikas Satversmes komentāri. VIII nodaļa. Cilvēka pamattiesības.* Autoru kolektīvs prof. R. Baloža zinātniskā vadībā. (Rīga, Latvijas Vēstnesis, 2011) p. 26.
585. Mits, M., *European Convention on Human Rights in Latvia. Impact on Legal Doctrine and Application of Legal Norms* (Lund: Media Tryck 2010).
586. *Latvijas Republikas Satversmes komentāri. VIII nodaļa. Cilvēka pamattiesības.* Autoru kolektīvs prof. R. Baloža zinātniskā vadībā. (Rīga, Latvijas Vēstnesis, 2011) p. 27.
587. Constitutional Court, Case No. 2003-04-01, 27 Jun. 2003.
588. Constitutional Court, Case No. 2007-03-01, 18 Oct. 2007, para. 11.
589. *Latvijas Republikas Satversmes komentāri. VIII nodaļa. Cilvēka pamattiesības.* Autoru kolektīvs prof. R. Baloža zinātniskā vadībā. (Rīga: Latvijas Vēstnesis, 2011) p. 31.
590. Constitutional Court, Case No. 2000-07-0409, 3 Apr. 2000.

Chapter 2. Methodology for Assessing a Restriction on Fundamental Rights

663. The Constitutional Court has repeatedly noted that:

> the assumption that no restrictions whatsoever can be placed upon the rights envisaged [in the *Satversme*] to a particular person would collide both with the fundamental rights of other persons guaranteed in other Articles of the *Satversme*, as well as with the State's obligation to defend a person's fundamental rights defined in Article 89 of the *Satversme*, and also with other norms of the *Satversme*.[591]

The State, by way of legislation, sets out the procedure for exercising fundamental rights and restrictions (requirements) on that exercise. Thus the State ensures implementations of fundamental rights and also protects other persons' rights and other constitutional values.[592]

664. According to Article 89 of the *Satversme*, the State protects human rights in accordance with the *Satversme*, laws, and international treaties binding on Latvia. The Court has concluded that this provision aims at achieving harmony between provisions of the *Satversme* and international human rights obligations.[593] Protections offered by the *Satversme* cannot be lower than those derived from international instruments. Otherwise this would lead to a violation of the principle of the rule of law enshrined in Article 1 of the *Satversme*. Therefore, when interpreting the *Satversme*, a harmonious solution should be sought.[594] In addition, it should be borne in mind that the *Satversme* can provide a higher protection of human rights in comparison with international human rights instruments.[595]

665. Article 116 of the *Satversme* provides:

> The rights of persons set out in Articles 96, 97, 98, 100, 102, 103, 106, and 108 of the *Satversme* may be subject to restrictions in circumstances provided for by law in order to protect the rights of other people, the democratic structure of the State, and public safety, welfare and morals. On the basis of the conditions set forth in this Article, restrictions may also be imposed on the expression of religious beliefs.

591. Constitutional Court, Case No. 2002-04-03, 22 Oct. 2002, para. 2.
592. Constitutional Court, Case No. 2005-12-0103, 16 Dec. 2005, para. 9.
593. For instance Constitutional Court, Cases No. 2003-04-01, 27 Jun. 2003, para. 1, Constitutional Court, Cases No. 2004-10-01, 17 Jan. 2005, para. 7.1.
594. Constitutional Court, Case No. 2004-18-0106, 13 May 2004, para. 5.
595. Constitutional Court, Cases No. 2001-06-03, 22 Feb. 2002, para. 3, and Constitutional Court, Cases No. 2005-02-01-6, 14 Sep. 2005, para. 10.

666. The Constitutional Court has emphasized, in particular, that any:

> arbitrary placement of restrictions to exercising of fundamental rights is inadmissible. Fundamental rights may be restricted only in cases provided for in the *Satversme*, when this is required to protect important public interests and if the principle of proportionality is complied with.[596]

The exercise of fundamental rights can be restricted only if such a restriction is admissible; that is, if it complies with certain criteria. Taking into consideration thus the structure of Article 116 of the *Satversme*,[597] the Constitutional Court in its judgments has established a set of criteria or methodology for review whether a restriction on fundamental rights is admissible.

667. The Constitutional Court in all its cases on the admissibility of a restriction on fundamental rights applies a uniform methodology. This methodology consists of a three-stage test in order to establish whether a restriction on fundamental rights is justifiable. The Court verifies first the scope of the respective fundamental right; secondly, whether the actions by the State can be qualified as a restriction on or a violation of fundamental rights, and, thirdly, whether this restriction or violation is justifiable.

668. The justification of a restriction or a violation of fundamental rights is verified in accordance with appropriate methodology, envisaged by Article 116 of the *Satversme*. The methodology used in the practice of the Constitutional Court for testing whether a restriction upon fundamental rights is justifiable is based upon the construct 'law – legitimate aim – proportionality'.[598]

669. Article 116 of the *Satversme* provides that fundamental rights can be restricted only 'in circumstances provided for by law'. Likewise, the restriction on fundamental rights must have a legitimate aim – the safeguarding of other persons' rights, the democratic order of the state, public security, welfare, and morals. The Constitutional Court, in interpreting Article 116 of the *Satversme*, has concluded that there is one more mandatory criterion for assessing a restriction of fundamental rights: the requirement that any restriction should comply with the principle of proportionality.

670. Restrictions on fundamental rights should be established by a law adopted pursuant to due process, in accordance with established procedures. The Constitutional Court has concluded that the concept of a 'law' encompasses not only an act adopted by the *Saeima*, but also any other generally binding (external) regulatory enactment, for example, a government regulation. Hence the concept 'law' includes

---

596. Constitutional Court, Case No. 2005-12-0103, 11 Apr. 2006, para. 9.
597. *Latvijas Republikas Satversmes komentāri. VIII nodaļa. Cilvēka pamattiesības.* Autoru kolektīvs prof. R. Baloža zinātniskā vadībā (Rīga, Latvijas Vēstnesis, 2011), pp. 737–782.
598. *Latvijas Republikas Satversmes komentāri. VIII nodaļa. Cilvēka pamattiesības.* Autoru kolektīvs prof. R. Baloža zinātniskā vadībā (Rīga, Latvijas Vēstnesis, 2011), pp. 737–782.

not only laws adopted by the *Saeima*, but also other generally binding (external) regulatory enactments, if they comply with certain criteria. Restrictions must be established by law or on the basis of law which is published or otherwise accessible, and must be defined with sufficient clarity so that the addressee could understand his or her rights and obligations.

671. The institution which has adopted a law restricting fundamental rights should demonstrate the purpose and the necessity of restricting fundamental rights. It must prove that indeed circumstances exist which require restrictions upon fundamental rights. As the Constitutional Court has noted, 'in establishing restrictions upon fundamental human rights, the obligations to demonstrate and substantiate the legitimate aim of such a restriction in the legal proceedings before the Constitutional Court first and foremost lies upon the institution, which has adopted the contested act'.[599]

672. In those cases, where the institution adopting a legal norm or a regulatory enactment is unable to substantiate the necessity for the respective restrictions, the Court must verify whether, in the particular case, a legitimate aim for the restriction on fundamental rights can be established. Article 116 of the *Satversme* provides an exhaustive list of legitimate aims for which a person's fundamental rights may be restricted. However, in applying the principle, the *Satversme* favours international commitments. Hence, the legitimate aims enumerated in Article 116 of the *Satversme* are expanded by such aims, which are not expressly referred to in it. For example, in its Judgment of 2 February 2010 in Case No. 2009-45-01, the Constitutional Court notes that:

> the *Satversme* has defined restrictions to the freedom of speech in a general way, whereas the EConvHR provides more concrete criteria. Therefore, with regard to admissible more extensive restrictions upon the freedom of speech, the norms of the *Satversme* should be interpreted in the meaning of Article 10 of the Convention. … [I]t follows from the finding by the Constitutional Court referred to above, that the aim of a restriction on the fundamental right to freedom of speech is to be recognised as being legitimate only if it complies with aims referred to not only in Article 116 of the *Satversme*, but also Article 10 of the Convention.[600]

673. The Constitutional Court has emphasized that:

> one of the most important pre-requisites for recognising a restriction on fundamental rights as justifiable is its proportionality to the social need for which it has been set down. This means that it must be assessed whether the public benefit gained by adopting the contested norm exceeds the damage to a person's fundamental rights.[601]

599. Constitutional Court, Case No. 2005-16-01, 8 Mar. 2005, para. 14.
600. Constitutional Court, Case No. 2009-45-01, 10 Feb. 2010, para. 9.
601. Constitutional Court, Case No. 2004-17-01, 26 Jan. 2005, para. 14.3.

The Constitutional Court has also recognized that the principle of proportionality should be recognized as one of the most important fundamental principles of a democratic state based on the rule of law. The principle of proportionality provides that any public power restriction of a person's rights and lawful interests should observe a balance between the interests of a person and those of the State or society.[602] Therefore, it must be verified whether, in establishing restrictions to fundamental rights, the elements of the principle of proportionality have not been violated as follows:

(1) first, its suitability for attaining its intended goal: whether the specific aim can be reached by the measures chosen by the legislator;
(2) second, the necessity of the selected measure: whether the established restrictions could be considered as being the more lenient measures (meaning that no other measure exists that would be equally effective, and yet less restrictive of a person's fundamental rights); and
(3) third, the adequacy of the selected measure: whether the benefit gained by society through establishing the restriction on fundamental rights exceeds any damage caused to the interests of an individual person.

674. The Constitutional Court is also developing in its case law a methodology for testing the admissibility of restrictions upon fundamental social, cultural, and economic rights. The criteria used to assess the compatibility of a legal norm with the fundamental right to social security may differ depending on whether the particular norm restricts the rights granted to a person or establishes the State's positive obligations.

675. The right in Latvia to social security and protection has constitutional value.[603] However, the special nature of social rights also defines the limits of judicial control in this field. In implementing social rights, the legislator enjoys a broad discretion insofar as it is reasonably linked with the economic situation of the State.[604]

676. In assessing whether the State has fulfilled its positive obligations which follow from a person's fundamental social rights, the Constitutional Court assess whether:

(1) the legislator has implemented measures that would ensure for persons the possibility of exercising their social rights;
(2) these measures have been duly implemented: whether persons have at least some minimum scope for exercising their social rights; and
(3) general principles of law have been complied with.[605]

602. Constitutional Court, Case No. 2001-12-01, 19 Mar. 2002, para. 3.1.
603. Constitutional Court, Case No. 2000-08-0109, 13 Mar. 2001.
604. Constitutional Court, Case No. 2006-07-01, 2 Nov. 2006, paras 13–14.
605. Constitutional Court, Case No. 2006-10-03, 11 Dec. 2006, para. 16.1.

677. For those cases where the contested norms have restricted the rights established by Article 109 of the *Satversme*, the Constitutional Court determines whether the restriction:

(1) has been established by law or is based upon law;
(2) can be justified by a legitimate aim;
(3) complies with the principle of proportionality.[606]

678. Cases where the contested norm affects the core of the right to social security, are assessed differently. The Constitutional Court has noted that, irrespectively of the economic situation and even under conditions of rapid economic recession, a certain minimum of basic obligations remain for the State, and the State has no right to depart from that. The right to social security of a minimum level is one among these basic obligations, and the purpose of this right is to ensure, to the extent possible, an existence worthy of human dignity.[607]

679. Therefore the Constitutional Court is determining not only the negative but also the positive obligations of the State. In choosing its methodology the Court is guided by the threefold obligations of the State in respect to each fundamental right: obligations to protect, to respect, and to fulfil. In the latter instance, the Court examines the scope of the State's obligations. Then the Constitutional Court assesses:

> whether the legislator, in exercising its discretion, has acted in accordance with the rule of law, i.e., in conformity with the norms and principles of the *Satversme*, and whether the rules on the functioning of the provisions have been adopted with sufficient justification, i.e., whether the particular regulation is aimed at implementing interests of public importance and protecting values of constitutional significance; … whether the principle of legal certainty and the principle of a socially responsible state have been complied with.[608]

606. Constitutional Court, Case No. 2004-21-01, 6 Apr. 2005, para. 10 and Constitutional Court, Case No. 2009-43-01, 21 Dec. 2009, para. 26.
607. Constitutional Court, Case No. 2009-43-01, 21 Dec. 2009, para. 30.
608. Constitutional Court, Case No. 2011-03-01, 19 Dec. 2011, para. 15.4.

Chapter 3. Civil and Political Rights

680. The *Satversme* prescribes the following civil and political rights:

– a right to know one's rights (Article 90);
– a prohibition on discrimination, the equality before the law and the courts (Article 91);
– a right to a fair trial and the presumption of innocence (Article 92);
– a right to life (Article 93);
– a right to personal freedom (Article 94);
– a prohibition on torture (Article 95);
– a right to private life (Article 96);
– the freedom of religion and faith (Article 99);
– a right to freedom of speech (Article 100);
– a right to hold a position in civil service (Article 101);
– the freedom of assembly and association (Article 102 and Article 103);
– the right to own property (Article 105).

681. By Article 90 of the *Satversme* 90, 'Everyone has the right to know about his or her rights.'

682. In interpreting this norm, the Constitutional Court has recognized that it introduces the catalogue of fundamental rights included in the *Satversme* and points to the significance the legislator has attributed to the enshrining of this fundamental right in the *Satversme*. Only a person who knows his or her rights is able to exercise them and, in a case of their unjustifiable breach, to defend them in a fair hearing. Thus, the *Satversme* envisages a person's subjective public right to be informed about his or her rights and obligations as well. Laws and other regulatory enactments should be publicly accessible. Likewise, a person should have access to case law. In a democratic State case law should be freely accessible to all interested parties. A norm should be worded in such a way that an individual, when necessary, would be able to understand how to regulate his or her actions accordingly.[609] The study of case law allows persons to obtain important information on the application of legal norms, and thus be able both to defend their rights more effectively and to form a better understanding of their obligations.[610]

683. When analysing the contents of Article 90 of the *Satversme*, the Constitutional Court has indicated that the article establishes the subjective rights of a person to be notified on his or her rights and duties.[611]

609. Constitutional Court, Case No. 2006-12-01, 20 Dec. 2006, para. 16 and judgment of the Constitutional Court in Case No. 2010-60-01, 30 Mar. 2011, para. 15.2.
610. Judgment of the Constitutional Court in Case No. 2012-06-01, 1 Nov. 2012, para. 7.2.
611. Judgment of the Constitutional Court in Case No. 2006-12-01, 20 Dec. 2006, para. 16.

684. Article 91 of the *Satversme* provides, 'All human beings in Latvia shall be equal before the law and the courts. Human rights shall be realised without discrimination of any kind.'

685. When interpreting Article 91 of the *Satversme*, the Constitutional Court has recognized that the legislator has incorporated two closely interconnected principles in this article: the principle of equality (in the first sentence), and the principle of prohibition of discrimination (in the second sentence.)[612]

686. The prohibition of discrimination limits the possibilities for justifying deviations from the principle of equality set out in the first sentence of Article 91. If unequal treatment is based upon a criterion covered by the prohibition on discrimination, then the justification is inadmissible.[613]

687. The second sentence of Article 91 contains the following catalogue of prohibited criteria:

(1) race;
(2) ethnicity, ethnic origin and belonging to a minority;
(3) language;
(4) birth and origin;
(5) gender;
(6) age;
(7) disability;
(8) sexual orientation;
(9) religious beliefs;
(10) political and other opinion;
(11) affiliation with a political party;
(12) social status and social origins;
(13) property;
(14) other similar circumstances.[614]

688. When interpreting the first sentence of Article 91 of the *Satversme*, the Constitutional Court has recognized that the principle of equality forbids State institutions from passing norms that, without reasonable grounds, work differently for persons who find themselves in similar and comparable situations. The principle of equality allows – and even demands – a differentiated attitude to persons who are in different circumstances, and allows a differentiated attitude to persons who are in equal circumstances if there are objective and reasonable grounds for this.[615] A

612. Constitutional Court, Case No. 2005-02-0106, 14 Sep. 2005, para. 9.2.
613. *Latvijas Republikas Satversmes komentāri. VIII nodaļa. Cilvēka pamattiesības.* Autoru kolektīvs prof. R. Baloža zinātniskā vadībā. (Rīga, Latvijas Vēstnesis, 2011) p. 88.
614. *Latvijas Republikas Satversmes komentāri. VIII nodaļa. Cilvēka pamattiesības.* Autoru kolektīvs prof. R. Baloža zinātniskā vadībā. (Rīga, Latvijas Vēstnesis, 2011), p. 104.
615. Constitutional Court, Case No. 2008-37-03, 29 Dec. 2008, para. 7.

differentiated attitude is not objective and well-grounded if it does not have a legitimate aim or if the chosen means and the defined aims are not proportionate.[616]

689. When assessing whether the contested norms comply with the first sentence of Article 91 of the *Satversme*, the Constitutional Court should assess whether the contested norms contain a regulatory framework establishing a different attitude towards persons in similar and comparable conditions, namely: (1) whether persons (groups of persons) are in a similar and, according to certain criteria, comparable situation; (2) whether the contested norms establish similar or differentiated treatment of these persons; (3) whether such an attitude has objective and reasonable grounds, namely, whether it has a legitimate aim and whether it observes the principle of proportionality.[617]

690. Article 92 of the *Satversme* reads:

> Everyone has the right to defend his or her rights and lawful interests in a fair court. Everyone shall be presumed innocent until his or her guilt has been established in accordance with law. Everyone, where his or her rights are violated without basis, has a right to commensurate compensation. Everyone has a right to the assistance of counsel.

691. The right to a fair trial has been defined rather succinctly. Only the fundamental principle in criminal law proceedings has been singled out: the presumption of innocence and the right to assistance by counsel.

692. It has been established in the case law of the Constitutional Court that the term 'fair court' established in the first sentence of Article 92 of the *Satversme* means, *inter alia*, due process, appropriate to the principle of the rule of law, under which the case is being adjudicated.[618]

693. In this light, Article 92 of the *Satversme* imposes an obligation on the State to establish a proper judicial system and adopt procedural norms according to which a court's dealing with cases ensures fair and objective adjudication.[619] The right to a fair court also means that a person has access to court. Namely, fairness of the court would be of no importance if access to court was not be ensured.[620]

694. Article 92 of the *Satversme* provides for both the responsibility to create a relevant judicial institutional system and the responsibility to adopt relevant procedural norms.[621]

---

616. Constitutional Court, Case No. 2002-15-01, 23 Dec. 2002, para. 3.
617. Constitutional Court, Case No. 2001-02-0106, 26 Jun. 2001, para. 4.
618. Constitutional Court, Case No. 2001-10-01, 5 Mar. 2002, para. 2 and Constitutional Court, Case No. 2006-12-01, 20 Dec. 2006, para. 9.3.
619. Constitutional Court, Case No. 2009-93-01, 17 May 2010, para. 8.2.
620. Constitutional Court, Case No. 2005-18-01, 14 Mar. 2006, para. 8.
621. Constitutional Court, Case No. 2007-24-01, 9 May 2008, para. 8.

695. However, Article 92 of the *Satversme* does not include a duty on the State to provide for the possibility of appellate and cassation proceedings for all decisions in all cases.[622]

696. The first sentence of Article 92 of the *Satversme* does not stipulate what kinds of cases should be reviewed according to what kinds of proceedings (administrative, civil, or criminal). When adopting the relevant procedural laws, the legislator enjoys a discretion in establishing the kinds of proceedings and the kinds of cases to be reviewed according to a particular procedure.[623] Likewise, the legislator can also determine the categories of cases which are not subject to appeal.[624]

697. This discretion of the legislator is, however, not absolute. The limits are determined by both efficiency considerations and the very substance of the right to a fair court. It is also necessary to take into consideration that the process by which cases are reviewed, should not deny a person the right to a fair trial nor substantially restrict the right of a person to protect his or her rights.[625]

698. It has been recognized in the case law of the Constitutional Court that equality of procedural rights is one of the elements of a fair trial. This principle means that both in civil procedure and criminal procedure the rights of the parties should be fairly balanced. Equality of procedural rights is a substantive element of the right to a fair trial and a manifestation of the principle of legal equality.[626]

699. The Constitutional Court has concluded that the notion 'to protect' in the context of Article 92 of the *Satversme* does not mean the right to endless judicial proceedings. On the contrary, it entails the right to proceedings which can be completed in a reasonable period of time with an effective court decision.[627] The aim to ensure quick and effective review of cases by reducing the workload of courts can be regarded as a legitimate aim for restrictions on the rights established in Article 92 of the *Satversme*.[628] Likewise, the right to a fair court can be restricted with a view to ensure the effective functioning of courts.[629]

700. Even though the *Satversme* does not directly envisage cases in which the right to a fair trial might be restricted, the right is not absolute.[630] The *Satversme* should be interpreted systemically. The presumption that no limitations could be imposed on the rights accorded in Article 92 of the *Satversme* to every person would be incompatible with the fundamental rights of other persons, guaranteed by the

622. Constitutional Court, Case No. 2001-08-01, 17 Jan. 2002, para. 4 and Constitutional Court, Case No. 2007-22-01, 2 Jun. 2008, para. 11.
623. Constitutional Court, Case No. 2005-18-01, 14 Mar. 2006, para. 16.3.
624. Constitutional Court, Case No. 2001-17-0106, 20 Jun. 2002, para. 6.3.
625. Constitutional Court, Case No. 2005-18-01, 14 Mar. 2006, para. 16.2.
626. Constitutional Court, Case No. 2009-85-01, 3 Mar. 2010, para. 12.
627. Constitutional Court, Case No. 2001-10-01, 5 Mar. 2002, para. 5.
628. Constitutional Court, Case No. 2004-10-01, 17 Jan. 2005, para. 8.4.
629. Constitutional Court, Case No. 2004-16-014 Jan. 2005, para. 8.2.
630. *Ibid.*, para. 7.1.

Satversme.[631] Thus, the right to access to courts can be restricted. It remains, however, to be determined of course whether the restriction is justifiable, namely: (1) whether it has been established by law; (2) whether it has a legitimate aim; (3) whether it is proportionate.[632]

701. In the Latvian legal system, the presumption of innocence has been established in two ways, in Article 92 of the *Satversme* as one of the fundamental rights of a person, and in Article 19 of the Criminal Procedure Law as the fundamental principle of criminal procedure.[633]

702. In accordance with the presumption of innocence established in Article 92, innocence is presumed unless evidence to the contrary exists. If a person is held guilty of committing an offence, even though there is no evidence in the case that would prove this person's guilt, the presumption of innocence is violated.[634]

703. The presumption of innocence consists of three elements:[635]

(1) it protects a person from a finding of guilt where guilt has not been proven in accordance with law. This is binding on the officials in charge of criminal procedure: investigators, prosecutors, judges;
(2) a person does not have to prove his or her innocence; the burden of proof lies on the officials in charge of the procedure (the investigator and the prosecution);
(3) all reasonable doubt concerning the offence must be assessed as being in favour of the accused person; proof established under the procedures determined by law shall be the basis of a conviction.[636]

631. Constitutional Court, Case No. 2002-04-03, 22 Oct. 2002, para. 2.
632. Constitutional Court, Case No. 2003-04-01, 27 Jun. 2003, para. 1.2.
633. Constitutional Court, Case No. 2005-22-01, 23 Feb. 2006, para. 4.
634. Constitutional Court, Case No. 2010-01-01, 7 Nov. 2010, para. 16.
635. On 12 Sep. 1996, the Saeima adopted the Law 'On the Insolvency of Undertakings and Companies' (henceforth – the Insolvency Law). In Item 4 of its first part of s. 14 (restrictions regarding administrators) it was determined that the person, who has been sentenced in regard of crimes against property, economic crimes, crimes while holding office in a State institution, crimes against the administration of justice or crimes regarding administrative procedures regardless of termination or extinguishment of a conviction may not be appointed administrators. On 1 Jan. 2003, the submitter of the constitutional claim Ingus Strautmanis acquired the qualification of 'a certified administrator'. On 13 Dec. 2004, the State Agency 'Insolvency Administration' issued a certificate, by which the submitter was conferred the right of performing the duties of the administrator of Corruption Combating and Prevention Bureau till 31 Dec. 2009. At the beginning of 2005, the Corruption Combating and Prevention Bureau initiated a criminal matter, in which – in accordance with the offence envisaged in Art. 183 (the second part) of the Criminal Law – the submitter was in the status of a suspect. Taking into consideration the above circumstance the Insolvency Agency addressed the court with a request to remove the submitter from the duties of the administrator. The Court removed the submitter from the duties of the administrator of several insolvency processes by applying Art. 14, Item 4 of the First Part of the Insolvency Law.
636. Constitutional Court, Case No. 2005-22-01, 23 Feb. 2006, para. 4.

704. The third sentence of Article 92 of the *Satversme* provides, 'Everyone, where his or her rights are violated without basis, has a right to commensurate compensation.' When interpreting the above-mentioned provision, the Constitutional Court has concluded that the protection of fundamental human rights is one of the most important guarantees of a State founded on the rule of law. The norm includes a general guarantee stating that if a State has infringed the rights of an individual, the latter has the right to compensation.[637]

705. As a norm of human rights, the third sentence of Article 92 of the *Satversme* should be applied directly. Besides, the norm does not envisage that a special law is needed to specify it. If a person finds that his or her rights have been groundlessly violated, he or she has the right to submit a claim, making reference just to the third sentence of Article 92 of the *Satversme*, to a court of general jurisdiction demanding commensurate compensation.[638]

706. When interpreting the term 'commensurate compensation' in the third sentence of Article 92 of the *Satversme*, it is important to ensure that the scope of this particular fundamental right would not be restricted without reason, or applied only to the field of substantive rights or compensation of losses. The term 'commensurate compensation' should first of all be interpreted as satisfaction appropriate for any kind of infringement of rights that includes both compensation for losses and indemnification of non-material (moral and individual) harm. Consequently, the third sentence of Article 92 of the *Satversme* includes a general guarantee of a fair trial: if rights or legal interests of a person are infringed, then the person has the right to receive commensurate compensation.[639]

707. The right to a fair trial is one of the most important rights. It includes also the right of a person to legal aid. The norm, incorporated into the *Satversme*, reads

637. Constitutional Court, Case No. 2011-21-01, 6 Jun., 2012, para. 6.
638. Constitutional Court, Case No. 2001-07-0103, 5 Dec. 2001, para. 1.
639. Constitutional Court, Case No. 2011-21-01, 6 Jun. 2012, para. 6. In this case, The Administrative Case Department of the Senate of the Supreme Court adjudicates a matter, in the frameworks of which the association 'Daugavas vanagi Latvijā' have contested a decision of the Riga City Executive Director to organize a procession and asked to compensate moral detriment – LVL 5,000 to each. The Administrative District Court [Administratīvā rajona tiesa] annulled the decision of the Executive Director and rejected the claim regarding compensation of detriment based on the Contested Norm. The Applicant, the Senate of the Supreme Court, holds that the legal regulatory framework included into the Contested Norm restricts the rights of persons in a non-proportional manner. By referring to the case law of the Constitutional Court of the Republic of Latvia stating that the right to compensation is a general guarantee, indicates that in practice it considers this right as an effective remedy. However, the Contested Norm restricts exercise of this right. Consequently, contrary to what has been established in the third sentence of Art. 92 of the *Satversme*, it prohibits the courts assessing circumstances of a particular case to consider whether an ungrounded infringement of rights has taken place entitling a person to a commensurate and fair compensation. Taking into account the aforesaid, the Senate asks the Constitutional Court to assess compliance of the Contested Norm with the third sentence of Art. 92 of the *Satversme* that establishes that everyone, where his or her rights are violated without basis, has a right to commensurate compensation.

as follows, 'Everyone has the right to the assistance of counsel.' The Court has had to define the content of the legal notion 'advocate'.[640]

708. The advocate who provides aid covered by State resources, must be qualified (with sufficient legal knoweldge as duly verified) in order to provide legal aid to a person. The requirements regarding the qualification of an advocate providing legal aid are defined in the Law on State Ensured Legal Aid.

709. The Constitutional Court has recognized that the State has an obligation to adopt such legal norms that regulate fairly the issues regarding compensation for legal aid costs. The State is obliged to establish such regulation of litigation costs as ensures accessibility to the courts.[641]

710. Article 93 of the *Satversme* reads, 'The right to life of everyone shall be protected by law.' The content of this article has been examined in only one ruling of the Constitutional Court.[642] Article 93 of the *Satversme*, similarly to the Universal Declaration of Human Rights and the International Covenant on Civil and Political Rights, does not declare a general principle of a right to life, but contains, like Article 2 of the EConvHR, a legal guarantee for the protection of the right to life. In contrast to Article 2 of the EConvHR, Article 93 of the *Satversme* does not provide an enumeration of those cases where the right to life could be restricted.

711. By Article 94 of the *Satversme,* 'Everyone has the right to liberty and security of person. No one may be deprived of or have their liberty restricted, otherwise than in accordance with law.' Even though, thus far, the Constitutional Court has not had the opportunity to interpret Article 94 of the *Satversme*, in Latvian constitutional law the right to liberty may be derived from the case law of the ECtHR.

712. Article 95 of the *Satversme* reads, 'The State shall protect human honour and dignity. Torture or other cruel or degrading treatment of human beings is prohibited. No one shall be subjected to inhuman or degrading punishment.' The Constitutional Court has interpreted Article 95 of the *Satversme* in conjunction with international acts for the protection of human rights.[643]

713. The Constitutional Court has recognized in its case law that the abovementioned article enshrines one of the most fundamental values of democratic societies and prohibits in absolute terms torture and inhuman or degrading treatment or punishment. Derogation from this is not allowed even in exceptional cases. Where treatment humiliates or debases an individual, showing a lack of respect for, or

640. Constitutional Court, Case No. 2003-08-01, 6 Oct. 2003, para. 1.
641. Constitutional Court, Case No. 2013-04-01, 7 Feb. 2014, para. 19.2 and 19.3. In this case, the Applicant – a limited liability company 'Gardie Visdari' – notes that a lawyer had represented its interests in civil law proceedings. The Applicant had won the case and wanted to collect the costs related to the lawyer's assistance.
642. Constitutional Court, Case No. 2009-12-03, 7 Jan. 2010.
643. Constitutional Court, Case No. 2002-04-03, 22 Oct. 2002, para. 5.

diminishing, his or her human dignity, or arouses feelings of fear, anguish, or inferiority capable of breaking an individual's moral and physical resistance, it may be characterized as degrading and also falls within the prohibition of Article 95.[644]

714. Article 96 of the *Satversme* provides, 'Everyone has the right to inviolability of his or her private life, home and correspondence.'

715. Article 96 of the *Satversme* directly points to three protected aspects of a person's life: private life, home, and correspondence. The concept of private life is central to Article 96. It comprises various elements of personal life. It protects an individual's physical and mental integrity, respect and dignity, name and identity, and personal data.[645]

716. When explaining the right to private life guaranteed in Article 96 of the *Satversme*, the Constitutional Court has indicated that this right applies to different aspects. It protects the physical and moral integrity, honour and reputation, use of a person's name and identity, and personal data of a person. The right to private life means that the individual has the right to his or her private home, the right to live as he or she desires in accordance with his or her nature and wishes regarding personal development, tolerating a minimum of interference from the State or other persons. The right includes the right of an individual to be different, and retain and develop virtues and abilities which distinguish him or her from other persons and individualizes him or her.[646]

717. Article 99 of the *Satversme* provides, 'Everyone has the right to freedom of thought, conscience and religion. The church shall be separate from the State.'

718. The Constitutional Court has underscored that:

> this freedom comprises different religious, non-religious and atheistic beliefs, as well as the right to accept or refuse religion. In the light of the particular Article of the religious beliefs can be interpreted in a broad manner. Moreover,

---

644. Constitutional Court, Case No. 2010-44-01, 20 Dec. 2010, para. 8.1. In this case, Art. 7(1) of the Law 'On Procedures for Keeping of Detained Persons' (hereinafter – the Law on Keeping Detained Persons) provides that a detention cell must be supplied with toilet facilities connected with a water-main, the facilities being separated from the rest of the premise by means of a wall, the height of which does not exceed 1.2 meters; whilst para. 1 of Transitional Provisions provide that requirements established in Art. 2(2) and Art. 7(3) and (5) shall be fulfilled before 31 Dec. 2013 (hereinafter also referred to as the Contested Norms). The Ombudsman (applicant) indicates that what has been established in Art. 7(5) Indent 1 of the Law on Keeping of Detained Persons is only one of the circumstances that testify non-compliance of places of temporary detention with standards of the human rights. The most important infringement of the human rights established in Art. 95 of the *Satversme* follows from the fact that the legislator has adopted para. 1 of Transitional Provisions of the above-mentioned law and thus it has extended the term, within which it is permitted that places of temporary detention do not comply with standards of the human rights.
645. *Latvijas Republikas Satversmes komentāri. VIII nodaļa. Cilvēka pamattiesības.* Autoru kolektīvs prof. R. Baloža zinātniskā vadībā. (Rīga, Latvijas Vēstnesis, 2011) pp. 237–238.
646. Constitutional Court, Case No. 2004–17–01, 26 Jan. 2005, para. 10.

not only the presence of religious beliefs but also expression of religious beliefs is protected.[647]

719. The Constitutional Court has noted that internal aspects of religious beliefs ('*forum internum*') and the right to devote oneself to religion or the freedom of expressing religious beliefs, being the right to the external expression of the freedom of religion ('*forum externum*'), are to be distinguished.[648]

720. The *Satversme* does not provide any explanation of the term 'expression of religious beliefs'. When interpreting the content of Article 99 of the *Satversme*, the Constitutional Court has to take into account international human rights instruments.

721. Article 100 of the *Satversme* reads, 'Everyone has the right to freedom of expression, which includes the right to freely receive, keep and distribute information and to express his or her views. Censorship is prohibited.'

722. It has been stated in the case law of the Constitutional Court that freedom of speech covers a broad field, and includes two aspects: a private and a public one. The public aspect to the freedom of speech applies to the right of every person to receive information and to express his or her opinion in any way: orally, in writing, visually, through artistic means of expression, and so on. These ways of information distribution and expression of opinions also include mass media – radio and press. Freedom of expression in its public aspect includes also the freedom of the press.[649]

723. Article 101 of the *Satversme* provides:

> Every citizen of Latvia has the right, as provided for by law, to participate in the work of the State and of local government, and to hold a position in the civil service. Local governments shall be elected by Latvian citizens and citizens of the EU who permanently reside in Latvia. Every citizen of the EU who permanently resides in Latvia has the right, as provided by law, to participate in the work of local governments. The working language of local governments is the Latvian language.

724. Article 101 of the *Satversme* envisages the right serving as a guarantee for the existence of democracy and aims to ensure the legitimacy of the democracy. However, the right is not absolute, since Article 101 of the *Satversme* includes the condition 'in the manner prescribed by law'.[650]

---

647. Constitutional Court, Case No. 2010-50-03, 18 Mar., 2011, para. 7.1.
648. Constitutional Court, Case No. 2010-50-03, 18 Mar., 2011, para. 7.2.
649. Constitutional Court, Case No. 2003-02-0106, 5 Jun. 2003, para. 1 and Constitutional Court, Case No. 2003-05-01, 29 Oct. 2003, para. 21.
650. Constitutional Court, Case No. 2000-03-01, 30 Aug. 2000, para. 1.

725. The first part of Article 101 of the *Satversme* is applicable to the right to request a national referendum if this is not expressly provided for in the *Satversme* or a law, and this request applies to the cases for holding a referendum, as guaranteed by the *Satversme*. A person may request the application of the constitutionally guaranteed procedure of a national referendum or request examination, whether the adoption of a particular law complies with the right to participation. A national referendum, however, may not be held if the constitution or a normative act in conjunction with the constitution does not provide for it. It shall be applicable, for instance, to the cases when deciding on a particular issue falls within the exclusive competence of the *Saeima*. Consequently, persons may not request the creation of participatory procedures which are not provided for in normative acts but are merely desirable.[651]

726. The first part of Article 101 of the *Satversme* covers a very broad field, and therefore this could be considered to be a composite right – the totality of a number of rights. In contrast to many other articles in Chapter VIII, the first part of this article identifies only a citizen of Latvia as the subject.[652]

727. The first sentence in the second part of Article 101 sets out which persons have the right to elect local government, according to the procedures set out by law. This enumeration is exhaustive. The wording of the sentence indirectly comprises also the principle of electability of local governments, by noting indirectly that local governments are elected. This sentence ensures the compatibility of the Latvian constitutional system with EU law.[653]

728. Article 102 of the *Satversme* reads, 'Everyone has the right to form and join associations, political parties and other public organisations.'

729. The Constitutional Court has recognized the freedom of association as one of the most essential political rights of a person.[654] This freedom is one of the preconditions for a democratic State order. The freedom of association ensures persons have the possibility of protecting their lawful interests through uniting in order to reach shared aims. By exercising the fundamental right defined in Article 102 of the *Satversme*, a person gains the possibility of participating in democratic processes.[655]

730. Article 102 of the *Satversme* protects the rights of everybody to unite in the most diverse of voluntary and social groups to reach freely chosen and legal aims. Hence the aim of this article is to ensure a manifestation of everyone's personality and privacy in the form of group membership. The freedom of association basically

651. Constitutional Court, Case No. 2008-35-01, 7 Apr. 2009, para. 13.3.
652. *Latvijas Republikas Satversmes komentāri. VIII nodaļa. Cilvēka pamattiesības.* Autoru kolektīvs prof. R. Baloža zinātniskā vadībā. (Rīga, Latvijas Vēstnesis, 2011) p. 383.
653. *Ibid.*, p. 392.
654. Constitutional Court, Case No. 2006-03-0106, 23 Nov. 2006, para. 7.
655. Constitutional Court, Case No. 2012-16-01, 10 May 2013, para. 17.

protects the field of an individual's personal freedom from interference by the State ('*status negativus*').[656]

731. By Article 103 of the *Satversme*, 'The State shall protect the freedom of announced peaceful meetings, street processions, and pickets.'

732. The Constitutional Court has noted that:

> freedom of assembly side by side with freedom of association and freedom of speech belong to the most important political rights of a person. Article 103 of the *Satversme* ensures the subjective rights of a person to participate in peaceful processions, meetings and pickets and freely express thoughts. Freedom of assembly is a vital element of a democratic society, which ensures the possibility to influence political processes, *inter alia*, also by criticizing the State power and protesting against the actions of the State.[657]

733. Article 105 of the *Satversme* provides:

> Everyone has the right to own property. Property shall not be used contrary to the interests of the public. Property rights may be restricted only in accordance with law. Expropriation of property for public purposes shall be allowed only in exceptional cases on the basis of a specific law and in return for fair compensation.

734. The Constitutional Court has recognized that the content of Article 105 of the *Satversme* is similar to the content of Article 1 of Protocol 1 to the EConvHR and determines both the right to enjoyment of property and the right of the State to restrict property rights. The fourth sentence of Article 105 of the *Satversme*, like Article 1 of Protocol No. 1 of the EConvHR, provides for the rights of the State to restrict the right to property de iure in certain cases.[658]

735. When interpreting Article 105 of the *Satversme* in connection with the above-mentioned norm of EConvHR Protocol 1, Article 1, the Constitutional Court has established that Article 105 of the *Satversme* provides for the peaceful enjoyment of the right to own property and the right of the State to restrict the use of property in accordance with the general interest.[659]

736. Analysing the notion 'property' included in Article 105 of the *Satversme*, the Constitutional Court has concluded that property rights include the right to gain

656. *Latvijas Republikas Satversmes komentāri. VIII nodaļa. Cilvēka pamattiesības*. Autoru kolektīvs prof. R. Baloža zinātniskā vadībā. (Rīga, Latvijas Vēstnesis, 2011) p. 404.
657. Constitutional Court, Case No. 2006-03-0106, 23 Nov. 2006, para. 7.
658. Constitutional Court, Case No. 2002-01-03, 20 May 2002, and Constitutional Court, Case No. 2005-10-03, 14 Dec. 2005, para. 8.
659. Constitutional Court, Case No. 2002-01-03, 20 May 2002.

all possible benefits from property, including income and interest,[660] as well as the right of the property owner to use his possessions in a manner that would ensure gaining greatest economic benefit possible.[661]

660. Constitutional Court, Case No. 2008-05-03, 12 Nov. 2008, para. 7 and judgment in Case No. 2008-36-01, 15 Apr. 2009, para. 10.
661. Constitutional Court, Case No. 2006-38-03, 26 Apr. 2007, para. 11.

Chapter 4. Economic, Social, and Cultural Rights

737. The *Satversme* envisages exercising the following economic, social, and cultural rights:

- the right to choose employment according with one's abilities and qualification (Article 106);
- prohibition against forced labour (Article 106);
- the right to receive commensurate remuneration for the work done, which is not below the minimum established by the State (Article 107);
- the right to weekly holidays and annual paid vacation (Article 107);
- the right to a collective agreement (Article 108);
- the right to social security (Article 109);
- the protection of the rights of parents and children (Article 110);
- the right to minimum health care (Article 111);
- a right to education (Article 112);
- a right to participate in cultural life, to use the results of scientific progress and its practical applications, to have protected moral and material rights derived from any scientific, literary, or art works authored by a person (Article 113);
- a right to live in a benevolent environment (Article 115).

738. Article 106 of the *Satversme* provides, 'Everyone has the right to freely choose their employment and workplace according to their abilities and qualifications. Forced labour is prohibited. Participation in the relief of disasters and their effects, and work pursuant to a court order shall not be deemed forced labour.'

739. The first sentence of Article 106 of the *Satversme* grants to a person the right to freely choose employment, taking into account the totality of abilities, knowledge, and skills that characterize the preparedness and suitability of a person for performing a particular job, and thus includes accounting for education, practical experience, and other knowledge, skills, and abilities which a particular person may have acquired and developed.[662]

740. The notion 'employment' is attributed to work in the private and the public sectors, and also to occupations in which legal relations are not based on a contract, regulated by the Labour Law.[663]

741. The case law of the Constitutional Court regarding assessment of the fundamental rights established in Article 106 of the *Satversme* applies mainly to vocational qualification requirements in the framework of the public service.[664] The Constitutional Court has concluded that officials implement the State power and therefore the State has the right to set forth certain qualification and education

662. Constitutional Court, Case No. 2007-08-01, 1 Nov. 2007, para. 7.
663. Constitutional Court, Case No. 2003-12-0106, 18 Dec. 2003, para. 7.
664. Constitutional Court, Case No. 2004-13-0106, 22 Mar. 2005, Constitutional Court, Case in Case No. 2006-29-0103, 10 May 2007 and Constitutional Court, Case No. 2007-08-0, 1 Nov. 2007.

requirements for these persons. The above-mentioned qualification and education requirements can also be applied to professions, the labour relations of which are established not only on the basis of a contract regulated by the Labour Law but also on the grounds of other civil law agreements.

742. The Constitutional Court has noted that:

> irrespective of the sector, public of private, where a person is employed, the State has the right to establish requirements, according to which a person, when selecting a particular employment, must prove his or her skills and qualification by having obtained vocational education. In order to meet the needs of inhabitants, it is necessary to implement most balanced and consistent policy possible. On the one hand, the legislator should adopt such legal regulation that persons who have freely chosen their occupation could earn their living. However, on the other hand, the legal regulation should be such to ensure that interests important for the society are protected. The legislator enjoys discretion to determine education necessary for each particular profession, as well as to set forth other requirements.[665]

743. Article 107 of the *Satversme* provides, 'Every employed person has the right to receive, for work done, commensurate remuneration which shall not be less than the minimum wage established by the State, and has the right to weekly holidays and a paid annual vacation.'

744. Article 107 of the *Satversme* does not expressly prescribe the minimum wage, but merely indicates that a minimum wage should be established. The authorization of the legislator to establish a minimum wage is thus included in the *Satversme*. Article 107, stating that the decision should be taken by legislator, prohibits employers from paying lesser wages than those established by the legislator.[666]

745. The right to weekly holidays, enshrined in Article 107 of the *Satversme*, should be ensured mandatorily: it cannot be substituted by remuneration instead of rest.[667]

746. The right to annual paid vacation included in Article 107 of the *Satversme* ensures the possibility of rest during the year. This norm contains two mandatory prerequisites: an annual vacation and a paid vacation.[668]

665. Constitutional Court, Case No. 2009-74-01, 18 Feb. 2010, para. 14.
666. Constitutional Court, Case No. 2005-03-0306, 21 Nov. 2005, para. 6.
667. *Latvijas Republikas Satversmes komentāri. VIII nodaļa. Cilvēka pamattiesības*. Autoru kolektīvs prof. R. Baloža zinātniskā vadībā. (Rīga, Latvijas Vēstnesis, 2011) p. 521.
668. *Ibid.*, p. 523.

747. Article 108 of the *Satversme* provides, 'Employed persons have the right to a collective labour agreement, and the right to strike. The State shall protect the freedom of trade unions.'

748. The Constitutional Court has noted that 'the second sentence in Article 108 of the *Satversme*, envisaging the freedom of trade unions, is to be recognised as being lex specialis in relation to Article 102 of the *Satversme*.'[669]

749. The concept of 'trade union', referred to in the second sentence of Article 108, means one of the ways in which the freedom of association manifests itself in the field of labour law.[670]

750. The Constitutional Court has emphasized that:

> in the context of the second sentence of Article 108 of the *Satversme* the State is obliged to refrain from interfering into the activities of trade unions. The legislator has the obligation to adopt such regulatory enactments that would allow persons to join in trade unions and thus exercise their right to association. These regulatory enactments should ensure that trade unions, as well their members have necessary protection against the employer's possible interfering into the exercise of the freedom of trade unions.

751. Article 109 of the *Satversme* provides, 'Everyone has the right to social security in old age, for work disability, for unemployment and in other cases as provided by law.'

752. The Constitutional Court has indicated that social rights are very important, but at the same time these are special, different human rights, since the implementation of these rights depend upon the economic situation and accessible resources in each State. Article 109 of the *Satversme* guarantees the right to a stable and predictable, as well as effective, fair and sustainable, system of social protection which ensures proportional social security. However, this norm also envisages and allows certain differences in the provision of social security.[671]

753. The State has established a social security system, comprising social insurance services, social assistance, and other measures. The State has a discretion in choosing the methods and mechanisms for implementing social security. Usually the decisions in this field depend not so much on legal, but rather on political, considerations which, in their turn, depend on the legislator's view of the principles for providing social services, the economic situation in the State, and the needs of all or some of the society for State assistance or support.[672]

---

669. Constitutional Court, Case No. 2013-15-01, 23 Apr. 2014, para. 8.
670. *Ibid.*, para. 9.
671. Constitutional Court, Case No. 2000-08-0109, 13 Mar. 2001 and Constitutional Court, Case No. 2009-88-01, 15 Apr. 2010.
672. Constitutional Court, Case No. 2009-08-01, 26 Nov. 2009, para. 15 and para. 21.

754. However, the discretion of the State is not absolute. With regard to those social insurance services, the receipt of which depends upon the contributions made by a person to the social insurance budget, the discretion of the State is narrower.[673] For those social assistance services where receipt of benefits does not depend upon contributions made, the State has broader discretion.[674]

755. Cases where a contested norm applies to the core of social security should be assessed in a different way. The Constitutional Court pointed out that even if the State reduced pension amounts for a period of time in the situation of rapid economic recession; there is still a definite body of fundamental rights that the State is not entitled to derogate from. One of the duties of the State is the duty to guarantee a minimum level of social security, and the aim of these rights is to ensure a life of worth and dignity.[675]

756. In cases where a contested norm restricts the rights established in Article 109 of the *Satversme*, the Constitutional Court investigates whether the restriction: (1) has been established by law or is based on a law; (2) has a legitimate aim; and (3) complies with the principle of proportionality.[676]

757. Article 110 of the *Satversme* says that the State 'shall protect and support marriage – a union between a man and a woman – the family, the rights of parents and rights of the child. The State shall provide special support to disabled children, children left without parental care or who have suffered from violence'.

758. It has been established in the case law of the Constitutional Court that the positive duty of the State to form and maintain social and economic protection system for families follows from the first sentence of Article 110 of the *Satversme*.[677]

759. Because the legislator, when implementing the positive duty of creating and maintaining the system of a family social and economic situation, has specified the right of a family to specific protection by determining several mechanisms (benefits, grants, and so on), these rights have become the rights of an individual. A person may require exercise of these rights from the State, as well as may defend the above rights in court.[678]

---

673. Constitutional Court, Case No. 2003-22-01, 26 Mar. 2004, para. 11.
674. Constitutional Court, Case No. 2011-20-01, 21 Jun. 2012 para. 12.
675. Constitutional Court, Case No. 2009-43-01, 21 Dec. 2009, para. 31 and 31.2.
676. Constitutional Court, Case No. 2004-21-01, 6 Apr. 2005, para. 10 and Constitutional Court, Case No. 2009-43-01, 21 Dec. 2009, para. 26.
677. Constitutional Court, Case No. 2005-09-01, 4 Nov. 2005, para. 9.3, Constitutional Court, Case No. 2006-07-01, 2 Nov. 2006, para. 13.1 and Constitutional Court, Case No. 2006-10-03, 11 Dec. 2006 para. 13.1.
678. Constitutional Court, Case No. 2005-09-01, 4 Nov. 2005, para. 9.3.

760. The Constitutional Court has noted that:

> one of the kinds of special family protection is provision of additional support due to childbirth. The State provides a special support for families with children aged up to two years. The necessity of such benefit is related to the fact that new-borns need special care. Usually these are parents of the child who undertake such care. Therefore they are no more able to earn living at the same level as before childbirth.[679]

761. Article 111 of the *Satversme* provides, 'The State shall protect human health and guarantee a basic level of medical assistance for everyone.'

762. The Constitutional Court has recognized that the State's obligation to respect, protect, and ensure a person's right to health follows from Article 111 of the *Satversme*. The obligation to respect the right to health means that the State should refrain from interfering with a person's rights and freedoms. It must abstain from such activities that restrict a person's abilities to care for his or her own health protection. The obligation to protect the right to health means that the State must protect a person from other persons interfering with his or her exercise of fundamental rights. On the other hand, the obligation to ensure the right to health means that the State must implement measures for the exercise of this fundamental right.[680]

763. An obligation of the State to ensure for everybody the highest possible level of health does not follow from this norm of the *Satversme*. However, the right to health comprises not only freedoms, but also rights. Freedoms, for example, mean that every person is free to control his or her own health. The Constitutional Court has also pointed to a person's right to implement measures that he or she deems to be necessary to ensure their health. By contrast, rights must be linked to the State's obligation to create an appropriate system of health protection. Thus, the State's obligation to ensure the existence and accessibility of healthcare institutions, services, equipment and medicines, as well as other circumstances that influence the possibility for persons to attain the highest level of health, corresponds to the right to health.[681]

764. The Constitutional Court has recognized that the obligation of the State to ensure accessibility to medicine follows from Article 111 of the *Satversme*. The State cannot refuse to fulfil the economic, social, and cultural rights included in the *Satversme*. However, the scope of implementation of these rights may depend upon

679. Constitutional Court, Case No. 2009-44-01, 15 Mar. 2010, para. 8.

680. Constitutional Court, Case No. 2002-04-03, 22 Oct. 2002, para. 1, Constitutional Court, Case No. 2003-15-0106, 23 Apr. 2004, para. 6 and Judgment of the Constitutional Court in Case No. 2008-37-03, 29 Dec. 2008, para. 12.1.2.

681. Constitutional Court, Case No. 2002-04-03, 22 Oct. 2002, para. 1, Constitutional Court, Case No. 2003-15-0106, 23 Apr. 2004, para. 6 and Constitutional Court, Case No. 2008-37-03, 29 Sep. 2008, para. 11.

the resources at the disposal of the State. Therefore, it is the task of the State to allocate resources and decide for whom, under what circumstances, and what kind of treatment shall be paid for. There are no universal criteria for setting priorities in this field. Thus, the State has a broad discretion in deciding these issues.[682]

765. Article 112 of the *Satversme* provides, 'Everyone has the right to education. The State shall ensure that everyone may acquire primary and secondary education without charge. Primary education shall be compulsory.'

766. The Constitutional Court has noted that:

> a systemic interpretation of the first and the second sentence in Article 112 of the *Satversme* allows concluding that the State has the obligation to ensure primary and secondary education free of charge. However, the *Satversme* does not envisage an equal obligation of the State with regard to higher education free of charge. The State must fulfil the obligation to ensure the rights of persons to acquire also higher education free of charge within the limits of its financial possibilities.[683]

767. Article 113 of the *Satversme* provides that 'the State shall recognise the freedom of scientific research, artistic and other creative activity, and shall protect copyright and patent rights.'

768. The Constitutional Court has found that 'the above-mentioned article includes two mutually related aspects: freedom of artistic creativity, and protection of works created as a result of creative activity.'[684]

769. Article 113 of the *Satversme* does not disclose the content of the term 'copyright' or that of the duty to protect copyright. The Constitutional Court has noted that the duty to protect copyright included in Article 113 of the *Satversme* concerns the protection of individual and material rights of subjects of copyright.[685]

770. The Constitutional Court has also underscored that the duty to protect the material rights of subjects of copyright included in Article 113 of the *Satversme* include the right of authors to material gain from the use of their works. However, this right is not absolute.[686]

771. Article 115 of the *Satversme* reads, 'The State shall protect the right of everyone to live in a benevolent environment by providing information about environmental conditions and by promoting the preservation and improvement of the environment.'

---

682. Constitutional Court, Case No. 2000-08-0109, 13 Mar. 2001, Constitutional Court, Case No. 2006-10-01, 11 Dec. 2006, para. 14.2 and para. 14.3.
683. Constitutional Court, Case No. 2010-57-03, 6 May 2011.
684. Constitutional Court, Case No. 2011-17-03, 2 May 2012, para. 12.
685. *Ibid.*, para. 12.2.
686. *Ibid.*, para. 12.3.

772. The Constitutional Court has noted that the right to live in a benevolent environment comprises, *inter alia*, the right of an individual (a person) as a member of society to have any decision by a public person linked to use of environment taken and implemented within the framework of an effective system for environmental protection (management). With regard to planning, it means that the development solution chosen by the local government should be sustainable.[687]

773. The right to live in a benevolent environment and the respective obligations of the State to care for the conservation of the environment, as established in Article 115 of the *Satversme*, is specified in laws and other acts, and these rights and obligations should be interpreted according to the international legal norms binding on the Republic of Latvia. For instance, the Aarhus Convention of 25 June 1998 on Access to Information, Public Participation in Decision-making and Access to Justice in Environmental Matters, ratified by the *Saeima* on 18 April 2002, grants the rights to the public to access environmental information, to participate in the environmental decision-making process and access to justice on environmental matters. The Law on Environmental Protection specifies the rights established in Article 115 of the *Satversme*, and even broadens the environmental rights of the society provided in the Aarhus Convention.[688]

774. Sustainable development is the integrated and balanced development of social welfare, environment, and economy, which satisfies the inhabitant's present social and economic needs and ensures complying with the requirements of environmental protection, without placing under threat the possibilities for satisfying the needs of future generations, and ensures safeguarding the physical person.

Selected Further Reading

Minority Rights Handbook. Latvian Human Rights Quarterly, No. 5-6, Human Rights Institute of the University of Latvia, Faculty of Law, 1998.

Constitution and Human Rights Yearbook. Latvian Human Rights Quarterly, No. 7-10, Human Rights Institute of the University of Latvia, Faculty of Law, 1999.

Mits, M. *European Convention on Human Rights in Latvia. Impact on Legal Doctrine and Application of Legal Norms*. Medya Tryck: Lund University, 2010.

687. Constitutional Court, Case No. 2008-38-03, 9 Jul. 2009, para. 9.2.
688. Constitutional Court, Case No. 2007-11-03, 17 Jan. 2008, para. 12.

Chapter 5. Ombudsmen

§1. Introduction

775. The Ombudsman's Office of the Republic of Latvia commenced its activities on 1 January 2007, when the Ombudsman Law came into force. Its history, however, spans over more than a decade.

776. Already in 1995, when the need to have an institution for human rights protection was discussed, an idea of creating an independent institution using the model of the Scandinavian Ombudsman was expressed during *Saeima* debates. In 1995 the State Office of Human Rights was established according to suggestions made by the UN High Commissioner for Human Rights. The Office failed to succeed in its operations and, therefore, the idea of another type of institution was introduced.

777. Although there were a number of suggestions tabled over the years, intensive work to create the institution of the Ombudsman started in August 2000. At that time, at the initiative of President Vaira Vīķe-Freiberga, a working group was formed to develop the concept of the institution of a Latvian Ombudsman. In 2003, another working group was established under the auspices of the Chancellery of the State President which was tasked to draft the law on the Ombudsman's Institution (the public rights advocate).[689]

778. The Ombudsman is an official approved in accordance with the procedures specified by law, who performs the functions and tasks specified by the law.[690] The Constitutional Court has noted that the Ombudsman has been granted jurisdiction allowing him or her to deal with the problems of exercising human rights where the courts, the legislator, or the executive power cannot deal with them with satisfactory efficiency.[691]

779. Romāns Apsītis, a former Justice of the Constitutional Court, was appointed as the first Ombudsman of the Republic of Latvia on 1 March 2007 with the absolute majority of the *Saeima* (seventy votes).

§2. Establishment

780. The Ombudsman is approved in office by the *Saeima* pursuant to the proposal of not less than five members of the *Saeima*.

689. President of Latvia stresses the importance of the Ombud institution for Latvia in the conference 'The Ombud Institution in a Democratic and Law-based State'. Available: http://www.president.lv/pk/content/?art_id=10364. See also Tiesībsarga 2007. ziņojums. Available: http://www.tiesibsargs.lv/files/content/Tiesibsarga%20gada%20zinojums_2007.pdf, accessed 10 Jul. 2015.

690. Ombudsman Law of 6 Apr. 2006, Art. 3.

691. Constitutional Court, Case No. 2013-15-01, 23 Apr. 2014, para. 7.

781. A citizen of Latvia having an unimpeachable reputation, who has attained 30 years of age, has a higher education, has knowledge and work experience in the field of law enforcement, and who in accordance with the requirements of the law is entitled to receive a special permit for access to State secrets may be approved as the Ombudsman. A citizen with dual citizenship may not be approved as the Ombudsman.[692]

782. Upon assuming office the Ombudsman gives the following oath (solemn vow) at the *Saeima* sitting:

> Taking upon the duties of the Ombudsman, I, ___________, am fully aware of the responsibility laid upon me, and swear (solemnly vow) to be honest and fair in the protection of the rights and freedoms of persons in accordance with the Satversme of the Republic of Latvia, laws and international agreements.[693]

783. The term of office of the Ombudsman is five years from the day when he or she takes the oath (solemn vow). The Ombudsman may be re-approved in office.[694]

784. The institution of Ombudsman is not mentioned in the *Satversme*. However, his functions in the legal system of Latvia as well as his status in the institutional architecture is important to ensure that human rights and good governance are observed.

§3. Legal Status

785. The Constitutional Court has noted that the Ombudsman's Office is an independent State institution, which ensures that the Ombudsman's functions are fulfilled. The Ombudsman's Office does not belong to the system of institutions of public administration subordinated to the Cabinet of Ministers that are defined in Article 58 of the *Satversme*. In contrast to the President of the State, the courts, and the State Audit Office, the Ombudsman's status has not been enshrined in the *Satversme*.[695]

786. The Ombudsman is independent in his or her activities and is governed exclusively by the law. No one has the right to influence the Ombudsman in the performance of his or her functions and tasks.[696]

---

692. Ombudsman Law of 6 Apr. 2006, Art. 5(2).
693. *Ibid.*, 2006, Art. 6.
694. *Ibid.*, Art. 7.
695. Constitutional Court, Case No. 2010-06-01, 25 Nov. 2010, para. 14.4.
696. Ombudsman Law of 6 Apr. 2006, Art. 4.

787. The office of the Ombudsman may not be combined with a membership in a political party.[697]

788. The Ombudsman appoints a Deputy Ombudsman. During absence of Ombudsman, his or her functions and tasks are performed by the Deputy Ombudsman, who during this period of time has the same powers as the Ombudsman.[698]

789. Administrative sanctions against the Ombudsman are permitted only with the consent of the *Saeima*.[699]

790. The Ombudsman's immunity from criminal proceedings is determined by the Criminal Procedure Law. Only the Prosecutor General may initiate criminal proceedings against the Ombudsman. The Ombudsman may be held criminally liable or arrested only with the consent of the *Saeima*. A decision on placing the Ombudsman under arrest, conveyance by force, detention, or subjection to a search is taken by a specially authorized Supreme Court judge. If the Ombudsman has been apprehended when committing of a serious or especially serious crime, a decision on conveyance by force, detention, or subjection to a search is not necessary, but the specially authorized Supreme Court judge and the Prosecutor General must be informed within twenty-four hours.[700]

791. If the *Saeima* has given its consent for the commencement of a criminal prosecution against the Ombudsman, his or her powers are suspended until such time as any conviction comes into effect or the criminal prosecution is terminated.[701]

792. The Ombudsman's powers terminate:

(1) upon the release from the office;
(2) upon the termination of the powers of the Ombudsman;
(3) if the Ombudsman's conviction of a criminal offence has come into legal effect; or
(4) due to the death of the Ombudsman.[702]

793. If a person approved as the Ombudsman has at that time already been approved to become a judge for an unlimited term of office in accordance with the Law on Judicial Power, he or she has the right to return in that previous position.[703]

---

697. Article 4(2).
698. *Ibid.*, Art. 16.
699. *Ibid.*, Art. 4(3).
700. Criminal Procedure Law of 21 Apr. 2005, Art. 120(2).
701. Ombudsman Law of 6 Apr. 2006, Art. 8.
702. *Ibid.*, Art. 9(1).
703. *Ibid.*, Art. 9(2).

794. If a person approved as the Ombudsman has at that time been performing State civil service, military service or was an official with a special service rank, he or she must be ensured the right to hold an equal position.[704]

795. The *Saeima* releases the Ombudsman from the office if he or she:

(1) resigns freely, notifying the *Saeima* in writing;
(2) is unable to perform the duties of office due by reason of health;
(3) has committed a shameful act incompatible with the status of the Ombudsman;
(4) without a justified reason does not perform the duties of office; or
(5) has been elected or appointed to another office.[705]

796. The matter regarding the release of the Ombudsman from office may be proposed by not less than one-third of the MPs of the *Saeima*.[706]

§4. Competence

797. The Ombudsman has the following functions:

(1) to promote the protection of the human rights of private individuals;
(2) to promote compliance with the principles of equality and of the prevention of any kind of discrimination;
(3) to evaluate and promote compliance with the principle of good administration in the State;
(4) to discover deficiencies in legislation and its application regarding issues related to the observance of human rights and the principle of good administration, as well as to promote the rectification of such deficiencies; and
(5) to promote public awareness and understanding of human rights, of the mechanisms for the protection of such rights, and of the activities of the Ombudsman.

798. A person may submit an application to the Ombudsman with regard to all the issues referred to above, requesting a solution to a problem. If a violation is identified and if it is necessary in the public interest, the Ombudsman may defend a private person's rights and interests before an administrative court and the Constitutional Court. The Ombudsman is also authorized to initiate verification procedures (including upon own initiative), to visit any company, organization, or institution which is being audited and familiarize himself with the materials necessary for verification. The Ombudsman has the right to visit, without special permit, closed institutions, to move around freely on the territory of the institution, visit all premises, and meet in private all persons who are held in closed institutions. The Ombudsman has the right to hear a child's opinion in private without other persons

704. *Ibid.*, Art. 9(5).
705. Ombudsman Law of 6 Apr. 2006, Art. 10(1).
706. *Ibid.*, Art. 10(2).

present, if the child so wishes. The Ombudsman has the right to participate in the meetings of the Cabinet of Ministers, in the capacity of an advisor.[707]

799. In the performance of the functions specified by this Law, the Ombudsman:

(1) accepts and examines submissions of private individuals;
(2) initiates verification procedures for the clarification of circumstances;
(3) requests that institutions clarify, within the scope of their competence and within the time limits provided for by the law, the necessary circumstances of the matter and inform the Ombudsman thereof;
(4) provides the institution with recommendations and opinions regarding the lawfulness and effectiveness of their activities, as well as their compliance with the principle of good administration;
(5) resolves disputes between private individuals and institutions, and disputes in respect of human rights between private individuals, in accordance with the procedures specified by this Law;
(6) facilitates conciliation between the parties to the dispute;
(7) provides opinions and recommendations to private individuals regarding the prevention of human rights violations in resolving disputes in respect of human rights issues;
(8) provides the *Saeima*, the Cabinet, local governments, or other institutions with recommendations in respect of the issuance of or amendments to the legislation;
(9) offers consultations regarding human rights issues; and
(10) conducts research and analysis of the situation in the field of human rights, and provides opinions regarding topical human rights issues.[708]

800. The law prescribes the Ombudsman's jurisdiction to submit an application to the Constitutional Court to request a review of the compatibility of legal norms with the *Satversme*. The only prerequisite for submitting such application to the Court is defined by Article 13(8) of the Ombudsman Law and Article 17(1)(8) of the Constitutional Court Law. The Ombudsman must first turn to the institution or the official who has adopted the contested act, and set a term for eliminating the identified deficiencies. The Ombudsman's right to approach the institution which has adopted the contested act, or to submit an application to the Constitutional Court, does not depend upon the number of persons petitioning the Ombudsman in connection with the alleged violations of human rights.

801. Until 1 June 2015, the Ombudsman had submitted five applications to the Constitutional Court with regard to which the Court has initiated cases.[709]

707. *Ibid.*, Art. 13.
708. Ombudsman Law of 6 Apr. 2006, Art. 12.
709. Constitutional Court, Case No. 2010-06-01, 25 Nov. 2010, Constitutional Court, Case No. 2010-44-01, 20 Dec. 2010, Constitutional Court, on Terminating Judicial Proceedings in Case No. 2011-12-01, 1 Mar. 2012, Constitutional Court, Terminating Judicial Proceedings in No.

802. The Constitutional Court has emphasized that it is the obligation of the *Saeima* to examine the Ombudsman's applications with the regard to the need to amend or adopt new legal acts on issues of exercising, ensuring, or protecting human rights as meticulously as possible. The interaction between the legislator and the national mechanism for human rights protection – the Ombudsman – should be aimed at the efficient prevention of the deficiencies of legal acts identified in the field of human rights protection.[710]

803. The Ombudsman may establish advisory councils and working groups for the development of specific projects or the preparation of other measures, including legislative ones. Membership in councils and working groups, as well as their terms of reference, are approved by the Ombudsman.[711]

804. To ensure the activities of the Ombudsman, an Ombudsman's Office has been established. The structure and internal working regulations of the Ombudsman's Office is regulated by the by-law of the Office approved by the Ombudsman.[712]

805. The Ombudsman's Office is financed by the State budget.[713] In terms of budget allocation, the Ombudsman Office is equal to other constitutional institutions.[714]

2012-15-01, 13 Dec. 2011, Constitutional Court, Case No. 2013-15-01, 23 Apr. 2014, Constitutional Court, Case No. 2014-08-03, 12 Feb. 2015.

710. Judgment of the Constitutional Court in Case No. 2010-44-01, 20 Dec. 2010, para. 14.1.
711. Ombudsman Law of 6 Apr. 2006, Art. 14.
712. *Ibid.*, Art. 18.
713. Ombudsman Law of 6 Apr. 2006, Art. 19.
714. Constitutional Court, Case No. 2010-06-01, 25 Nov. 2010, para. 14.4.

Selected Bibliography

§1. Before the 2001 State Restructuring

Andersons, E. *Latvijas vēsture. Ārpolitika. 1920-1940,* Vol. I (Stockholm, Daugava, 1982).
Dišlers, K. *Ievads Latvijas valststiesību zinātnē.* (Rīga, A. Gulbis, 1930).
Dišlers, K. *Konvencionālas normas valststiesību novadā.* (Rīga, Tieslietu Ministrijas Vēstnesis, 1933, No. 11/12).
Dišlers, K. *Latvijas valsts varas orgāni un viņu funkcijas.* (Rīga, Tieslietu Ministrijas Vēstnesis, 1925).
Kronvalds A. *Kopotie raksti. I.* (Rīga, Valters un Rapa, 1937).
Lēbers, D. A. (ed.), *Latvijas tiesību vēsture (1914-2000).* (Rīga, Fonds Latvijas Vēsture, 2000).
Karulis, K. *Latviešu etimoloģijas vārdnīca.* (Rīga, Avots, 1992).
Lēbers, D.A. *Ministru kabinets: komentārs Latvijas Republikas Satversmes IV nodaļai 'Ministru kabinets'.* (Rīga, Tiesiskās informācijas centrs, 1998).
Jundzis, T. *4.maijs. Rakstu, atmiņu un dokumentu krājums par neatkarības deklarāciju.* (Rīga, Fonds Latvijas Vēsture, 2000).
Feldmanis, I, Freimanis, A. A., Lerhis & A, Ziemele, I, *Latvijas valsts Okupacijas gados (1940-1991), Dokumenti par Latvijas valsts starptautisko atzisanu, neatkaribas atjaunosanu un diplomatiskajiem sakariem (1918-1998).* (Rīga, Latvijas arhivistu biedriba, Latvijas Republikas Arlietu ministrija, Latvijas Valsts vestures arhivs, NORDIK, 1999).
Cielēns, F. *Baltijas federācija.* (Latvju Ziņas, 10 *December* 1947, No. 95).

§2. After the 2001 State Restructuring

Balodis, R., Kārkliņa, A. *Divdesmit gadi kopš Latvijas Neatkarības deklarācijas: valststiesību attīstības tendences un risinājumi.* (Jurista Vārds, 27 April 2010, No. 17/18).
Endziņš, A. *Latvijas konstitūcijas apskats, kas rada šaubas un jautājumus.* (Rīga, Jurista Vārds, 1 May 2005, No. 8).
Ijabs, I. *Demokrātija Latvijā.* 'Latvieši un Latvija', III sējums 'Atjaunotā Latvijas valsts'. (Rīga, Latvijas Zinātņu akadēmija, 2013).
Kusiņš, G. *Parlamentārās tradīcijas Latvijā.* (Rīga, Jurista Vārds, December 25 2012, No. 52).
Latvijas Republikas Satversmes komentāri. Ievads. I nodaļa. Vispārējie noteikumi.

Autoru kolektīvs prof. R. Baloža zinātniskā vadībā. (Rīga, Latvijas Vēstnesis, 2014).

Latvijas Republikas Satversmes komentāri. VI nodaļa. Tiesa. VII nodaļa. Valsts kontrole. Autoru kolektīvs prof. R. Baloža zinātniskā vadībā. (Rīga, Latvijas Vēstnesis, 2013).

Latvijas Republikas Satversmes komentāri. VIII nodaļa. Cilvēka pamattiesības. Autoru kolektīvs prof. R. Baloža zinātniskā vadībā. (Rīga, Latvijas Vēstnesis, 2011).

Latvijas Satversmes Sapulces stenogrammu izvilkums (1920–1922). Latvijas Republikas Satversmes projekta apspriešana un apstiprināšana. (Rīga, Tiesu namu aģentūra, 2006).

Lazdiņš J. *Valsts prezidenta institūta tapšana Latvijā.* (Likums un Tiesības, 2001, No. 6),

Lerhis, A. *Latvijas Republikas ārlietu dienests. 1918-1941.* (Rīga Latvijas vēstures institūta apgāds, 2005).

Levits, E. *Aktuālās judikatūras apskats.* (Rīga, Likums un Tiesības 2005, No. 1).

Neimanis, J. *Judikatūra un tās saistošais spēks.* (Rīga, Jurista Vārds, 8 March 2005. No. 9).

Osipova, S, Strupišs, A., Rieba, A. *Tiesu varas neatkarības un efektivitātes palielināšanas un nostiprināšanas rezerves.* (Jurista Vārds, 9 March 2010, No. 10).

Pastars E., Pleps J., *Satversmes lasīšana Satversmes tiesā.* (Rīga, Jurista Vārds, 20 November 2007, No. 42).

Pleps, J. *Baltijas vienotības ideja Latvijas valststiesiskajā domā.* (Rīga, Jurista Vārds. 31 July 2012, No. 31).

Pleps, J. *Bīskaps Rancāns un Satversme. Valsts prezidenta vietas izpildīšana.* (Jurista Vārds, 3 March 2009, No. 9).

Pleps, J. *Latvijas valsts konstitucionālie pamati.* 'Latvieši un Latvija', III sējums 'Atjaunotā Latvijas valsts'. (Rīga, Latvijas Zinātņu akadēmija, 2013).

Pleps, J. *Satversmes iztulkošana.* (Rīga, Latvijas Vēstnesis, 2012).

Pleps, J., Pastars, E., Plakane, I. *Konstitucionālās tiesības. Papildinātais un pārstrādātais izdevums.* (Rīga, Latvijas Vēstnesis, 2014).

Valsts prezidenta Konstitucionālo tiesību komisijas 2008. gada 30.aprīļa viedokļa '*Par Saeimas priekšlaicīgu vēlēšanu mehānisma pilnveidošanu*'. Valsts prezidenta Konstitucionālo tiesību komisija. Viedokļi: 2008-2011 (Rīga, Latvijas Vēstnesis, 2011).

Valsts prezidenta Konstitucionālo tiesību komisijas 2011. gada 10.maija viedokļa *'Par Valsts prezidenta funkcijām Latvijas parlamentārās demokrātijas sistēmas ietvaros'* Valsts prezidenta Konstitucionālo tiesību komisija. Viedokļi: 2008-2011 (Rīga: Latvijas Vēstnesis, 2011).

Vilka I. *Administratīvi teritoriālais iedalījums un pašvadības. 'Latvieši un Latvija', III sējums 'Atjaunotā Latvijas valsts'.* (Rīga, Latvijas Zinātņu akadēmija, 2013).

Ziemele, I. *Piezīmes pie sagatavotā lēmuma projekta* (Rīga, Jurista Vārds, 30 January 2007, No. 5).

Ziemele, I., Krūma, K., *Eiropas Savienības pilsonība un Latvijas nepilsoņi* (Latvijas Vēstnesis, Jurista Vārds, 2003).

§3. Publications in English

Balodis, R. 'Latvia', Encyclopedia of World Constitutions. Volume II', edited by Robbers, G., U.S. Facts on File, 2007.

Crawford, J. *Creation of States.* New York: Oxford University Press Inc., 2006.

Jennings, R. & A. Watts (eds). *Oppenheim's International Law.* 9th ed. vol. I. London: Longman, 1992.

Kruma K. *Access to Electoral Rights.* Latvia, European University Institute, Florence, Robert Schuman Centre for Advanced Studies, EUDO Citizenship Observatory, June 2013.

Kruma, K. *Country Report: Latvia.* European University Institute, 2013.

Krūma, K. *An Ongoing Challenge. EU Citizenship, Migrant Status and Nationality. Focus on Latvia.* Lund: Media Tryck, 2012.

Kruma, K. *EU Citizenship, Nationality and Migrant Status. An Ongoing challenge.* Leiden: Martinus Nijhoff Publishers, 2014.

Kruma, K. *Latvia: Comprehensive Citizenship Reform on the Agenda in Parliament and in a Referendum Campaign, http://eudo-citizenship.eu/news/citizenship-news/700-latvia,* 2 September 2012.

Kruma, K. 'Latvian Integration Policy: Lost in Translation'. In *A Re-definition of Belonging? Language and Integration Tests in Europe*, edited by van Oers Ricky, Ersbøll Eva & Kostakopoulou Dora. Leiden, Martinus Nijhoff Publishers, 2010.

Loeber. D. A. *Legal Consequences of the Molotov – Ribbentrop Pact for the Baltic States on the Obligation 'to Overcome the Problems Inherited from the Past'.* vol. 1. London, The Hague: Baltic Yearbook of International Law, 2001.

Mits, M. *European Convention on Human Rights in Latvia. Impact on Legal Doctrine and Application of Legal Norms.* Lund, Media Tryck, 2010.

Mits, M. *Internationalisation of Public Law: the Case of Latvia.* vol. 18(1), *Revue Européenne de Droit Public*, 2006.

Muižnieks, N. *Latvian-Russian Relations: Domestic and International Dimensions.* Rīga, LU Apgāds, 2006.

Muižnieks, N. 'Russian Foreign Policy Towards "Compatriots"'. In *Latvia.* Rīga, LU Apgāds, 2006.

Rodiņa, A. & J. Pleps. *Constitutionalism in Latvia: Reality and Developments. New Millennium Constitutionalism: Paradigms of Reality and Challenges.* Yerevan: NJHAR, 2013.

Ronen, Y. 'Status of Settlers Implanted by Illegal Territorial Regimes'. *British Yearbook of International Law* 79/1 (2009).

Strik, T. et al. The INTEC Project: Synthesis Report. 'Integration and Naturalisation Tests: The New Way to European Citizenship'. In *Which Integration Policies for Migrants? Interaction between the EU and Its Member States*, edited by Pascouau Y. & T. Strik. The Netherlands: Wolf Legal Publishers, 2012.

Taube, C. *Constitutionalism in Estonia, Latvia and Lithuania. A study in comparative constitutional law.* Upsala, Iustus Förlag, 2001, 46–55.

William, H.J. & III. Hough. 'The Annexation of the Baltic States and Its Effect on the Development of Law Prohibiting Forcible Seizure of Territory'. *NewYork Law School Journal of International and Comparative Law* 6(2) (1985).

Selected Bibliography

Ziemele, I. *State Continuity and Nationality: The Baltic States and Russia. Past, Present and Future as Defined by International Law.* Leiden, Martinus Nijhoff Publishers, 2005).

§4. CASE LAW

I. Constitutional Court

A. Judgments

Case No. 01-05(98), 27 November 1998
Case No. 03-04-(98), 30 July 1998
Case No. 03-05(99) of 1 October 1999
Case No. 04-07(99), 24 March 2000
Case No. 2000-03-01, 30 August 2000
Case No. 2000-07-0409, 3 April 2001
Case No. 2000-08-0109, 13 March 2001
Case No. 2001-02-0106, 26 June 2001
Case No. 2001-04-0103, 21 December 2001
Case No. 2001-06-03, 22 February 2002
Case No. 2001-04-0103, 21 December 2001
Case No. 2001-06-03, 22 February 2002
Case No. 2001-08-01, 17 January 2002
Case No. 2001-09-01, 21 January 2001
Case No. 2001-10-01, 5 March 2002
Case No. 2001-17-0106, 20 June 2002
Case No. 2002-04-03, 22 October 2002
Case No. 2002-06-01, 4 February 2003
Case No. 2002-08-01, 23 September 2002
Case No. 2002-15-01, 23 December 2002
Case No. 2002-18-01, 5 March 2003
Case No. 2003-02-0106, 5 June 2003
Cases No. 2003-04-01, 27 June 2003
Case No. 2003-05-01, 29 October 2003
Case No. 2003-08-01, 6 October 2003
Case No. 2003-12-0106, 18 December 2003
Case No. 2003-15-0106, 23 April 2004
Case No. 2003-22-01, 26 March 2004
Case No. 2004-04-01, 5 November 2004
Case No. 2004-06-01 of 11 October 2004
Cases No. 2004-10-01, 17 January 2005
Case No. 2004-13-0106, 22 March 2005
Case No. 2004-15-0106, 7 March 2005
Case No. 2004-16-014 January 2005
Case No. 2004-18-0106, 13 May 2005
Case No. 2004-19-01, 15 February 2005

Case No. 2004-21-01, 6 April 2005
Cases No. 2005-02-01-6, 14 September 2005
Case No. 2005-03-0306, 21 November 2005
Case No. 2005-09-01,4 November 2005
Case No. 2005-12-0103, 16 December 2005
Case No. 2005-13-0106, 15 June 2006
Case No. 2005-18-01, 14 March 2006
Case No. 2006-03-0106,23 November 2006
Case No. 2006-04-01, 8 November 2006
Case No. 2006-05-01, 16 October 2006
Case No. 2006-07-01, 2 November 2006
Case No. 2006-10-03, 11 December 2006
Case No. 2006-12-01, 20 December 2006
Case No. 2006-29-0103, 10 May 2007
Case No. 2007-01-01, 8 June 2007
Case No. 2007-03-01, 18 October 2007
Case No. 2007-04-03, 9 October 2007
Case No. 2007-08-01, 1 November 2007
Case No. 2007-10-0102, 29 November 2007
Case No. 2007-23-01, 3 April 2008
Case No. 2007-22-01, 2 June 2008
Case No. 2007-24-01, 9 May 2008
Case No. 2008-03-03, 24 September 2008
Case No. 2008-09-0106, 16 December 2008
Case No. 2008-35-01, 7 April 2009
Case No. 2008-37-03, 29 December 2008
Case No. 2008-40-01, 19 May 2009
Case No. 2009-04-06, 30 October 2009
Case No. 2009-05-01, 7 October 2009
Case No. 2009-08-01, 26 November 2009
Case No. 2009-11-01, 18 January 2010
Case No. 2009-12-03, 7 January 2010
Case No. 2009-43-01, 21 December 2009
Case No. 2009-44-01, 15 March 2010
Case No. 2009-45-01, 22 February 2010
Case No. 2009-74-01, 18 February 2010
Case No. 2009-85-01, 3 March 2010
Case No. 2009-88-01, 15 April 2010
Case No. 2009-93-01, 17 May 2010
Case No. 2009-94-01, 13 May 2010
Case No. 2010-06-01, 25 November 2010
Case No. 2010-17-01, 29 October 2010
Case No. 2010-22-01, 27 April 2011
Case No. 2010-40-03, 11 January 2011
Case No. 2010-44-01, 20 December 2010
Case No. 2010-50-03, 18 March, 2011
Case No. 2010-57-03, 6 May 2011

Case No. 2010-60-01, 30 March 2011
Case No. 2011-01-01, 25 October, 2011
Case No. 2011-03-01, 19 December 2011
Case No. 2011-11-01, 3 February 2012
Case No. 2011-17-03, 2 May 2012
Case No. 2011-20-01, 21 June 2012
Case No. 2012-02-0106, 18 October 2012
Case No. 2012-06-01, 1 November 2012
Case No. 2012-16-01, 10 May 2013
Case No. 2012-24-03, 7 November 2013
Case No. 2013-04-01, 7 February 2014
Case No. 2013-06-01, 18 December 2013
Case No. 2013-15-01, 23 April 2014
Case No. 2014-03-01, 5 February 2015
Case No. 2014-08-03, 15 February 2015

B. Decisions

Decisions of 10 May 2007 on the Applicant's Request in Case No. 2007-10-0102
Decision of 16 April 2008 on Terminating Judicial Proceedings in Case No. 2007-21-01
Decision of 20 January 20009 on Terminating Judicial Proceedings in Case No. 2008-08-0306
Decision of 8 March 2011 on Terminating Judicial Proceedings in Case No. 2010-52-03
Decision of 1 March 2012 on Terminating Judicial Proceedings in Case No. 2011-12-01
Decision of 19 December 2012 on Terminating Judicial Proceedings in Case No. 2012-03-01
Decision of 13 December 2011 on Terminating Judicial Proceedings in No. 2012-15-01

II. Other Court

Judgment by ECHR in Case 'Podkolzina v. Latvia', No. 46726/99, April 2002
Judgment by ECHR in Case 'Jutta Mentzen alias Mencena v. Latvia', No. 71074/01, 6 April 2005
Judgment by ECHR Case of *Ždanoka v. Latvia*, No. 58278/00, 16 March 2006
Judgment of Department of Administrative Cases of the Senate of the Supreme Court of the Republic of Latvia in Case No. SKA-216, 23 November 2004
Judgment of the Administrative Cases Department of the Supreme Court's Senate. See case No. SKA 221, 11 April 2006
Judgment of Department of Administrative Cases of the Senate of the Supreme Court of the Republic of Latvia in Case No. 162/2007 of 10 May 2007

Judgment of Department of Administrative Cases of the Senate of the Supreme Court of the Republic of Latvia in Case No. SKA-68/2013, 22 February 2013

Judgment of the Administrative Cases Department of the Supreme Court in Case No. SA/-1/2014, 12 February 2014

Decision by the Department of Administrative Cases of the Supreme Court Senate in Case No. SKA-528/2009. 29 June 2009

Decision by the Department of Administrative Cases of the Supreme Court Senate in Case No. SKA-32/2009, 23 March 2009

Decision by the Department of Administrative Cases of the Supreme Court Senate in Case No. SKA-589/2010, 12 October 2010

Decision by the Department of Administrative Cases of the Senate of the Supreme Court of the Republic of Latvia in Case No. SKA-68/2013, 22 February 2013

Judgment of Department of Civil Cases of the Senate of the Supreme Court of the Republic of Latvia in Case No. SKC 12/2009, 29 April 2009

Decision by the Department of Civil Cases of the Senate of the Supreme Court of the Republic of Latvia in Case No. SKC 12/2009, 29 April 2009

Judgment of the Regional Court of administrative cases in Case No. A42051204 (AA43-1868-07/9), 28 April 2008

Selected Bibliography

Table of Legislative Instruments

Listed are legislative instruments, treaties, conventions, resolutions, and intergovernmental agreements discussed in the text. Only certain relevant national and international legislative instruments have entries for specific articles. All references include amendments to date. A listing below should not be understood to characterize the bindingness or legal nature of the instrument so listed.

Table of Legislative Instruments

Index

The numbers here refer to paragraph numbers.

Index

Index

Index

www.ingramcontent.com/pod-product-compliance
Lightning Source LLC
Chambersburg PA
CBHW071442230926
51846CB00001B/311
* 9 7 8 9 0 4 1 1 8 2 7 5 3 *